Roy Jenkins

Roy Jenkins

A RETROSPECTIVE

Edited by

ANDREW ADONIS

AND

KEITH THOMAS

OXFORD

UNIVERSITY PRESS

OXFORD
UNIVERSITY PRESS

Great Clarendon Street, Oxford OX2 6DP

Oxford University Press is a department of the University of Oxford.
It furthers the University's objective of excellence in research, scholarship,
and education by publishing worldwide in

Oxford New York

Auckland Bangkok Buenos Aires Cape Town Chennai
Dar es Salaam Delhi Hong Kong Istanbul Karachi Kolkata
Kuala Lumpur Madrid Melbourne Mexico City Mumbai Nairobi
São Paulo Shanghai Taipei Tokyo Toronto

Oxford is a registered trade mark of Oxford University Press
in the UK and in certain other countries

Published in the United States
by Oxford University Press Inc., New York

British Library Cataloguing in Publication Data

Data available

Library of Congress Cataloging in Publication Data

Data available

ISBN 0-19-927487-8

1 3 5 7 9 10 8 6 4 2

Typeset in Bembo by
Jayvee, Trivandrum, India
Printed in Great Britain
on acid-free paper by
Biddles Ltd.,
King's Lynn, Norfolk

ANDREW ADONIS

Andrew Adonis is Special Adviser to Tony Blair (since 1998) and was Head of the Downing Street Policy Unit (2001–3). An Oxford history graduate, he was from 1988 to 1998 successively Fellow in Politics at Nuffield College, Oxford, Public Policy Editor of the *Financial Times*, and columnist and leader-writer on *The Observer*. His books include studies of the Victorian aristocracy, the rise and fall of the poll tax, the English class system, and the development of modern British government and politics. His biography of Roy Jenkins is forthcoming.

KEITH THOMAS

Keith Thomas, like Roy Jenkins, was educated at a South Wales grammar school (Barry) and at Balliol College, Oxford. He is an Oxford historian who was a college tutor at St John's and, later, President of Corpus Christi. In 2001 he returned to All Souls College, where he was a Fellow in the 1950s. He has been President of the British Academy (1993–7), a Trustee of the National Gallery (1991–8), and a Trustee of the British Museum (since 1999). His writings on social and cultural history include *Religion and the Decline of Magic* (1971) and *Man and the Natural World* (1983). He was knighted in 1988.

Preface

Roy Jenkins died on 5 January 2003. He had been a commanding figure in British politics and cultural life for the previous four decades. His political impact was greater than that of many prime ministers of the time and he gained more applause for his literary work than do most historians and biographers. His name is synonymous with the liberalization of society since the 1960s and the development of social democratic politics between the death of his mentor, Hugh Gaitskell, and the premiership of his friend and, some would say, protégé Tony Blair. He was a progressive Home Secretary, a powerful and effective Chancellor of the Exchequer, and the first (and only) British President of the European Commission. He pioneered the Social Democratic Party and helped to reshape British Politics in the 1980s and 1990s. He was a notably successful Chancellor of Oxford University. At the age of 80 he published his best-selling life of Churchill, fifty years after his first biography, *Mr Attlee*. His energy and self-discipline were accompanied by an exceptional zest for life.

This book is not an overall assessment of Roy Jenkins's historical importance, but a collection of essays by those who knew him intimately at the different phases of his career. Their recollections and appraisals take us from his childhood in a Monmouthshire mining valley to his mellow and productive old age in rural Oxfordshire. In this way, they supplement his own vivid autobiography, *A Life at the Centre* (1991). There are contributions by politicians, civil servants, historians, and personal friends. We have asked them to avoid hagiography and to be candid in their judgements. The result is a book which we hope is both a contribution to history and a lasting tribute to an extraordinary and many-sided man.

Andrew Adonis
Keith Thomas

Contents

List of Illustrations

List of Figures

Roy Jenkins, 1920–2003

1920	Born Abersychan, Monmouthshire
1931	Abersychan Secondary School
1937	University College, Cardiff
1938–41	Balliol College, Oxford
1942–3	Second Lieutenant, Royal Artillery
1943–5	Bletchley Park Headquarters Staff
1945	Married Jennifer Morris
1948–50	MP (Labour), Southwark
1948	*Mr Attlee: An Interim Biography*
1950–77	MP (Labour), Stechford, Birmingham
1954	*Mr Balfour's Poodle*
1958	*Sir Charles Dilke: A Victorian Tragedy*
1964	*Asquith*
1964–5	Minister of Aviation
1965–7	Home Secretary
1967–70	Chancellor of the Exchequer
1970–2	Deputy Leader of the Labour Party
1974–6	Home Secretary
1977–81	President of the European Commission
1982–3	Leader of the Social Democratic Party
1982–7	MP (SDP), Glasgow Hillhead
1987	Created Lord Jenkins of Hillhead
1987–2003	Chancellor of the University of Oxford
1988–98	Leader of the Social and Liberal Democratic Peers
1991	*A Life at the Centre*

1993	Appointed to the Order of Merit
1995	*Gladstone*
2001	*Churchill*
2003	Died, East Hendred, Oxfordshire

Roy Jenkins

PITA KARAKA

Pita Karaka, Roy Jenkins's cousin, was brought up in south Wales, living much of the time with Roy and his parents. After the Second World War she lived for thirty years in India, marrying the leading weekly newspaper editor D. K. Karaka, who was briefly imprisoned during Indira Gandhi's emergency. She now lives in Tunbridge Wells.

HUGH BRACE

Hugh Brace was born in Talywain, north of Pontypool. His father was a builder and his mother a pianist. After Abersychan School he studied physics at Birmingham. He fought in the Middle East and Italy during the war. Afterwards, he entered the Patent Office in London and retired as a senior patent official in 1980.

Chapter 1

Youth

I

PITA KARAKA

My father died when I was 3 and my aunt—Roy's mother—persuaded my mother to come back to live in south Wales with her two daughters. My sister was 18 months older than I and every time she was ill—measles, scarlet fever, shingles, or whatever—I was packed off to live with my aunt. The stays became increasingly frequent and long. My mother died when I was 17, and I then went to live with my aunt and uncle entirely, until I left Wales at the age of 21. I was 5½ years older than Roy, who was an only child, so I was more elder sister than cousin.

What are my memories? Roy's mother—my Aunt Hattie—was very ambitious for him, from the earliest age, and made a

This chapter consists of two edited extracts from interviews with Andrew Adonis.

tremendous fuss of him. She was also utterly devoted to Uncle Arthur—Roy's father—a miner's agent who went to Ruskin College, Oxford, and became an MP. Uncle Arthur was mild, extremely good-looking with blue-grey eyes and a prominent forehead. Although somewhat reserved, he had great strength of character. Roy modelled himself on his father in so many ways. As Roy grew up, they moved into steadily larger houses in Pontypool—though always taking the same name, Greenlands, with them. They had a servant always. They never moved to London: as an MP Uncle Arthur stayed in hotels part of the week and spent the rest of the time at home. Aunt Hattie rarely went to London.

Neither of them spoke Welsh, though Roy's father taught himself some, which was pretty hard in those days since no one spoke it at all in our valley. They both adored Roy. I remember when he had to go into hospital for appendicitis, about the age of 10, Uncle Arthur nearly died because he was so frantically worried. Most people just take things like that for granted: not Uncle Arthur, who was in a great state. I rarely heard a raised voice or a cross word in the house. If there was a slight argument, there would be silence and that's all.

The main thing about Roy as a child was his addiction to numbers. He was always silent and counting or working out some sum. He was like that ever after! And also addicted to trains. He used to love going down to Pontypool Road station to see the engines and take notes of them. And to look at the timetables—something else that stayed with him, arriving for trains the minute they were due, not a minute before. He also read a lot from Uncle Arthur's library and used to play cricket with him in the garden. And he loved rugger.

The most famous incident in Roy's youth was the imprisonment of his father for three months when he was 6, in connection with a picketing dispute in the miners' lock-out after the General Strike. I believe Aunt Hattie's version of it. She said he stood in front of them and tried to calm them down. He was regarded as a ringleader, but he hadn't an ounce of aggressiveness in him. I can't believe he was egging them on; that's the last thing he would be doing. While he was in Cardiff gaol everyone tried to look after Aunt Hattie. She closed the house, and went with Roy to live with friends in Newport. I went over to be company for Roy in the strange house.

Aunt Hattie told Roy nothing about why his father was away. He had been away before, fighting the compensation cases, so his absence wasn't totally surprising. Whether Roy realized it, I don't know. I didn't tell him a word. Aunt Hattie took it all very badly. Absolutely knocked out. She needed a lot of support at that time, otherwise she would have stayed in her own house. But she couldn't, and could never bear to talk about it.

Roy went to the local council school and then on to grammar school. He picked up things so quickly in the junior school. He loved working hard, which was very fortunate for Uncle Arthur and Aunt Hattie. At the time I didn't know if he had any girlfriends. Years later when some television people asked me about his girlfriends, I said I didn't know; so I asked Roy afterwards and he said 'Yes, I did,' and he gave me the names of four or five of them, all from school.

He loved me reading to him, before he could read. He knew exactly what he wanted me to read and if I missed a word he would remind me of what the word was, as he knew all the stories off by heart. He treated me like a sister. He'd give me worms to hold. Later Roy had a bike and would go riding with the boy next door. Roy's father was lucky to have a car. He would take us out every Sunday, driving around Monmouthshire and sometimes beyond.

It was always assumed Roy would go on to university. If Uncle Arthur could go to university with absolutely no backing at all except his own brain, there was no question that Roy would go too. It was a natural progression. It all seemed to be very much taken for granted that he was clever enough to do so, and Oxford was often talked about. By the time he went, in 1938, I was in London and working. I only went down there once or twice and I didn't see much of him.

As soon as my twenty-first birthday came up in July of '36, I shot off to London and escaped from Wales. My aunt was so nervous about it. She arranged for me to go to a Christian hostel at 116 Baker Street, which was a lovely place and I thoroughly enjoyed it. I started working as a stenographer, and two years later married. I separated during the war, and went to India after the war, where I married again, to an Oxford-educated Parsee who became a weekly magazine editor. He had been President of the Oxford Union, which was very amusing because Roy always wanted to be President of the Union and he didn't make it. He and Roy got on extremely well and Roy used to write for my husband's magazine in its early days. It was his beginning in journalism.

Every time I came home from India, which was every two years, I would always land on Roy and Jennifer. And I lived with them, in their basement flat in Ladbroke Square, for a time after my husband died in 1976.

II

HUGH BRACE

I was Roy's closest friend at his secondary school in Abersychan. We went there on scholarships from different primary schools. Out of my primary class of forty or fifty, two got scholarships. I think Roy was third and I was fifth in the scholarship competition, which covered a wide area extending down the valley almost as far as Newport. Roy was by far the youngest in our class, not yet 11 when he started. His father and headmaster must have pushed him hard to get him in that year: he would have taken the eleven-plus when he was only 10½, whereas I was 11 and a bit.

There were four secondary schools in the area; ours was the most modern—built only a few years before—and the only co-educational, with more girls than boys. West Monmouth School, a Haberdashers' School, had the established reputation and was more fashionable. But Roy's father was impressed with J. C. James, the headmaster of Abersychan School, and I think that is why Roy went there. He was also one of the school governors—but then he was also a governor of 'West Mon' and most of the other major institutions in the area. Our fathers had things in common, although mine was older. Both taught themselves Welsh. Mine was a builder in a very small way: he was a tremendously avid reader—like Roy's—and might have been an academic if he had had the education, but he left school at 14.

J. C. James was a fine headmaster, strict in discipline and very cultured. He taught Roy and me Latin, just the two of us. By sixth form I was into the sciences, Roy the arts. Not all the teaching was good. The French was particularly bad—a second-rate French mistress; my French never recovered and Roy's was never marvellous. The history teacher was all right, but no more. It wasn't an intensely competitive school. The sixth form was quite small. Most of the sixth form went on to university but mostly within Wales: Bangor, Aberystwyth, and other Welsh colleges. Roy's father wanted to get him into Oxford, as he himself had been to Ruskin. For a year in between school and Balliol, because he was so young, he went to one of the Cardiff colleges as a kind of crammer. By then he had lost any trace of Welsh accent, though I don't remember much trace of it in the sixth form and there was no Welsh taught in the school. I went to Birmingham. I only remember one other going to Oxford, seven years before us. It was a rarity.

There was no debating society as such, but there were debates held from time to time and Roy obviously took part. Rugger was the main game—Roy played in the scrum—and cricket in the summer. He was quite a good bowler. I remember him saying that he had been slow to achieve a certain elegant untidiness in his game. We had no swimming: there was no pool within a couple of miles. A tennis court was laid out while we were in the sixth form, and we played. The girls played too.

Roy's mother was quite a character in the town. She was chairman of a local bench of magistrates and was involved in all sorts of activities. She was a pillar of the chapel, unlike his father, who went about once a year under protest, rather like Roy in later life.

Roy was not especially gregarious. Apart from me, his only other particular friend was Derek Powell, who lived next door to him and was a few years older. I remember Roy going round with the girls a bit in the sixth form, one in particular. We both had bikes and were always out riding weekends—there were a lot of interesting places around Monmouth, Raglan, and Abergavenny. I did some much longer journeys—down to Southampton once—but Roy did not go that far although he was a great one for planning journeys. He took a tremendous interest in maps generally. He used to plan train journeys—complete with times and interchanges—to Jerusalem and Constantinople, and he could recite all the stations on the Paris Métro at a very young age. He had been to Paris twice with his father, and to Belgium. Nobody else in the school had been there. He was, as I saw it, a seasoned traveller.

We were in different places in the war, and did not see much of each other until it was over. I remember going up to London, just after he was elected an MP, for the State Opening of Parliament. I think he wanted to be a politician from the very start. He was immersed in it, took it for granted. Clement Attlee and a string of other Labour politicians of the 1930s were often in his father's house, down in south Wales for the great miners' conferences. Politics came absolutely naturally to him.

Ronald McIntosh

Ronald McIntosh was educated at Charterhouse and Balliol College, Oxford, and served in the merchant navy from 1939 to 1945. He held senior posts in the Department of Economic Affairs, the Cabinet Office, and the Treasury before being appointed Director-General of the National Economic Development Office and a member of NEDC in 1973. He was made a KCB in 1975. From 1978 to 1990 he pursued an active business career as chairman of APV plc and a director of S. G. Warburg and other companies.

Chapter 2

Balliol

Ronald McIntosh

R
oy Jenkins and I first met in October 1938 at the
beginning of our freshman term at Balliol. We got on
well straight away and remained close friends for
sixty-five years.

Balliol was a good place to be in that last year of peace before
the Second World War. It had a wider social and ethnic mix
than most other colleges, with strong contingents from North
America, India, and (thanks to a seventeenth-century bene-
faction) Glasgow. Perhaps because of this it had an open and
tolerant atmosphere where people were accepted on their own
merits as human beings and not because of school or other
connections. This was not so common in pre-war days as it may
have since become.

Relations between Fellows and undergraduates were good—
somewhat detached, as was the custom in those more hier-
archical days, but easygoing and founded on mutual respect.
The Senior Common Room was a strong one. The doyen was

Cyril Bailey, a much admired figure who was perhaps the most distinguished Oxford classicist of his day. In Humphrey Sumner, Dick Southern, and Christopher Hill the College had three historians of unusual quality, all of whom became heads of houses after the war. And there were outstanding tutors in mathematics, English, and the law. We freshmen appreciated the intellectual distinction which these and other Fellows brought to the college community we had joined, but for most of us interest in the SCR more or less stopped there.

Tutorials and lectures were a novel and quite agreeable way of filling a morning, but in what seemed increasingly likely to be the last year of European peace, academic work was not the first priority. The real business of university life was—as it probably always has been—to get to know one's peers and sit up half the night discussing the great questions of life. Though not noted for its architectural beauty, Balliol was well designed for this purpose. With around 260 undergraduates (of whom over eighty were in their first year) it was one of the largest colleges and big enough to be more or less self-sufficient socially. Freshmen all lived in college, where the centrally situated buttery, with a good stretch of lawn for outside drinking, provided a natural meeting point. It was an intrinsically friendly place.

The general style of the College was greatly influenced by Sandy Lindsay, a humane and liberal-minded Scot who by 1938 had been Master for nearly fifteen years. Lindsay had strong views about the responsibilities which young men who were educated at privileged places like Balliol had towards their less fortunate fellow citizens and society at large. His views were in tune with those of young men who had grown up in the decade of the Jarrow hunger march and the Spanish Civil War, and when we went up, Balliol was a highly political place— more so, I would guess, than any other college at the time.

The prevailing ethos was definitely left of centre: but there were relatively few Communists in the College and Conservative supporters of the 'Middle Way' advocated by Harold Macmillan (whose son Maurice was one of the 1938 entry) were generally comfortable with Lindsay's ideas. As the Michaelmas term began, the ink was scarcely dry on the Munich Agreement and political discussion focused almost entirely on issues of foreign rather than domestic policy. When Lindsay agreed to stand in the Oxford by-election of November 1938, as an independent candidate on an anti-Munich platform, he received overwhelming support from undergraduates of all political persuasions—including, paradoxically, the pacifists, of whom Balliol had quite a few. During the ensuing year party-political differences among undergraduates were not very important; what mattered was the position an individual took on Chamberlain's appeasement policy.

Roy Jenkins fitted happily into this college environment. A naturally gregarious character, he was always at ease with himself socially and had no hang-ups about being a Welsh miner's son, which in those days could have been a handicap in some colleges. His family background was in fact a source of strength to him. By the time he went to Balliol, his father was already Clement Attlee's parliamentary private secretary and his parents were people of some consequence in the Valleys. His mother, Hattie, had a strong, outgoing personality and high ambitions for her son. His father, Arthur, was a gentle person who was liked and respected by his fellow MPs of all parties. Both naturally took a keen interest in their only child's progress at Oxford. Rather more unusually, they got to know well some of his close friends at Balliol during his first year there and had them to stay at the family home in Pontypool during vacations—thus perhaps sowing the seed for the social-cum-family occasions which were an important part of their son's life at his own Oxfordshire home in later years.

Like his father, Roy was well liked. In his first year his social life took place very largely within his own college, where he formed lifelong friendships with Neil Bruce and Madron Seligman (who became respectively a foreign correspondent with the BBC and a Member of the European Parliament) as well as myself. In his second and third years, when his involvement in undergraduate politics widened his contacts in the University, he made lasting friendships with men from other colleges—most notably Tony Crosland, whose relationship with him is brilliantly captured in Giles Radice's book *Friends and Rivals*. Other lifelong friendships made at this time which he particularly valued were those with Nicko Henderson (sometime British Ambassador in Paris and Washington) of Hertford and Mark Bonham Carter, who until his death in 1994 was probably Roy's closest friend.

Among his contemporaries Roy was generally regarded as good company, with a well-developed sense of fun and a lively, though not scholarly, mind. Though popular—in 1940 he was elected President of the Junior Common Room—he was not a dominant personality among his peers, who evinced mild surprise when in 1941 he got his First. Since, with hindsight, it is apparent that he had an intellect of great breadth and quality, it is perhaps reassuring that the examiners were more perceptive than his contemporaries.

Roy was not a natural athlete and showed little interest in organized sport—his love of tennis and the fiendish behaviour on the croquet lawn which played a large part in his middle years were not, as I recall, in evidence during his time at Oxford—but he took an active part in other college pursuits. These included a celebrated production of Aristophanes'

The Birds, which the Balliol Players (an undergraduate group whose self-confidence was not always matched by the quality of its acting) took on tour in southern England during the long vacation of 1939. Roy was an enthusiastic member of the chorus and gave an impressive imitation of a bird about to leave the ground, which those who knew him only in later life might find hard to credit. As an undergraduate he also showed the meticulous interest in the minutiae of travel and timekeeping which remained with him all his life; the widely held belief that his favourite bedtime reading was Thomas Cook's Continental Railway timetable was not necessarily apocryphal.

It was, however, politics that took centre-stage in his interests from the start. Whereas few of the rest of us knew—or with war looming particularly cared—what career we would follow when we left university, Roy was always clear that he was going to be a Member of Parliament. To prepare himself for this he gave priority to achieving his ambition to become President of the Oxford Union. He made his maiden speech in January 1939 and was elected to membership of the Library Committee (the bottom end of the greasy pole of Union politics) before his first year was up.

Roy was a good Union debater, but he never achieved the complete mastery of Union audiences which he displayed in the House of Commons during the 1960s, and the presidency, which he would have dearly liked to attain, eluded him. Though he held in turn the offices of Secretary and Librarian, he was twice defeated in elections for President—first by James Comyn of New College and then by Bahadur Singh of St Catherine's. Perhaps the members had simply become fed up with having Balliol Presidents—there were twenty-three of them between the wars.

In September 1939 war came and our ways parted for a time.

I went off to sea the following month, while Roy went back to Oxford to await his call-up to the Army and (later) Bletchley and in the meantime pursued his political interests with enthusiasm. We continued to see one another when leave allowed: but I have no first-hand knowledge of the turbulent internal politics of the Oxford University Labour Club, which occupied a great deal of Roy's attention in the first year of war. The Club, in which Denis Healey and Iris Murdoch were prominent, was at that time dominated by Communists. Following the Nazi–Soviet Pact of August 1939, the British Communist Party opposed Britain's participation in what, for it, had ceased to be an anti-fascist struggle and become an imperialist war. With Tony Crosland and others, Roy decided to split the Club, and in what was almost a dry run for the formation of the SDP forty years later, created a breakaway—and highly successful—social democratic organization. Healey, whose own break with Communism was still two or three months away, opposed the move—more, according to his memoirs, from inertia than conviction.

By the time I went back to Balliol in 1946, Roy had left Bletchley and his life had been enriched by his marriage to Jennifer Morris the year before. He was very anxious to find a seat in the House of Commons, and when in 1948 the opportunity arose to fight a by-election in Southwark he took it eagerly, even though it was known that the seat would disappear at the next general election. Along with one or two Balliol friends I canvassed for him in Southwark and was much struck by his ability to relate to and communicate easily with the man and woman in the street in that down-to-earth south London borough. The next time I canvassed for him was at Hillhead some thirty-four years later when, as an older and much grander political figure, he exhibited the same sympathetic interest in the concerns of a very different set of constituents. By blood, upbringing, and inclination Roy was a thoroughly political animal.

My friendship with Roy was a personal one and not political—though I cannot remember any important political issue on which we took significantly different views. His gift for personal friendship was one of his most notable characteristics. The breadth of his intellectual interests and his ever-present sense of the absurd made him extraordinarily good company among close friends. If in his public utterances a hint of pomposity could sometimes be discerned, there was no trace of it in private. Indeed, in personal conversation he often indulged in an engaging form of self-deprecation, it being understood by those who knew him well that such self-deprecation was not to be taken too seriously. He put a lot of hard work into his friendships, as he did with every activity he cared about, and both gave and received enduring loyalty. Certainly for me, our long friendship was, as Roy himself might have put it, most agreeable. Though the full extent of his abilities may not have been obvious in his undergraduate days, Roy grew over the years into one of the outstanding personalities of his generation—a man of rich and many-sided talent whose urbane wit and civilized values made him a companion of rare worth.

Asa Briggs

Asa Briggs, social and cultural historian, was Vice-Chancellor of the University of Sussex from 1968 to 1976 and Provost of Worcester College, Oxford, from 1976 to 1991. He was Chancellor of the Open University from 1978 to 1994. He is the author of many volumes, including five in the series *The History of Broadcasting in the United Kingdom* (1961–95). In 1976 he was made a life peer.

Chapter 3

Bletchley

Asa Briggs

Bletchley Park, to which Roy moved in April 1944, was a place of secrets, granted great publicity only almost half a century later. It was a site of national importance in the history of Intelligence. Yet the secrecy which had once protected it almost destroyed it, and at the beginning of the 1990s it was in danger of being converted into a housing estate.

It was at Bletchley Park, then in its prime, that I got to know Roy. I had preceded him there by two years, neither of us arriving there directly from our universities, Oxford in his case, Cambridge in mine. The Park, surrounding an ugly and pretentious would-be country house, was conveniently located half-way between the two universities, and was then accessible by rail to both. At its peak around 10,000 people worked there, all pledged to secrecy. They included members of the three Forces, women and men, civilians, and from 1943 Americans. They had been recruited on a personal basis, which, whatever its oddities or its biases, worked well. At the very least they helped Britain to win the war more quickly than it otherwise would have done. Some of its historians and historians of the war have judged that its role in winning the war was decisive.

Neither Roy nor I, neither of us born cipher-breakers, thought in terms of belonging to an elite, and, although we were both dependent on machines, not yet called electronic, as well as on colleagues, we were doing significantly different kinds of cryptographic work at Bletchley, rather more aware of what each other was doing than most people at Bletchley were allowed to be. The code word Ultra was added to the Most Secret security classification on all reports produced within the Park. It was not there, however, that most of the machines were located: they were scattered about the surrounding countryside.

An exception, an absurdly modest way of describing it, was Colossus, forerunner of the post-war digital computer, dependent not on transistors, not yet invented, but on valves, no fewer than 1,500 of them. A prototype was installed on 8 December 1943, the first design having been prepared—at great speed—the previous February. It was with the cooperation of Colossus that Roy's section at Bletchley, the so-called Newmanry, set out to break intercepted Wehrmacht messages.

Max Newman, born in 1897, was Mathematics Fellow at St John's College, Cambridge, from 1923 to 1945. The ciphers he and his colleagues were seeking urgently to break were called, as a group, Fish. Much imagination was applied to naming them: one was called Tunny, another Sturgeon. Newman was exactly the right man in the right place, but the formal name of the section to which Roy was attached was Major Tester's section. For Roy, Tester was a 'shadowy figure, neither much encouraging nor admonishing, nor, indeed, performing great feats of cryptography himself'.

I was just as blunt about some of my own colleagues at Bletchley, who, nonetheless, included some who were as clever and imaginative as Newman, very few of them honoured at the end of the war. The section to which I belonged was the oldest of them. Located in Hut 6, it was concerned through their many vicissitudes with the breaking of Enigma machine ciphers, which have received more attention from historians, playwrights, and novelists than any other. We broke them with the help of the so-called 'bombes', electro-mechanical devices, in a network of outstations, operated mainly by Wrens.

It was Gordon Welchman, Mathematics Fellow at Sidney Sussex College, the Cambridge don who took me to Bletchley, who first clearly appreciated long before I arrived the import-ance of regular organization through 'sections', but there was a cryptographic genius in our background too, Alan Turing, the brilliant figure on whom artistic imagination has played. Backed by Welchman, it was he who devised the 'bombes' which enabled the team of cryptographers in Hut 6, of whom I was one—and we were a real team—to break Enigma messages. We worked in a watch, with shifts from nine to four, four to twelve, and twelve to nine. The length of the stints was sometimes nominal.

I was far more settled and happy in my work with Enigma ciphers at Bletchley than Roy was with Fish. Puma, covering Luftwaffe operations in Yugoslavia, was my favourite 'key'. Nevertheless, Roy's personal position inside Bletchley was dif-ferent from mine in two important respects, one of them which might have been important proving to be surprisingly unim-portant. He was a uniformed officer, I was a Warrant Officer Class I. When I was made one in August 1943, dizzily leaping from the rank of Lance-Corporal, it was because I could not then be spared as a cryptographer to go through officer training, and I was told this face to face by Colonel (later Brigadier) Tiltman, cryptographer as well as chief military officer, for whom I had the highest respect and admiration.

In fact, rank never mattered within Bletchley Park, only outside it, including the adjacent military camp at Shenley Road, commanded by Colonel Fillingham of the Durham Light Infantry, who, to his chagrin, was never allowed himself to go into Bletchley Park. The difference between civilians and uniformed personnel did not matter either. Again to Fillingham's chagrin, we ourselves often wore civilian clothes. I cannot remember seeing in uniform Warrant Officer Class I P. J. H. Solomon-Benenson, later founder of Amnesty.

I personally spent a lot of my leisure time in uniform at another camp, the American camp at Little Brickhill, commanded by Captain William (Bill) Bundy, where I made the first American friends of my life and tasted my first American food and drinks. An adopted little brown dog remains as much the symbol for me of an extremely informal American camp as it is for those Americans who worked there and have survived. Unlike me, Roy already knew Americans when he arrived at Bletchley. He had met them at Balliol. One of them, Philip M. Kaiser, who wrote a lively 'political and diplomatic memoir', *Journeying Far and Wide*, was President of its Junior Common Room before Denis Healey and Roy Jenkins. Neither Roy nor I, however, visited the United States until 1953.

The other difference between Roy and myself in 1943 did matter. Before he arrived at the Park—'Station X' which meant Station Ten—he was already engaged to Jennifer (May 1943), later Dame Jennifer, whom he married on 20 January 1945. And this affected our daily lives. While I delighted, not without a share of cares, in meeting bevies of girls, large numbers from Scotland, whose presence made Bletchley a very different environment from male-dominated Oxford and Cambridge, Roy did not feel the heart throbs that for most of the people working in the Park determined their moods almost as much as their success in 'breaking codes'. (This was the description usually applied then and later to the unlikely occupation in which we were both engaged.)

There were many people at Bletchley who were employed in Intelligence, working to and through the Foreign Office, rather than in breaking codes. They analysed information as well as passed it on. There was no curtain, however, between the Newmanry and Hut 6 or Hut 3, where the 'intelligent' worked, many of them already well-known figures in Oxford, Cambridge, and other universities, but since there was an intelligence dimension to our own work they were required to ask us more questions than we were allowed to ask them. We had no overall picture. Some of them did, and some of them were in communication with 'on high', even with the highest, Winston Churchill. Neither Roy nor I looked in that direction. We had other things to talk about when we met, including memories of our grammar school and university education and, above all, our prospects for the future.

In 1931 Roy himself had been sent to Abersychan Secondary School, later to become a grammar school, not to the better-known West Monmouth School. He never knew why. His father, who became Labour MP for Pontypool in 1935, was a Governor of both institutions. He might well have chosen West Monmouth, for he wanted Roy to go to Oxford, as he had done—and West Monmouth School had far closer ties to Oxford than Abersychan. I had no choice, although Denis Healey, born in Keighley, went not to Keighley Grammar School, as I did, but to Bradford Grammar School. His father was head of the Keighley Technical School, which shared the local Grammar School premises. Denis's wife, Edna, whom he met while at Oxford, taught my sister at Keighley Girls' Grammar School. It was her first teaching appointment.

Denis himself had a completely different Oxford career while at Balliol from Roy, although both were already politicians in a way that I never was or wanted to be. Denis remained dedicated to the Oxford Labour Club, which included Communists: Roy, along with his friend from Trinity College, Anthony Crosland, created a breakaway Oxford University Democratic Socialist Club. Roy's political alignments were markedly different from Denis's, although in Roy's autobiography, *A Life at the Centre*, there is a photograph of the two of them together at a Blackpool Labour Party Conference in May 1945.[1]

There was one political intermediary who had been at school at West Monmouth and who briefly played an important part in both Roy's life and mine in 1943 and 1944: Ivor Thomas, later Ivor Bulmer-Thomas. Born in 1905, the son of a brickyard worker, he had gone up to Oxford, becoming both a mathematical and classical scholar, and in 1935 he had created a minor sensation when he almost defeated the National Liberal politician Sir John (later Lord) Simon, MP for Spen Valley, who thought of himself as a statesman not as a politician: Simon was also an even more important figure in Oxford than he was in Yorkshire.

Ivor Thomas was MP for Keighley during the war—in 1942 he had succeeded a prominent Labour politician, H. B. Lees Smith, who died in office—and he went on to pursue an unusual political career of his own. He left the Labour Party for the Conservatives in 1948, crossing the floor of the House. In a

---

[1] See Illus. 3.

constituency which had produced Philip Snowden, who remained with Ramsay MacDonald in 1931 and became 'Iron Chancellor' in the new National Government, this was treated as a second act of treachery. This was familiar history to me. After the end of afternoon lessons in Keighley Grammar School, I often worked in the Snowden Library, then housed in the Carnegie Public Library opposite the school, in the Library's reference department. Ivor Bulmer-Thomas was to take Roy to a far more famous historical library, that of Benedetto Croce, in Naples in 1952, where Roy met the aged Croce himself. A. D. Lindsay, Master of Balliol when Roy was an undergraduate there, had written an introduction to one of his books.

In January 1945 Ivor Thomas, David Ginsburg, and I were to serve as the 'oddly assorted' trio of ushers, as Roy was later to describe us, at Roy's wedding to Jennifer at the Savoy Chapel. Clement Attlee, whom I then met for the first time, made a highly appropriate speech. I admired him greatly, and saw him on many occasions later in public and in private. Roy was to write his first book, *Mr Attlee*, about him in 1948. In 1945 I had already met Michael Ashcroft, whom Roy had known at Oxford and who worked at Bletchley Park, who was his best man. We all had lunch at Boulestin—along with Roy's parents—before the ceremony. I took to Roy's father at once and found it easy to talk to him. I also liked Jennifer's father, Sir Parker Morris, who was then Town Clerk of Westminster.

Before Roy arrived at Bletchley, Ivor Thomas wrote to me about his impending arrival, warning me, unnecessarily and wrongly, that 'the difference in rank may make acquaintance difficult'. Like me, Roy arrived at Bletchley Park via a curious cryptographic course in Bedford, where, on the eve of tackling complex electronic technology, we were taught about substitution, 'playfair', and a cluster of hand ciphers, some centuries old. Rank mattered just as little there as in the Park itself. My fellow students in 1943 included Alexander Lieven, who, because of his princely Russian origins, was never allowed to work in the Park, and Alexander Hyatt-King, Head of Music in the British Museum, who never wished to do so and escaped Bletchley's clutches.

Roy's included an erudite student from the Museum, Charles Beckingham, whom I got to know and who subsequently became a Professor of Islamic Studies, and, straight from school, Francis Dashwood, a future friend of mine, who emerged from the eighteenth-century Hell-Fire Club setting of West Wycombe Park. The German language figured on the Bedford syllabus, and, like me (and Edward Boyle, another student in my time), Roy was a zealous reader of *Die Zeitung*, the little weekly newspaper published by and for German refugees, none of whom could ever have entered Bletchley Park.

When we were together in the Park, Roy and I talked as much about economics and politics as about history, and I was already co-authoring my first book, *Patterns of Peacemaking*, parts of which he read in proof. I would never have been able to forecast that he would subsequently become a lively writer of historical biographies, some of which were to become best-sellers. One of the economists whom we frequently discussed was Keynes, whom we had both read before we joined the Forces—I as part of the preparations for a London B.Sc. (Econ.) degree which in utmost pre-Bletchley secrecy I took in the summer of 1941 in parallel with my Historical Tripos. If I had revealed my intentions inside Sidney Sussex College, I would never have been allowed to proceed with it.

Roy and I did discuss Harold Laski together, however, for with him contemporary politics and the academic study of politics converged, and I had been in correspondence with Laski after winning the Gerstenberg Studentship for the London School of Economics in 1941. Before that I had heard him lecturing to crowded Saturday morning audiences, including lots of 'housewives', in Mill Lane in Cambridge. Roy had attended no lectures in Oxford after his first year, although he was taught by, among others, G. D. H. Cole, academic socialist, who had nothing in common with Laski, and John Fulton, who was to be Principal of the then University College of Sussex when I joined it as its first academic appointment in 1960.

The first post-war university college, Keele, was founded by Lindsay, who was Master of Balliol from 1924 to 1949 and who was another of Roy's tutors. Whether or not he was responsible for opening the gates of Bletchley Park to Roy—and I do not believe that he was—he provided an atmosphere in Balliol which allowed Roy as an undergraduate fully to develop his talents. Nonetheless, he was disappointed that, despite his First, Roy's mark in general philosophy, which Lindsay had taught him, was the lowest any Balliol undergraduate had received since the introduction of Modern Greats in 1924.

Roy was able to tell me much about Modern Greats (economics, politics, and philosophy) when I was considering in the autumn of 1944 whether to accept a Fellowship in Modern Greats at Worcester College, Oxford. The comparative advantages and disadvantages of an academic career figured in much of our talk together. But so, too, did the comparative advantages and disadvantages of a political career. Roy, like his father before him, but in very different circumstances, was determined to pursue one. Oxford, where he shone in the Union without becoming President, had prepared him for it. Cambridge had never impelled me in the same way. I played too much bridge with two mathematicians and another historian to have an undergraduate political career there. One of the mathematicians was Howard Smith, who preceded me to Bletchley and after the war turned to diplomacy and finally intelligence again. We were all academically ambitious, however, and, after coming to the conclusion that bridge was holding us back, dramatically threw away our packs of cards. Nevertheless, politics interested me and, indeed, could arouse me, and in 1944, watched over by Ivor Thomas, I received several letters from constituency Labour parties inviting me to become a candidate for their seats, some of which I might well have won at the next general election. I fully understood Roy's motives and aspirations, but, unlike him, I had only just become a member of the Labour Party in 1944—and it was a brief membership—though I had been pursued by Hugh Dalton, who took an intense interest in young servicemen whom he liked the look of and in whom he put his political trust.

Roy has described in his own autobiographical accounts how he failed to win the nomination for Aston—he was beaten by Woodrow Wyatt, a Worcester College man—and for Sparkbrook, a safe Labour seat, where he was beaten by one vote by a local alderman. He also failed to win nomination for Moseley and, further away, Middlesbrough. Instead at the end of April 1945, while still at Bletchley, he was offered what proved to be an unwinnable constituency, Solihull, where he was adopted on 3 June. He spent five weeks before polling day holding well-attended schoolroom meetings, in the process becoming more and more sanguine about his prospects. I helped him in the campaign, particularly in its last stages, for the only time in my life using a megaphone to address passers-by from a party van, telling electors that they had not had the chance of a vote for ten years and that now was the time for them to use it. I was also the last speaker at Roy's eve of poll meeting in July, 'holding on' when the candidate did not arrive at the planned time.

I felt almost as deflated as Roy did, although I knew how much it meant to him, when he was defeated by around 5,000 votes—around 26,000 to 21,000—by a good Conservative candidate. By then, with rooms in Worcester College, I was preparing for my Class B release from the Army, which came just in time for me to arrive in college for the beginning of the new Michaelmas term. I had already left Bletchley in July, not without a touch of irony, to join Colonel Fillingham as a 'real RSM' at a new Army Formation College, preparing soldiers for civilian life. It was not far from Bedford, so that in a sense my wheel had come full circle.

Roy stayed in the Army at Bletchley until 1 January 1946, and I saw him on more than one occasion in Oxford in the interval before our ways diverged. He was busy reading all the biographies he could while still 'a politician without a profession'; and with a further touch of irony by the time that he won Stechford, Birmingham, a secure seat, in February 1950—with a majority of 12,400—I was already engaged in writing volume II of *A History of Birmingham*, which was to appear two years later.

Alan Watkins

Photo: Express Newspapers

Alan Watkins was born in 1933 and educated at Amman Valley Grammar School and Queens' College, Cambridge. He has been a journalist since 1959, writing political columns successively for the *Sunday Express* (as 'Crossbencher'), *The Spectator*, the *New Statesman*, the *Sunday Mirror*, *The Observer*, and the *Independent on Sunday*. He has also written *The Liberal Dilemma* (1966), *Brief Lives* (1982), *Sportswriter's Eye* (1989), *A Slight Case of Libel* (1990), *A Conservative Coup* (1991), *The Road to Number 10* (1998), *A Short Walk Down Fleet Street* (2000), and, jointly, *The Making of the Prime Minister 1970* (1970).

Chapter 4

Backbencher

ALAN WATKINS

In the summer of 1959 I was 26 years old and had just started to work for the *Sunday Express*. My duties were ill-defined. I was not an ordinary reporter. I was, I suppose, a very junior feature writer. Clearly, however, I was not as junior as all that: in my very first week on the paper, without previous journalistic experience of any kind, I had been required to write the political 'Crossbencher' column, then in its silver age, because the regular author of the column, Wilfred Sendall, was on holiday, and the editor of the paper, John Junor, had forgotten about his short absence. I would go down to the House of Commons on Tuesday, Wednesday, and Thursday afternoons and was more or less Sendall's deputy, continuing to write the column in his absence until I took it over completely in 1963.

It was in these circumstances that I decided to ask Roy Jenkins to lunch. He was then 38, usually described in the papers as an 'economist', but best known as the author of *Mr Balfour's Poodle*, which was about the battle between

Asquith's government and the House of Lords before 1914, and *Dilke*, about the Victorian politician who became involved in a sexual–political scandal involving Joe Chamberlain on its periphery. He was also known to be a friend of the Labour leader, Hugh Gaitskell. The phrase 'the Hampstead set' was not then in general use, referring as it did to Gaitskell and political friends of his who would meet from time to time at his house in Frognal Gardens, London NW3. It was to see the light of day in one of Sendall's 'Crossbencher' columns only a few months after my lunch with Roy. In any event, it was thought Roy would occupy a fairly prominent position in any government formed by Gaitskell after the election, which was due in the autumn and in which Labour was expected—not only by its own supporters—to stand an excellent chance.

While Roy shared this general optimism, which turned out to be unfounded, he did not expect any great political reward from Gaitskell, or so he subsequently told us. He wrote this, admittedly, about the period in the early 1960s when Gaitskell was still alive and was expected to be the next Prime Minister, even though he had failed to win the 1959 election. But there is no reason to suppose that Roy's feelings about his prospects under Gaitskell were very different before 1959. This was not, however, the view of his colleagues or of observers of the political scene. We all thought he would go far. This was not the main reason I asked him to lunch. I asked him principally because he had the reputation also of being an interesting and amusing politician. His reputation for lunch was, I think, less well developed then than later. It was not that he did not enjoy a good (though preferably simple) meal, accompanied by a generous quantity of wine and a congenial companion. But these were less puritan times. A politician of the day— Anthony Crosland, Richard Crossman, Denis Healey, and

Iain Macleod come to mind—would think nothing of enjoying a large aperitif beforehand, sharing a bottle of wine with the meal and having some brandy afterwards with his coffee. He would then go either to the House of Commons or to his department, where he would put in a long afternoon's work or, if he went to the House, even make a speech. Tomato juice and mineral water and, much worse, the bringing along of press officers, came in during the 1980s, to the detriment of politics and journalism alike. Roy belonged to an earlier and better age.

We met at L'Épicure restaurant in Frith Street, Soho. It was owned by two Cypriots who wore back coats and striped trousers and did rather good generalized continental food, with much flourishing of spirit flames. Roy was wearing an expensive, heavy blue suit, a Paisley silk tie with a metal tie-clip (even then going out of fashion, and sported by Tories such as Peter Thorneycroft), and a blue shirt with upturned collar-points and gold cufflinks. This, I was to discover, was his customary garb. In particular, he made no concessions to the weather. Rain or shine, it was all the same to Roy. If it was warm—the summer of 1959 was warm—he tended to be overheated. And his clothes, good though they were, always seemed too tight for him. Yet the general impression he conveyed was of assurance and ease. It was only gradually I discovered that he was quite shy, giving his confidence to someone only if he had known that person for a long time.

Junor had several principles of lunching, which he conveyed to the younger members of his staff whether they asked for them or not. One was always to order from the table d'hôte menu, because that would shame one's guest into doing likewise, so saving the company money. L'Épicure, though it was one of Junor's favourite resorts, had no such menu. To start with, Roy ordered half an avocado pear, in those days still a somewhat exotic commodity. When it arrived, its surface bore some brownish streaks. It looked more or less all right to me. Roy was less pleased. 'Do you mind', he said, 'if I send this back? I think it's seen better days.' 'Not in the least,' I said, affecting an insouciance I was far from feeling, for Roy was the first politician I had taken to lunch and I was not sure how best to proceed in the circumstances. There was no need to worry, because he assumed control of the proceedings with complete confidence. 'Could you possibly ... better days ... thank you so much ...' An exchange was offered with no further trouble. About the wine he made no fuss at all. Another of Junor's principles of lunch was to have no truck with vintages or wine waiters but to order the house wine, red or white but on no account rosé: 'Only poofs drink rosé.' Crosland used to say, 'Let's leave the vintages to Roy', before requesting a carafe of the house wine or a bottle of retsina, which he liked because it reminded him of holidays in Greece.

We talked about Harold Wilson and Iain Macleod. Politicians commonly talk about people rather than about detailed policies or large and general notions, and Roy was no exception. He enjoyed a good gossip about who was up and who was down. Neither Wilson nor Macleod, he predicted, would ever lead his own party, and for exactly the same reason in both cases: both inspired distrust among their colleagues. About Macleod he was probably right. Wilson proved Roy wrong in 1963, when he comprehensively defeated George Brown and James Callaghan after the death of Hugh Gaitskell. There is no doubt that Wilson was distrusted, by Roy and his friends and by much of the party as well. On 13 August 1959 Crossman records in his diary that he had said he was 'sick' of 'anti-Harold talk' by Roy and others. Gaitskell replied that Roy was 'very much in the social swim these days'. He was 'sometimes anxious about him and young Tony [Crosland]. We, as middle-class socialists, have got to have a profound humility.' That was 'all right for us in the upper middle class, but Tony and Roy are not upper and I sometimes feel they don't have a proper humility to [sic] ordinary working people'.

Clearly, class-consciousness flourished in the Labour Party as luxuriantly as it did elsewhere. Gaitskell and Crossman had both been to Winchester; their fathers had been, respectively, a senior colonial civil servant and a High Court judge. Crosland had been at Highgate and Jenkins at Abersychan Secondary School; their fathers, respectively, a senior home civil servant and a coal-miner who had become a union official, a Labour MP, and parliamentary private secretary to the Leader of the party, Clement Attlee. In Labour terms it was manifestly Roy who was the aristocrat. His father had been not only a miner but a Welsh miner. He had even been to gaol for sedition. Neither then, at the beginning of his parliamentary career, nor later, when he stood a chance of becoming Leader of the Labour Party, did Roy exploit this background for his own ends. He was adversely criticized for this reticence in a kind of pincer attack. On the one side, people would say he was positively foolish in not making greater use—in fact he made no use at all—of a valuable asset. As one ambitious Labour MP put the matter to me, 'If my father had been a Welsh miner who'd gone to prison you wouldn't have heard the end of it.' On the other side, he was attacked for renouncing his background for snobbish reasons. The story went that at Oxford, when he was asked where he came from, he used to reply, 'The Marches.'

What is indisputable is that he had the highest regard for Arthur Jenkins, and would often pay him tribute in conversation. He was, Roy would say, a highly cultivated man who could speak French better than his son ever managed to do. He was also a generous man. Because Roy had attended a Welsh local government school, followed by a brief spell at University College, Cardiff, and had clearly been a clever boy, it was generally assumed that he had won a scholarship to Balliol. Not at all, Roy said. At a time when local authorities were not as generous as they subsequently became, his father paid the fees. In April 1946 he died at the relatively early age of 64. Roy was overwhelmed by grief. This did not, however, prevent him from putting in for his father's seat at Pontypool. He reached the shortlist and was one of the last two, but the nomination went to a local solicitor, D. Granville West, who duly won the by-election.

Roy remained determined to get into the House as soon as he could. A vacancy arose in Southwark Central. Owing to redistribution, this seat was to disappear before the general election, to be replaced by a combined seat incorporating Southwark Central. The member for this seat was George Isaacs, Minister of Labour in the Attlee government. Anxious to secure the nomination for the new seat, Isaacs persuaded the London Labour Party to lay down that whoever was chosen to fight the by-election should undertake not to contest the nomination for the new seat. Roy gave this promise. 'Only someone as crazed as I was to get into the House of Commons, and also, in a curious way, as confident of his ability ultimately to fall on his feet, was likely to be attracted. Few were,' Roy recalled in his memoirs. He won the by-election on a reduced turnout, and was an MP by the early afternoon of 30 April 1948. He remembered 'feeling at a loose end, although contentedly so'. On the following Tuesday he was introduced into the House of Commons by the London area whip, which was usual, and by the Prime Minister, which was not. He was only

27 and the youngest member, a position he was to retain until displaced by Sir Edward Boyle in November 1950.

Inevitably he was labelled an Attlee loyalist. Not only had his father been parliamentary private secretary to Attlee: he had also recently published *Mr Attlee: An Interim Biography*. This, Roy's first proper book, is a perfectly respectable piece of work within its self-evident limitations: the family connection and Attlee's happily continuing survival. But though Roy was in no sense disloyal, his heroes of the period were Sir Stafford Cripps and Ancurin Bevan. Cripps was the Iron Chancellor, rich but ascetic (his self-denial brought about partly by ill health), a former hero of the Left who had helped finance their local paper, *Tribune*, and had, with Bevan, been expelled from the party before the war for his advocacy of the popular front. He was something of a national hero, too, admired for his integrity while mocked on the music-hall stage and elsewhere for an alleged fondness for carrot juice. His wife, shortly to become his widow, Isobel, Lady Cripps, used to have a regular Thursday appointment for afternoon tea with Hugh Massingham, the admired political columnist of *The Observer*, when she would divulge party secrets which would find their way into print.

For a lengthy part of his early political life—it was no mere passing phase—Roy was a convinced, even a dogmatic, egalitarian. He believed in redistributive taxation, achieved not only through income tax but through a capital levy as well. He published a *Tribune* pamphlet entitled *Fair Shares for the Rich: The Case for a Capital Levy* (1951). The title was thought up by Michael Foot. Roy, though (or perhaps because) he was a careful and sensitive writer, would not have possessed the journalistic headline-writing skill required to assemble those particular words. His essay 'Equality', in *New Fabian Essays*

(1952), has the same theme. It begins: 'The desire for greater equality has been part of the inspiration of all socialist thinkers and of all socialist movements.' He even devoted a large part of his maiden speech on 3 June 1948 to the same subject, when he defended Cripps's 'special contribution', a form of capital levy. It was, he said,

a question of righting the balance and putting rather more on the shoulders of the rich, who were looked after so well by successive Conservative governments, and putting less on the shoulders of the poor, who were not so well looked after by the same . . . governments. If the Labour government abandoned this policy in its financial plan it would not only be politically foolish but morally wrong and socially unjust.

In his memoirs in 1991 Roy described his *Tribune* pamphlet as

the apogee of my excursion to the left, not particularly because of the *Tribune* association, but much more because of the almost Robespierrean nature of its contents. It was a harsh and rigid doctrine which I preached, and one which now seems to me (as it would have for at least three decades past) to pay little or no regard to historical continuity or to the organic relationships of society, let alone to that now overworked concept of incentive.

And yet, in the 1950s and for long after, being in favour of high taxation, whether of capital or of income, was by no means a sufficient condition of being on the left in internal Labour Party terms. On the contrary, the Left believed in nationalization, in a foreign policy independent of the United States, and in Bevan as leader of the party in preference to Gaitskell. It was the Right who adopted redistributive taxation as proof of their socialist spirit, together with a planned economy and a reform of the education system. The Left had never been specially interested in this last subject, regarding it as an obsession of guilt-infested, middle-class socialists which diverted them from matters of greater concern to the workers. Nor, come to that, did the Left or the Bevanites—for present purposes the terms may be regarded as interchangeable—worry themselves unduly, or, indeed, at all, with the details of how existing nationalized industries should be modified or how further nationalization should be carried out. That was left to figures such as Crosland and Austen Albu. The Bevanites were content to demand further nationalization—the favoured candidates varied from party conference to party conference—while simultaneously lamenting one aspect of the administration of the existing nationalized industries. This was that they tended to be run by former captains of industry or soldiers of the Queen. It was high time, the Left would say, for 'our people' to be put in charge: a sentiment guaranteed to win long and pro-longed applause at the conference.

So at the time there was nothing specially leftist about favouring high taxation, as Roy did. As he wrote in his memoirs of his contribution to *New Fabian Essays*:

It was revisionist in . . . the Gaitskell–Crosland sense of the 1950s in that it treated nationalisation as a secondary question, unimportant for its own sake, although probably a necessary concomitant of a further advance to equality. The essay was also incipiently Gaitskellite by virtue of its dismissal of Communism as having nothing to do with equality either in theory or in practice.

Even so, at the beginning of his long parliamentary life Roy was attracted to Bevan. Bevan was then, it should be remem-bered, not a troublesome figure in opposition whose object was to topple the leader of his party but a highly regarded Minister of Health. He 'was not nearly so physically remote [as Cripps]', Roy recalled in his memoirs, although in a more florid way he was just as disdainful. He must have been very quick in the discharge of official business (and he was by no means a bad administrator), for he sat in the smoking room nearly every parliamentary day from 5.30 until 7.30 or 8.00 expatiating to a large circle of intimates and would-be intimates on politics and life. I, for a time, joined the category of would-be intimates.

Roy thought Bevan was 'petulant and vain' but 'on the frontier of being a great man'. He regretted not having known him better, he remarked in his review of the first volume of Michael Foot's life of Bevan in 1962. The period of admiration on Roy's part came to an end with Bevan's resignation from the government in April 1951 (he had been Minister of Labour since January of that year). Two junior ministers, Harold Wilson and John Freeman, resigned with him. Roy regarded Bevan's behaviour towards both the government and the Chancellor, Gaitskell, as intolerable. Bevan's motive in behaving as he did was almost certainly his anger—'pique' is too weak and loaded a word—at being leapfrogged by Gaitskell in the party queue of seniority. The reasons which he gave for his action varied from speech to speech. Nevertheless, what it is fair to take as his real reason (as distinct from his real motive) was valid then and remains persuasive today. It was not so much charging in the National Health Service ('teeth and specs'), but rather the level of rearmament in 1950–1 undertaken in response to the Korean War, which had made such charging necessary. Roy and Crosland had both of them supported the rearmament programme. Forty years later Roy would admit that the rearmament had been 'perhaps excessive'. Others arrived earlier at the same conclusion, which is now fairly generally accepted.

The events of 1951 were to turn Roy into a convinced follower and friend of Gaitskell. It was the most important political relationship of his life. Before this came about, he had been compelled to find a seat. He made several false starts, met with various rebuffs, suffered a minor nervous breakdown, and took himself off to a psychiatrist, who, he related in his memoirs, 'thought that I might nonetheless survive for a normal span provided that I led a quiet life'. It was doubtful whether the life of a Labour MP favoured such a prospect. The possibility that he might not be one for very much longer was what brought about the visit to the psychiatrist in the first place. But Roy found a resting place at Stechford, Birmingham, which he won in the general election of 1950 and continued to represent until January 1977. He was a popular and, in an old-fashioned way, an assiduous Member, paying monthly rather than weekly visits to the constituency. He once said to a fellow Labour MP for the city as their train to London was pulling out of New Street station, 'Don't you always feel an enormous sense of relief at this point?'

Before the 1951 election Roy had briefly been parliamentary private secretary to Philip Noel-Baker, Secretary of State for Commonwealth Relations, not because he was at that stage of his life interested in foreign affairs or, still less, in the Commonwealth, but because he wanted to get his foot inside the door of a real ministry. He did not foresee—few did—that he would spend thirteen years in opposition, mostly on the backbenches. He continued to make regular interventions in the House on financial matters. These were still egalitarian in tone. He denounced the 1952 Budget as probably the first of the century deliberately to increase the purchasing power of 'the fairly well-to-do' and to reduce that of the 'lower income group'. In 1954 he introduced a motion opposing takeover bids (then coming into a fashion that lasted for the rest of the century) and calling for an inquiry.

In this earlier period of backbench opposition he was also

active as an opponent of Bevanism, though Bevan himself he continued to treat with a wary respect. With Anthony Crosland, Douglas Jay, Patrick Gordon Walker, Woodrow Wyatt, and the whole Shadow Cabinet—which included Hugh Gaitskell—he voted for stern measures to be taken against the '57 varieties' who had rebelled against the official line on defence in March 1952. When, a year after this episode, Crossman complained to him about the lack of freedom of speech inside the party, he replied (according to Crossman's diary) that he and his friends felt that 'every speech' and 'every action' must now be considered as 'part of the power fight' within the party. That was why they hated Bevanism. Before it began, one could have free speech. Now, the party could no longer afford it. He and his friends felt that 'every force of demagogy' and 'every emotion' were against them. In the constituency parties, which were now 'opposition-minded', the Bevanites had it all their own way. Perhaps one had to wait for the tide to turn, as it did in the 1930s, away from the 'opposition-mindedness' of 1931 towards 'constructive' policies. 'The electorate is extremely Conservative-minded and we can never win except with the kind of attitude represented by the right-wing leadership.'

Crossman was an unreliable ally but, as far as I have been able to confirm, an accurate recorder of events. The revisionist view of the 1930s sounds characteristic of Roy. Equally, there was a feeling of being placed at an unfair disadvantage on account, not only of Bevan's oratorical prowess, but also of the journalistic skill of *Tribune*, Foot, Crossman, and Driberg (though the last two wrote for other publications). Indeed, *Forward*, originally a publication supporting the Independent Labour Party, was reinvigorated as a weekly paper supporting the Gaitskellites, specifically as a counterweight to *Tribune*. The

Gaitskellites were specially obsessed by *Tribune* and would encourage the circulation of (entirely true) stories about Foot's admiration for and friendship with Lord Beaverbrook and the flow of journalists from *Tribune* to Express Newspapers, as exemplified by the careers of Robert Pitman and Robert Edwards.

Roy's exertions on behalf of Gaitskell ceased when he was, in Roy's phrase, 'safely elected' as Leader of the party in December 1955. It was a more comprehensive victory than most people had expected, with Gaitskell obtaining an absolute majority on the first ballot, which made further ballots unnecessary: he received 157 votes to Bevan's disappointing 70 and Herbert Morrison's pitiable 40. In 1953 Spedan Lewis read a slim volume which Roy had published in that year, *Pursuit of Progress*, was impressed by it, and invited him to join the John Lewis Partnership as an adviser, a position he retained throughout his period of opposition, ending up as a director of financial operations of the company. The connection was not rewarded munificently, but it enabled Roy and his wife, Jennifer, to live more comfortably than they would have been able to if they had relied on his parliamentary salary and on his books and journalism.

Roy by then had a regular column in an Indian paper at £5 an article. He contributed several pieces to *The Spectator*, in what was perhaps its golden age, when it was owned by Ian Gilmour, as it was for most of the time Roy was in opposition. He was a friend of both Gilmour and his wife, Caroline, but his articles would have been worth the space irrespective of the claims of friendship. In any case, editors and, though perhaps to a lesser extent, proprietors are immune from sentimentality in this respect. Another friend, David Astor, editor and proprietor of *The Observer*, persuaded him to try his hand at longer pieces, of investigation rather than comment, as well as book reviews (which had previously been Roy's strong suit, as they were Crossman's likewise). The subject he first investigated was the takeover fight involving Courtaulds and ICI. The fruit of his labours was a Granada *What the Papers Say* award, which came as a genuine surprise to him (and he was not given to false modesty). His last excursion in this genre was into the British aircraft industry and its tribulations. More than any other factor, this was responsible for Wilson's appointment of him as Minister of Aviation in 1964.

But it is by his books that Roy would want to be judged. The title of *Mr Balfour's Poodle* was criticized by Randolph Churchill for 'frivolity'—usually a charge levelled against others by Anthony Crosland. It derived from a sentence of Lloyd George's to the effect that the House of Lords was not the watchdog of the constitution but Mr Balfour's poodle. The book was accordingly placed in the 'Pets' section of several bookshops, the sales no doubt benefiting thereby. *Dilke*, his next book, had its genesis at a dinner in the House after the publication party for *Mr Balfour's Poodle*. The guests, besides Jennifer, were Caroline and Anthony Wedgwood Benn, as he still called himself, who naturally, in view of his possible accession to a peerage, took a great interest in the affairs of the Upper House. Mark Bonham Carter, unhyphenated and yet to become Liberal MP for Torrington—he adopted the hyphen to appear above his principal rival on the ballot paper—was working for Collins the publishers and having dinner with someone else. Roy did not then know him well but later came to know him and his wife, Leslie, much better. Bonham Carter suggested the Dilke project, which attracted Roy because he was keen to begin a new book and had fallen out with his publishers, Heinemann. The *froideur* had arisen because Roy had agreed to write the life of Ernest Bevin, only to find that Arthur Deakin, the General Secretary of Bevin's union, the then mighty Transport and General Workers', expected to be able to censor its contents. He had gone so far as to nominate a friendly labour correspondent to help in the enterprise; to become effective though unacknowledged co-author. No self-respecting writer would put up with such terms. In addition Alan Bullock had appeared on the scene as a possible biographer of Bevin (as he later became). Heinemann seemed to regard him more favourably than they did Roy, who withdrew from the project, to general relief and happy consequences all round.

The deserved success of *Dilke* encouraged him to write another biography. He wanted a bigger subject, preferably a Prime Minister from the radical or, at least, the progressive side. He lighted on H. H. Asquith, the last Liberal Prime Minister, for though the title is often bestowed on Lloyd George, the Welshman was Prime Minister of two successive coalition governments between 1916 and 1922. There had been a substantial 'life and letters' biography of Asquith by his son Cyril and the journalist J. A. Spender. And Asquith had written two perhaps undervalued volumes of memoirs. Certainly Roy did not think much of them. Whatever their merits, there was no modern biography and Roy set to work with the active encouragement of Asquith's daughter Lady Violet Bonham Carter and her son Mark, whose firm again published the book.

Lady Violet played the role traditionally assigned to the widow of the deceased subject. She treated him with some imperiousness, not calling him 'Mr Jenkins', still less 'Roy', but 'Mr Roy Jenkins', as in 'Mr Roy Jenkins, I believe I left my bag in the other room. Would you be so kind as to fetch it for me?' There was no scandal involving Asquith such as that which had overtaken Dilke. Nevertheless, there were various aspects of Asquith's life over which he would have to tread delicately: his probably platonic affair with a friend of Violet's, Venetia Stanley, who married one of his Cabinet colleagues, Edwin Montagu; his sexual importunity towards young women generally in his later years; not perhaps least, his excessive drinking, remarked upon in the George Robey number:

> Mr Asquith says in a manner sweet and calm.
> Another little drink won't do us any harm.

Over all these matters truth battled with tact, and tact invariably won, though Roy was never untruthful.

He served the cause of books, even of literature, in another way. He was responsible for the Obscene Publications Act of 1959. The genesis of this measure lay in five cases in 1954. Reputable publishers and equally reputable novelists were prosecuted for obscenity. There had been two convictions, two acquittals, and on one book the jury had twice disagreed. The bill was drafted mainly by Norman St John-Stevas, a young barrister and author of a highly regarded work, *Obscenity and the Law*. The bill sought to correct various defects. The law was uncertain. The intention of the author was irrelevant: he or she could not be asked about it. No defence was possible on grounds of literary or artistic merit. No expert evidence could be called. There was no clarity about whether isolated passages were to be judged; or was it the general effect? And no maximum penalty was laid down.

For five years, from 1954 to 1959, Roy pursued the issue. He was helped by others: Hugh Fraser and Lord Lambton, who sponsored successive versions of the bill; the broadsheet press, which showed an uncommon and perhaps surprising liberalism; the Society of Authors, which acted as a pressure group.

He was helped most of all by Sir Alan Herbert, the Society's chairman, and by the new Home Secretary, R.A. Butler. There was to be a by-election in the Harrow East constituency, which was held by the Conservatives. Herbert announced his intention of standing as an Independent if the government did not modify its obstructive attitude towards the bill. Moreover, he made clear, he would be standing as a kind of Independent Conservative, supporting the government in most areas except that of law reform. Butler's attitude changed immediately, partly because, up to a point, he agreed with Roy, and partly because he got on with him. The bill's sponsors obtained most of what they wanted and the bill duly became law. Most of the credit belongs to Roy.

In 1957–64 [Roy wrote in his memoirs] my position in the political hierarchy hardly advanced at all. I was elected neither to the Shadow Cabinet nor to the National Executive Committee of the Labour Party. I occupied a very minor front bench position for a few months or so, but resigned from it in irritation at a suggestion that it should inhibit me from speaking unequivocally (from a back bench) about Britain's membership of the Common Market.

Roy was being untypically modest about his contribution to politics after 1955, the year when, with Gaitskell now leader, he perhaps surprisingly interested himself less in the House of Commons. He remained close to Gaitskell, and helped him in his unsuccessful campaign against Clause IV of the party constitution, even though he was opposed to that choice of battle and would have preferred the clear rejection of specific proposals for nationalization or renationalization. Though he was a late convert to Europe, he had, since 1961, been the leading campaigner outside the Conservative Party (then in pro-European mode) for British entry into the Common Market.

He was dismayed by Gaitskell's rejection of entry at the Brighton Conference of 1962, though it did not affect his personal liking for him. He was devastated by Gaitskell's death only a few months later, at the beginning of 1963. He could summon up little enthusiasm for George Brown as a potential successor, and even less for his duly elected successor, Wilson.

There then came an offer to edit *The Economist*. Roy was temped to accept, for it was a paper of influence, particularly in the United States, despite (or perhaps because of) a certain cocksureness of tone which it was prone to adopt, particularly about subjects of which it was largely ignorant. Perhaps that would have changed under Roy's regimen. But first, before making any decision, he had to learn what, if anything, Wilson had in store for him, for it was then, in 1964, generally assumed that Wilson would shortly be propelled into Downing Street with a large majority (which he did not obtain, as it turned out). But Roy did not know what Wilson's plans for him were. The wife of the former French ambassador, on whom Roy called in Paris on his way back from a holiday further south, suggested, 'Why not ask him and find out?' On his return to London, this is what he proceeded to do. Wilson was highly impressed by the *Economist* offer—more impressed, Roy thought, than Gaitskell would have been—but he wanted to form the strongest possible government, of which Roy would inevitably and rightly be a member. At the same time Roy discovered that the paper's offer was not as firm as it had first seemed. He was more the journalists' choice than that of the top people. In particular that paladin of laissez-faire economics, Lord Robbins, the Chairman of the Board, was uneasy at the prospect of Roy as editor.

I had by then advanced from my earlier position when I had entertained Roy to lunch at L'Épicure and was writing the

'Crossbencher' column on a regular basis. I had wind of the *Economist* offer and put it to him over the telephone. He denied it, said there was no truth in it. Maybe the offer had by now already trickled into the sand. I did not bear the slightest resentment. But the episode clearly weighed on Roy's mind. For years afterwards he would refer to it, apologize for it, and say that, in the circumstances, he could have adopted no other course. I did not demur. He was an honourable politician and a decent man.

ROY HATTERSLEY

Roy Hattersley is a politician-turned-writer. Elected to Parliament in 1964, he served in Jim Callaghan's Cabinet and was Deputy Leader of the Labour Party from 1983 to 1992. He was made a life peer in 1997. He has written 'Endpiece', his *Guardian* column, for over twenty years, as well as contributing to *The Times*, *The Observer*, and the *Daily Mail*. He is the author of fifteen books, including *Who Goes Home?* (1995), *A Yorkshire Boyhood* (1983), *Blood and Fire* (1999), and *A Brand from the Burning* (2002; a biography of John Wesley). In 2003 he became a Fellow of the Royal Society of Literature.

Chapter 5

Birmingham

R OY H ATTERSLEY

The relationship—intense if not passionate, loyal while it lasted—began inauspiciously. On his first visit to Birmingham, Roy Jenkins, like so many visitors to the city, lost his way. And the enterprise which took him to the West Midlands ended in failure. In the summer of 1937 Dick Crossman, then a Fellow of New College, Oxford, was the Labour candidate in the by-election which had followed the death of Austen Chamberlain. Arthur Jenkins— President of the Welsh miners' union, member of the Labour Party's National Executive, and Member of Parliament for Pontypool—supported Crossman at one of his public meetings and young Roy, on holiday from Abersychan Secondary School, went along with his father for the experience and the ride. His map-reading did not prove up to the task of navigating Birmingham's notorious one-way system. And Crossman lost. But the city impressed itself on Roy Jenkins's young mind. A couple of months before he died, he expressed his astonishment at my inability—despite representing a Birmingham seat for over thirty-three years—to feel exalted by my association with the whole conurbation, rather than just the fraction of it that I thought of as mine.

The enchantment which was born during that first visit survived the war. A few months before the end of hostilities, Captain Jenkins of the Royal Artillery offered himself as Labour candidate for Aston. He was on the losing side again. Woodrow Wyatt was chosen to fight (and win) the seat in 1945.

According to Birmingham folklore, Jenkins lost because he chose to spend the night before the selection conference, with Jennifer Morris (soon to become Mrs Jenkins) in a city centre hotel. Wyatt stayed with a party worthy. It was a mistake which Jenkins was careful never to repeat. After 1950, within three weeks of becoming the prospective Labour candidate for Stechford, he arranged to lodge, during his visits to the city, with Austin and Dora (Dink) Hitchman in 'a small but comfortably furnished semi-detached house . . . in the heart of the constituency'. The friendship endured and survived Jenkins's resignation from the Labour Party and foundation of the SDP. Dink remained Labour. But her devotion to Jenkins—a guest in her home in good times and bad—remains strong. She never asked for payment. Jenkins thought that to offer it would be to make her his landlady rather than his friend.

Despite the rebuff of Aston, Birmingham retained its attraction. So Jenkins turned his attention to Sparkbrook, the seat of Leo Amery, the Secretary of State for India and the last of the radical imperialists. The constituency preferred Percy Shurmer, a city councillor, co-operative society insurance agent, and the organizer of a children's choir (called The Snowdrops) which sang at old people's outings and chapel socials.

With the general election only weeks away, Jenkins wisely decided that it was better to fight in a Tory stronghold than not to fight at all. He became candidate for Solihull, lost by 5,000 votes, and was established as a figure in the West Midlands Labour Party.

There followed a brief metropolitan interlude when Roy Jenkins became first the Labour candidate in the Southwark by-election and then the Member of Parliament for that constituency. But he knew, from the start, that it was only a temporary refuge. The Boundary Commission had decreed that Southwark must be wiped off the political map. If he was to remain an MP after 1950, it was necessary for him to find another seat. Birmingham came to his rescue.

During his candidature in Solihull, Roy Jenkins had become a friend of Jim Cattermole, a Birmingham party organizer. Indeed, they became so close that, when Cattermole moved to Labour headquarters at Transport House in London, he lived with the Jenkinses until he found suitable accommodation. Cattermole had retained his connections with the West Midlands. He proved an invaluable guide when a new constituency—proposed by the Boundary Commission, which had extinguished Central Southwark—was to be created in Birmingham. It was to be called Stechford.

A sitting Member of Parliament—Wesley Perrins, a Black Country trade union official of the old school—had first claim on the seat. For Stechford was to be largely made up of Yardley, the constituency which he had represented since 1945. But Perrins did not enjoy Parliament. Indeed he was almost certainly one of those Members—like Percy Shurmer of Sparkbrook—who had fought the 1945 general election in the certainty that they could not win. In 1949 he was offered the chance of becoming the regional secretary of his union—

the Municipal and General Workers. After some weeks of doubt and hesitation, he decided to leave Westminster.

Perrins's decision to leave the Stechford seat vacant was Roy Jenkins's first piece of good fortune. The second was the inclusion, within Stechford's boundaries, of suburbs which had been part of the Solihull constituency. Within that small, middle-class area lived Joseph Balmer, a city councillor and solicitor who was to go on to be alderman, Lord Mayor, and knight. Balmer had known and admired Jenkins in Solihull and was—as an influential member of the new seat—as crucial to his selection in Stechford as Jim Cattermole. Jenkins was selected as candidate on the second ballot. He, and that constituency, lived happily—if not quite ever after, at least for twenty-seven years.

Part of the rapport between Jenkins and his constituency was the result of his ability to make and keep friends. Cattermole drove Balmer to Jenkins's country house for a celebration of Sir Joseph's eightieth birthday in 1992. Dink Hitchman took Jenkins on a tour of the new Birmingham before he wrote his chapter on the city for his book *Twelve Cities* (2002). But his enduring popularity—at times when he was, at best, a controversial figure with most Labour activists—was the result of the seriousness, indeed solemnity, with which he treated the business of being a Birmingham Member of Parliament. He quickly acquired the 'Second City' pride which had inspired Joseph Chamberlain.

I suspect that, during his Birmingham years, 'Radical Joe' was often on Roy Jenkins's mind. At the beginning of the 1964 election campaign—when I was fretting about my chances of winning Sparkbrook from the Tories—he told me that my real opponent was Chamberlain, the man who had convinced the Birmingham working classes that they were natural

Conservatives. At the reception during which he introduced the Labour candidate to the local press, he pointed out that Chamberlain had hoped to become a Sheffield MP and that I had made the journey in the opposite direction. The real comparison was between Chamberlain and Jenkins. Both abandoned the party which they had joined in youth and served with subsequent distinction. Each—after a period of tranquillity—had difficulties with the leadership of his adopted party. But—most important—they shared a historic characteristic. Chamberlain in the nineteenth century and Jenkins in the twentieth were—prime ministers aside—the most influential politicians of their respective eras, with parallel gifts and almost identical confidence in their own judgement.

Stechford was lucky to find Roy Jenkins, but he was equally lucky to find Stechford. Labour Members of Parliament rarely live in perfect peace with their constituency parties. And there were, throughout his quarter of a century in Birmingham, moments of particular potential friction. In 1951 the Stechford party was the standard-bearer of Bevanism. The resolution which appeared in its name on the agenda of the Annual Labour Conference explicitly endorsed Bevan's disagreements with the party leadership. But no one complained when Jenkins espoused the diametrically opposed course. In February 1954 the Parliamentary Labour Party and the Stechford constituency management committee both discussed German rearmament on the same day. In the parliamentary Labour Party a motion in support of the proposition was carried by one vote. At Stechford, a resolution against was won, on a show of hands, by thirty-four votes to nil. Jenkins, having voted in favour at Westminster, was—in a sense—responsible for the Westminster result. So he naturally expected trouble when some local Birmingham activists sought to 'discuss the relations of the Member with the constituency'. A proposal to that mild effect was defeated by thirty votes to two.

Jenkins fought nine elections as candidate for Stechford. In 1955 his majority was under three thousand. In the second election of 1974 it was over twelve. And, like most long-serving MPs, he developed an affection for the people who had supported him which transcended formal loyalty. Virtue is sometimes its own reward. The warmth he felt for Stechford prevented him from making the decision which would have ended his political career and denied him a place in history.

In 1963 Roy Jenkins was by no means sure that he would be found a place in the government which everybody expected Harold Wilson soon to form. So, when he was invited to be editor of *The Economist*, the temptation to turn his back on Westminster must have been immense. But he declined, with the explanation that he could not bring himself to tell his constituents that he was abandoning them in favour of a more congenial existence. He stayed, became Minister of Aviation, and played a dominant part in politics for the rest of the century.

By the time of the 1964 general election, Roy Jenkins had assumed the role of Birmingham senior Labour MP, though both Julius Silverman and Victor Yates could have laid claim to the title. Both men accepted Jenkins's leadership without question and the young candidates—particularly Brian Walden, who knew him well through the Gaitskellite Campaign for Democratic Socialism—looked to him for guidance. His style guaranteed some confusing moments. When he suggested that I met Honor Balfour, a *Time-Life* journalist who wanted to discuss the campaign in marginal seats, I asked how I should recognize her in the Grand Hotel lounge. He told me, 'You can't miss her. She looks just like Cissy Ormsby-Gore.' And when he took Walden and me to pay our respect to Harold Wilson—the morning after the party Leader's great Bull Ring speech—we were turned away by a retainer who explained that the next Prime Minister was 'having Marcia trouble'. I had no idea what that meant and Jenkins clearly thought it would be improper to explain. The previous night Lord Hailsham had asked, 'Are there no adulterers on the opposition front bench?' Marcia Williams (Wilson's secretary, now Lady Falkender) was forcibly arguing that she and her boss had been libelled and that they must both sue.

Although he was often accused by metropolitan journalists of being detached from his constituents, the charge was not made against him in the city—at least no more often that it is made against every Member of Parliament from time to time. That was, I believe, because he was meticulous in his duties rather than excessive in his attendance. He was always an energetic participant in the scramble for votes on the day of municipal elections. One year he drove to Stechford via Sparkbrook and charged into the Committee Rooms to pump all the party workers by the hand. Carried away by the enthusiasm of the moment, he rushed up to two painters, who were redecorating the Labour Club, and expressed—much to their astonishment—his gratitude for all that they were doing to secure a Labour victory.

Jenkins was also very good at funerals. He was second only to Denis Howell (as his autobiography proclaimed, Made in Birmingham) in the hierarchy of mourners at the obsequies for Victor Yates, the long-serving MP for Ladywood. Like me, he was clearly alarmed at the prospect of helping to bear the coffin from church door to altar rail. But he gamely did his best. Indeed he kept us on a steady course as we swayed, like a drunken bridegroom, down the aisle. In the train, on the way back to London, he described the day—whether or not with irony remains a mystery to me—as his first all-day funeral since Martin Luther King. Twenty years later he was the one politician of his generation who made the journey from London to Birmingham for Denis Howell's funeral. Roy Jenkins showed Birmingham—Birmingham institutions and Birmingham icons—proper respect. And it was genuine.

Perhaps Jenkins never realized how well liked he was. Walter Burleigh, the Labour Party's deputy regional organizer in the West Midlands, recalls a meeting which had been called to consider whether or not Jenkins should be readopted to fight the 1974 general election. There is no doubt that, at the time, Jenkins had caused offence to great sections of the Labour Party. He had led the rebellion over entry into the European Common Market, in which sixty-four Labour MPs had voted with the Tory government for entry. And he had resigned the deputy leadership of the party in order to continue the campaign. But, on the eve of the general election, he was back in the Shadow Cabinet and had destroyed Anthony Barber, the Conservative Chancellor, at the end of a debate on government economic policy.

That night Roy Jenkins had every reason to expect that Stechford would endorse his candidature with unanimity if not spontaneous acclaim. And so they did. But Burleigh recalls that, having addressed the General Management Committee, Jenkins sat anxiously on the edge of his seat, reluctant to leave the room while the vote was taken. That was, in its way, an indication of his acceptance that he was dependent on the goodwill of his local party—a point of view not always held by sitting Members. In Jenkins, that feeling represented a sort of modesty. It was not always recognized outside the constituency, but his relationship with Stechford made him safe and secure in Birmingham for more than half a century.

Philip Allen

Philip Allen entered the Civil Service in 1934, serving in the Home Office, the Offices of the War Cabinet, the Ministry of Housing and Local Government, and the Treasury, and ending as Permanent Under Secretary of State, Home Office (1966–72). Subsequently, he served on two Royal Commissions and chaired many public bodies and voluntary organizations. He was chief counting officer for the 1975 EEC referendum and was made a GCB in 1970 and a life peer in 1976.

Chapter 6

A Young Home Secretary

PHILIP ALLEN

Roy Jenkins's first period of office as Home Secretary lasted less than two years—from 23 December 1965 to 29 November 1967. Short as it was, it is not too much to say that it had a marked and lasting effect on the country's culture and social values. Many politicians would have been content to have achieved as much in a lifetime.

The Home Office has never been an easy department, and had hardly covered itself in glory under Roy's two predecessors, Henry Brooke and Frank Soskice. I had known Roy's father when I worked with Clement Attlee during the war, and had taken an interest in following Roy's career. I was not alone in looking to the appointment of this young reforming Home Secretary as giving hope for better things to come.

Roy had set out a programme of liberal reform, most of it on topics within the purview of the Home Office, in a Penguin Special written for the 1959 general election. Capital punishment had been abolished, but much remained to be done. He accepted his appointment as Home Secretary with pleasure and enthusiasm.

Not all members of the Home Office were equally pleased. Some perturbation was caused at the outset by Roy insisting on the current principal private secretary being ousted and replaced by David Dowler, his principal private secretary at his previous post as Minister of Aviation, with promotion to assistant secretary being thrown in. Dowler, extremely able as he was, did not exactly help by acting in a somewhat abrasive manner in dealings with his new colleagues, of whatever rank. Another alien import was John Harris, quite clearly more than just an adviser on public relations. It was the appointment of a non-civil servant adviser from outside, even though at that stage only on a part-time basis, unlike anything the Office had known since the days of Herbert Morrison. It has to be said, too, that some of the old hands saw Roy himself as an over-ambitious young politician aiming primarily for publicity and with a programme of active reform to that end which might disturb the even tenor of their official lives.

Trouble was not long in coming.

When work resumed after the Christmas break, Roy, with his clear ideas of what he wanted to do, lost no time in putting the wheels in motion in his new Office, only for those early days to be overshadowed by rows with Sir Charles Cunningham, the Permanent Under Secretary of State *in situ*. There were arguments about some staff appointments and changes of organization, but the main struggle took place over the form of policy submissions. It was Cunningham's practice to limit what was put to the Home Secretary to a beautifully written memorandum of his own composition. There were no background documents, there was no indication whether there were any differences of opinion within the Department, no contemplation that the Home Secretary might want to weigh up other possible courses. Although Cunningham fought hard, rather surprisingly so, to keep this system in defiance of Roy's wishes, in the end he had to give way, as he was bound to. But it did not make for harmony in the Office to have the Minister and his senior official in more or less open conflict.

Cunningham reached the pensionable age of 60 in May. He would have liked an extension, as the Office well knew, but Roy would not agree. So after a few weeks Cunningham left and I moved back from the Treasury to succeed him. Morale in the Office had sunk quite low in Frank Soskice's time, and in the light of the events I have narrated, it was still not altogether a happy department.

Anyway, there was work to be done, and to be done at once.

Roy had inherited a place in the legislative programme for the next session for a bill introducing a system of parole into prisons, and had decided to take the opportunity of turning it into a major criminal justice bill. Criminal justice bills were not then two a penny, and here was an opening both for catching up and for taking new initiatives.

Much preparation had been done. In July Roy chaired a series of meetings, each of them attended by the relevant experts, to weigh up possible candidates for inclusion in the bill, meetings at which all, including the most junior, were encouraged to speak up. It was a procedure which ensured that the Home Secretary was well versed in all the arguments on each issue, and when the time came he took a much more active part in the committee stage of the bill than was perhaps the general practice of senior ministers. The meetings were also an opportunity for a fair number of officials to see Roy at work at first hand and to appreciate that, as in the days of Rab Butler, we now had a minister who knew where he was going.

The parliamentary timetable meant that Roy had to be ready with his main proposals before the summer break, and this he managed to do. They covered a wide range. There were some aimed at reducing the numbers of those going to prison, something which in those days was thought to be desirable. They included putting restrictions on imprisonment in default of payment of fines, encouraging more use of bail, and introducing suspended sentences. Then there were proposals likely to have the opposite effect—banning the defence of the 'sprung alibi'; and, of great and lasting importance, the introduction of majority verdicts by juries. Later on Roy wrote that he was doubtful whether the Home Office was in favour of this last reform, but that is not my recollection. I think that we were all persuaded by the arguments for change. Other proposals in the bill were for improving the committal system from magistrates' courts; requiring a licence to hold a shotgun; giving more independence to the Parole Board than had originally been contemplated; improving legal aid; and, of particular importance to Roy, putting an end to corporal punishment in prisons. Flogging in prisons, to use his preferred more pejorative phrase, was anathema to him, and he had been greatly relieved when he had been able to find convincing enough reasons for refusing to confirm an award of birching made by visiting justices at Maidstone Prison.

All of this amounted to a considerable package of reform. When the Criminal Justice Act eventually received Royal Assent in July 1967, it had 106 sections and seven schedules, modest perhaps by modem standards but formidable enough then.

Just before the 1966 summer break the House of Commons took the second reading of the Medical Termination of Pregnancy Bill, a Private Member's Bill introduced by David Steel.

Roy persuaded the Cabinet that, although the government would remain neutral, parliamentary time and the services of parliamentary counsel would be made available, and ministers would be free to express their own personal views. (He had himself been given help with parliamentary time and drafting by a Conservative government when he promoted the Obscene Publications Bill in 1959.)

Roy spoke eloquently in support of the bill, while making it clear that the government's collective attitude was one of neutrality, and help was indeed given with drafting and allowing parliamentary time. It was not until October 1967 that the bill eventually reached the statute book, considerably amended and having changed its title on the way, as the Abortion Act 1967. It legitimized abortion in the interest of the mother, and of the child, with carefully framed safeguards.

In December 1966 Leo Abse introduced the Sexual Offences Bill, removing from the ambit of the criminal law homosexual behaviour in private between consenting adults. This too was a Private Member's Bill, and ministers agreed that it should be treated in the same way as David Steel's bill. So the government's public attitude was again one of neutrality, and Roy again spoke in warm support. There had been a number of debates, in both Houses, since the Wolfenden Committee some years before had recommended a change in the law, and there had been indications that there was increasing support for a change. The bill had an easier, and quicker, passage than did David Steel's bill and became law in July 1967, on the same day as the Criminal Justice Act.

I suppose that these last two measures, dealing with abortion and homosexual behaviour, are those most associated with Roy's first term of office as Home Secretary. They would never have become law without him.

During the summer break Roy, John Harris, David Dowler, and I paid a fortnight's visit to the United States. We saw quite a lot that was of professional interest to us, and learned one or two things. There were, though, lighter moments. The New York Police Commissioner (who, it may now sound surprising to say, greatly admired the British police) laid on a grand parade of his force in Roy's honour, but a burly police officer would not let us through to headquarters as there was to be a visit by a VIP, and it was quite difficult to persuade him that Roy was the VIP. On another occasion the rest of us watched with interest as the elegant member of Brooks's was seen standing in a queue at a Californian prison, tray in hand, to receive the same dreary lunch as was being served to the prisoners, accompanied by what was described as wine, made in the prison and served from some kind of bucket.

Among other events, Roy and I spent one and a half hours in a Chicago police patrol car without a single crime being reported, a happening without precedent in that great city; we had a weighty discussion with J. Edgar Hoover, the long-running head of the FBI; there was a dinner with Robert McNamara and other notables; and we went to the most westerly point that Dilke visited in the United States.

There were two quite important developments.

In the first place Roy, perhaps encouraged by his experiences at Bletchley Park, took a keen interest in the developments which were going on in the United States in the use of computers; and later set in train research projects which in due course led to the provision of the police national computer. (The police themselves were rather sceptical at this early stage, and the Home Office had to make the running.) It was also an initiative taken by Roy which led to each Metropolitan Police officer being equipped with a two-way telephone.

The second was not quite so happy. Information came from home that the police had raided an exhibition of drawings in a shop in Regent Street because a member of the public had complained that they were obscene. The sponsor of the Obscene Publications Act was furious, and angry messages of disapproval went winging back to New Scotland Yard. It did not augur well for relations with the Commissioner of Police of the Metropolis.

Roy from the start took a keen interest in the police and quite soon after his appointment announced a plan for the drastic reorganization of the service. The number of separate forces in England and Wales had already been reduced from over 180 to 117. Roy proposed to reduce that figure to forty-nine, using powers already on the statute book. He felt that a small force could no longer muster the resources needed to tackle crime effectively. The statute provided for a quasi-judicial inquiry to be held where there was serious objection, the crucial inquiry being the one held by a QC to examine the proposal to merge eleven borough forces in Lancashire into the county force. The QC found in favour, and the whole scheme went through without modification.

Roy was anxious to improve relations with the Police Federation (which represents the rank and file). A pay increase greatly helped. In addition, he appointed Federation nominees as members of one or two committees set up to review aspects of police conditions of service. The most important of these committees was one, chaired by Dick Taverne, then a Home Office minister, charged with considering the possibilities of attracting some of the increasing number of graduates to the police service. The Federation had a long memory, and still bitterly resented Lord Trenchard's scheme for creating a services-style officer class in the Metropolitan Police by starting selected recruits at the inspector level after completing a course at the Hendon Police College. Somehow, Dick persuaded them that times had changed and got them to agree to a scheme whereby a graduate would start at the bottom and spend a period on ordinary duty as a constable, but was then guaranteed a place on a special course at the Police Staff College at Bramshill and, if all went as it should, accelerated promotion to the rank of inspector. The chief officers of police, the superintendents, and the local authorities all went along with this proposal. Roy readily gave his approval, and the Taverne scheme, after a fairly slow start, worked well. It was a change of considerable significance for the future of the police service.

In London, where the Home Secretary was the police authority, my fears about relations with the Commissioner of Police proved to be justified. The Commissioner, Sir Joseph Simpson, a product of Lord Trenchard's Hendon scheme, had been Chief Constable of Surrey. He was intelligent, open-minded, and of complete integrity, but there were differences of approach between him and the Home Secretary over such issues as homosexual behaviour and obscene publications, and the need for the Metropolitan Police to start recruiting black applicants; and it was not helpful that the Commissioner was strangely inarticulate in the Home Secretary's presence. The two of them never got on.

Following precedent, it fell to Roy to address the annual meeting of the Metropolitan Police Joint Branch Boards. Three policemen had been shot dead at Shepherd's Bush and there were angry calls for the restoration of capital punishment. A pay award had been postponed, and there were other grievances. There was a lot of noise and shouting, and although Roy spoke up vigorously and won some support, he found it a distinctly disagreeable occasion.

One consequence of the reorganization of the provincial forces was that Robert Mark, who had caught Roy's eye, lost his post as Chief Constable of Leicester when the city force was absorbed by the county force. Roy astonished the New Scotland Yard hierarchy by appointing Mark as one of the four Metropolitan Police Assistant Commissioners. It was slightly odd that he started as the head of the Traffic Department when it was known that he was opposed to parking meters, which were just beginning to take our streets over. But never mind; there was now someone at New Scotland Yard who was *persona grata*. (Mark later went on to become Commissioner.)

In October 1966 there blew up a sudden storm, something always likely to happen in the Home Office. Just after we had set up a Tribunal of Inquiry into the Aberfan disaster, there came the news that the spy George Blake had escaped from Wormwood Scrubs prison. He was serving a sentence of forty-two years, the longest so far imposed by a British court, and had been responsible for the death of a number of British agents. The escape was serious news. Roy at once called a meeting at the Home Office on a Sunday morning, but it was pretty futile and Roy was not at all pleased by the contributions of the police and security representatives. Blake, as we now know, had gone to ground not all that far from the prison, but he was not traced. The publicity, naturally enough, was enormous.

Roy felt that it was essential to announce straightaway that there would be an inquiry into the escape, and decided that the inquiry should go wider and examine prison security in general. He welcomed David Dowler's rather unexpected suggestion that Lord Mountbatten should be asked to chair the inquiry, and after a lot of consultation on the Monday morning, he was in a position to make a statement in the House of

Commons that afternoon. The announcement of the Mountbatten Inquiry did not go down well. Quintin Hogg, the
Conservative Shadow Home Secretary, tried to move the
immediate adjournment of the House, and when the Speaker
refused, put down a Motion for the following Monday which
would be treated as a vote of censure.

It so happened that Roy and I, with our wives, were due to
pay an official visit to Jersey that weekend. I fear that Roy's
thoughts were addressed more to the vote of censure than to
the affairs of the Bailiwick. I remember that I had to ask him to
redo part of an interview with the local Robin Day when he
had answered 'Yes' to a question which, as he agreed, would
have been better answered with a 'no'. We went back early so
that Roy, who, unlike some other ministers, liked to write his
own speeches, could concentrate on this one. He listened to
comments and suggestions on his draft on the Monday but did
not make many alterations. By the time the debate came on, on
the evening of 31 October, he was keyed up in a way I had not
previously seen.

The Opposition Motion was that the House deplored the
refusal of the Secretary of State to set up a specific inquiry as a
matter of urgency into the escape of George Blake. Quintin
Hogg opened, and Enoch Powell wound up, for the Opposition. No minister spoke in the debate until Roy rose to his feet,
after some two hours of debate, to give the closing speech. He
spoke with great vigour. He began by arguing that the terms of
the Motion were misconceived. The Mountbatten Inquiry was
already launched into an investigation of Blake's escape and
would produce a quick report on this part of its remit, far
quicker for example than would a Tribunal of Inquiry, which
some speakers had advocated. Then, in a meticulously detailed
recital of the history of the case, he demonstrated that it had

been Rab Butler's original decision to move Blake to Worm-wood Scrubs and gradually to relieve special restrictions on him except for those relating to visits and correspondence, and that it had been Henry Brooke's decision to keep Blake at Wormwood Scrubs, after consulting the security service, even after a report by another prisoner that an escape plot was being hatched, without additional restrictions. Roy ended with a bitter attack on Edward Heath, the Leader of the Opposition, for having mismanaged the previous application for an adjournment of the House and now this Vote of Censure.

The cold print of the Hansard record gives no impression of the fact that this proved to be a notable parliamentary occasion. The House was packed, and the backbenchers behind Roy were cheering their heads off and waving their order papers. The whole atmosphere was one of great drama. The Motion was defeated by 331 votes to 230, the Opposition had been humiliated, and Labour morale had been boosted at a time when it was at a low ebb. It is perhaps rather remarkable that the greatest parliamentary triumph in the whole of Roy's career should have been occasioned by the escape of a prisoner and a failure to recapture him.

The problems of prison security had not been solved by this debate and escapes continued, although the total for the year turned out to be not all that exceptional. Enormous press interest was aroused by the escape from Dartmoor of a prisoner called Frank Mitchell, who was dubbed 'the mad axe-man'. Robert Mark, who was helping Lord Mountbatten, was sent to investigate and reported that Mitchell was not a murderer, was not dangerous, and had got away from an outside working party. (Mitchell himself came to an untimely end.) All this excitement was followed by the publication, just before Christmas, of the Mountbatten Report, which led to more publicity—and more escapes (but not, like Blake's, from secure accommodation). I think it was Solly Zuckerman who suggested that the Christmas toast at the Home Office should be 'to absent friends'. Anyway, following the Mountbatten Report, spy prisoners were moved, other serious offenders had their situation reviewed, and other steps were taken to tighten up on security. Argument about Lord Mountbatten's main long-term recommendation—that there should be one super-secure prison to house all the most serious prisoners, rather than keeping them in small secure units in prisons round the country—went on long after Roy's departure.

In March 1967 Roy had to cope with a crisis of a very different kind. The *Torrey Canyon*, an oil tanker sailing under a Liberian flag, ran aground on some rocks off the Scillies. Some crude oil was spilt, but there was a lot more in the wreck, and the possibility of serious pollution of the Cornish coast was alarming. Roy was nominally in charge as Chairman of the Emergencies Committee, but there was the complication that the Prime Minister went to his cottage on the Scillies for his Easter break and was, as it were, the man on the spot. Roy and other ministers went to the Scillies for a meeting with the Prime Minister, but as I understood it, responsibility still remained with Roy. The crucial question was whether the ship should be bombed in the hope of burning up the oil, with the risk of a major disaster if the operation went wrong. After considering technical advice, Roy went ahead with the bombing. It worked. There naturally followed grumbling that the bombing ought to have been done earlier, but it was one of those crises that dominate the headlines but, when over, rapidly lose their public interest.

I turn to a totally different topic. In 1940 an order was made setting time at one hour in advance of Greenwich Mean Time

(GMT) throughout the year. In 1941 double summertime was introduced. The orders were made under emergency powers, which lapsed when the war was over. Roy was quite keen on going back at any rate to the provisions of the 1940 order for summertime throughout the year. He knew that the farmers and the Scots would object, but there were the arguments that it would be helpful to business, especially to firms dealing with Europe, it would be beneficial for leisure, and slightly to our surprise, the experts said it would mean fewer traffic accidents. As a first step, an order was made, under an existing statute, for summertime in 1968 to start on 18 February and run to 27 October. Then, just before Roy left, Lord Stonham, a Home Office minister, moved the second reading in the House of Lords of the British Standard Time Bill, which simply provided that British Standard Time should be one hour in advance of GMT throughout the year. The bill was amended during its passage. The Act in the end provided that this change should operate only until 31 October 1971 unless an Order in Council were then made directing that the change should be made permanent. In the event, organized opposition succeeded in getting a vote in 1971 against continuing the Act. So that was the end of the experiment, which is now forgotten. But it is an interesting thought that, as so much of the opposition came from Scotland, it might well have been, if we had then had Scottish devolution, that Roy would be remembered as the creator of a perpetual difference in time zones north and south of the border.

Roy was anxious to play an active part in improving race relations. The Race Relations Act 1965 had made it unlawful for persons responsible for places of public resort, such as pubs and hotels, to practise discrimination on grounds of colour, race, or ethnic origin, and had provided for the setting up of a

Race Relations Board with the responsibility, through local conciliation committees, of securing compliance with this provision. It had also made it a criminal offence to publish any written matter or use any words in a public place which were intended to stir up hatred on grounds of colour, race, or ethnic origin. Roy appointed his friend Mark Bonham Carter as the first chairman of the new Board and thought that he proved to be an outstanding holder of the office. I was not quite so sure about his organizing ability; but certainly, despite his puny resources, he tackled his vast subject with enthusiasm. It is not easy to assess the impact of the work of such a Board, but Roy soon came to the conclusion that it needed more powers, and also that the area of racial discrimination covered by the 1965 Act should be extended. He put in a bid for a place in the pro-gramme for such a bill, but it had to await his successor's arrival, and passed into law in 1968. Roy made a number of speeches about race relations, but I think that he left in 1967 feeling that he might have done more.

The Gaming Act 1960 had for the first time legalized casinos in this country, but, regrettably, had failed to make adequate provision for supervision and enforcement. Casinos sprang up in hundreds, and provided easy pickings for the unscrupulous. There had recently been signs of the Mafia moving in, and one or two individuals with Italian-sounding names had been deported without much fuss. One decision, though, hit the headlines. George Raft, a well-known film actor, was a front man at a West End casino, and there was a lot of publicity when he was refused permission to return to this country after a visit back to New York. The decision was challenged in the courts, but in vain.

Reform of the gaming laws was not high on Roy's personal agenda, but he accepted the strong urgings of the police that here was a source of crime and that their powers were inadequate, and commissioned Dick Taverne to work out, with the Department, proposals for the new legislation. What was necessarily a rather long and complicated set of proposals was put together, but there was nothing complicated about the main proposal, which was to create a new Gaming Board with draconian powers of control over casinos, bingo clubs, and gaming machines. Roy accepted these conclusions, and obtained a place in the legislative programme. So at the tail-end of the Queen's Speech at the Opening of Parliament on 31 October 1967 it was duly announced that there would be legislation to reform the law on gaming.

The bill was enacted in 1968, and proved effective. It was based on the concept that permission could be given, under strict controls, for such facilities for gaming as were needed to meet an unstimulated demand. A generation later it had become government policy actively to encourage a gambling culture in this country.

Roy was not all that keen on some of the ceremonial aspects of the post of Home Secretary, such as reading out the names of knights bachelor at investitures, or dictating the oath when the Queen was swearing in a new bishop. He had taken the precaution of equipping himself with a new morning coat, although I believe that he still carried his father's hat, which did not fit him. There was one occasion, though, when he put on his morning coat with some relish. Mr Kosygin, the Soviet premier, was on an official visit to the country, and expressed a wish that, on his way to a reception at the Houses of Parliament, he should stop and lay a wreath on the Cenotaph. The Cenotaph was immediately opposite the front door of the Home Office, and Roy prepared to act as host. After the ceremony Mr Kosygin unexpectedly expressed a wish to see the

Minister's office, so the whole Soviet deputation swept into the Home Office, mounted to Roy's room on the first floor, expressed particular interest at seeing an open coal fire, and eventually proceeded, well behind its timetable, to the waiting throng at Westminster. Roy sent his guest copies of his books. His guest sent him, what was perhaps of more immediate use, caviar and vodka.

While I am on a sartorial note, I recall one evening when I had to go and see the Home Secretary on something which had just cropped up, and found him wrestling with the studs in a shirt he was putting on for a white-tie dinner. He was furious, and vowed he would never use a stiff shirt again. I believe that from then on, although unlike some of his colleagues he would wear a white tie if that was what his host wanted, he wore a soft shirt.

Stage censorship still existed, the responsibility of the Lord Chamberlain, Lord Cobbold, a former Governor of the Bank of England. A select committee had recommended its abolition, and Roy would dearly have liked to introduce legislation to implement this recommendation, but in the end it had to be left to a Private Member's Bill in 1968.

Capital punishment in the United Kingdom had been abolished by the time Roy took office, and he stoutly resisted any calls for its reintroduction, as for example after the murder of policemen. But there was one unhappy leftover. An inquiry by Mr Justice Brabin had established that it was almost certain that Timothy John Evans had been hanged for a murder he had not committed. It was a disquieting conclusion for those who had been involved. Roy decided, as a gesture, to recommend a posthumous Free Pardon for Evans.

Capital punishment still existed in the Bailiwick of Jersey (and did so until 1986). Roy used to tell the story of how the

Jersey court had imposed the death sentence on a conviction for murder, and it became his responsibility to decide whether to recommend a conditional pardon substituting a sentence of life imprisonment. Naturally, he was anxious to do so, and having been advised that a reprieve could be recommended if there was a scintilla of doubt about the convicted man's guilt, informed the Bailiff accordingly. 'A scintilla of doubt?' said the Bailiff incredulously. 'It is an open and shut case.' Roy, somewhat shaken, reaffirmed his view that there was a scintilla of doubt, whereupon the Bailiff said, 'If you had told me, Home Secretary, that you thought capital punishment was barbarous and obscene and should never be allowed to happen, I should have agreed with you entirely.' Roy used to say that, thereafter, he always gave the real reasons for his decisions.

Roy quite enjoyed driving, and was fond of his Armstrong-Siddeley Sapphire. He learned without enthusiasm that Barbara Castle had decided to introduce universal speed limits and pondered with me whether there were any Home Office objections which could be advanced. We had to conclude that there were not.

There was one last late-summer storm before Roy left the Home Office. An inquiry had been held by a QC into allegations of cruelty and mismanagement at Court Lees, in Surrey, an approved school for delinquent boys, and had found that the allegations were justified. Roy consulted the experts, and decided that the only proper course was to make other arrangements with the Surrey authorities for the boys, and to close the school. The Board of Governors came up to the Home Office, and, at another Sunday morning meeting, made their protest; and there was a good deal of adverse publicity. It would be difficult to deny that the timetable was to some extent influenced by Roy's holiday plans, but he was able to argue with conviction in the subsequent debate that the Governors had been given adequate time to consider their position. Having heard their case, Roy stuck to his decision, and left for his holiday. I was left to cope with, among others, the local MP and *The Times* leader writer, efforts to keep Roy informed of what was going on being somewhat handicapped by the rather poor telephone connections with southern Italy. The debate that followed in due course was rather bad-tempered, but Roy made a convincing speech and won the division, although it was not an occasion comparable with the Censure debate. Some of the staff at the school took legal proceedings, which went on for some time, but public interest soon died down.

The speech which Roy made on this occasion was the last he made in his first term of office as Home Secretary. A fortnight later he was Chancellor of the Exchequer.

The Prime Minister, in appointing Roy as Home Secretary, would have been well aware of his ambitions, and could well have hoped that lustre would be added to his administration by a programme of liberal reform. Roy himself greatly relished the opportunity. Although in no way pompous, he was not unconscious of being, at an early age, her Majesty's Principal Secretary of State for the Home Department, and head of a great department of state with a history of nearly two centuries and some most illustrious names among his predecessors. But it was much more important that this was the department most relevant to his programme of modernization and reform.

Looking back as he went to the Treasury, he had abolished corporal punishment in prisons; he had provided for a system of parole; he had introduced majority verdicts; he had reorganized the police service; he had introduced fresh blood into the Metropolitan Police, at the top and the bottom; he had prepared the way for strengthening the law relating to race relations and for the abolition of theatre censorship; and he had a direct responsibility for new laws legalizing abortion in defined circumstances, and decriminalizing homosexual conduct in private between consenting adults. Ben Pimlott put it well in his life of Harold Wilson:

The effect of this exceptional period of reform was to end a variety of judicial persecutions of private behaviour; quietly to consolidate a mood change in British society; and to provide a legal framework for more civilised social values. For hundreds of thousands, if not millions, of people directly affected—and millions who benefited later, without knowing when, or how, their liberation came about—these were the important changes of the Wilson administration.[1]

Roy was a little unhappy that he had perhaps concentrated too much on security in prisons, rather than trying to improve facilities for, say, education. He never had the opportunity to tackle the licensing laws or the laws on elections, two topics which were then the concern of the Home Office, and on which he had strong views. Riots, and Northern Ireland, which were both to feature so prominently in the experience of his immediate successor, did not appear on the agenda.

My colleagues and I were interested in Roy's relations with the Prime Minister. We now know that they were pretty frigid for a time when the Prime Minister suspected that Roy was involved in a plot, with others, to replace him, and that there was a continuing disagreement about the case for the devaluation of sterling. It is only fair, however, to record that the Prime Minister made no attempt to intervene when Roy was having his problems over prison escapes, and indeed got up during the

---

[1] Ben Pimlott, *Harold Wilson* (1992), 487.

censure debate to volunteer that he had concurred in Lord Mountbatten's appointment. And he acquiesced in the proposals for special facilities for the Private Members' Bills on homosexual conduct and abortion, although the latter would not have been very welcome to the large Roman Catholic element in his constituency.

I found Roy easy to work with, very approachable, and always ready to listen. He had a lively sense of humour, could laugh at himself, and, as the Jersey capital case illustrated, was not averse to telling revealing anecdotes about himself. We had some differences of opinion about appointments—I thought that he was too much inclined to look for youth rather than experience—but nothing serious. Years later he told me that he realized that he had made a mistake when he had advocated the appointment of Sir Eric St Johnston, the ebullient Chief Constable of Lancashire (and later H.M. Chief Inspector of Constabulary), as the next head of MI5. He admitted that he had sulked for a time when he had been talked out of the proposal, but he had been wrong. He then added, with a smile, that any minister should be allowed at least one error.

We had no great problems about staff within the Office. When there was a vacancy in the post of Deputy Under Secretary of State, he asked me if I would bring in an official who had worked closely with him in the Minister of Aviation. I always thought that there should be more movement between departments, and made no objection. In the event, although this individual was pleasant and competent, I could not in all honesty say that he made a greater contribution than a local candidate would have done, but he had the special qualification that he was close to the Secretary of State. Roy indeed depended very much on dealing with people he knew, liked, and trusted. I had not myself had experience of a minister surrounding himself with familiar faces in this way, but it was for Roy to decide how best he wished to operate. David Dowler and John Harris were particularly important to him. Dowler came with him from the Ministry of Aviation and went with him to the Treasury. He had an instinctive understanding of Roy's thinking and likely reaction, and although he was not conciliatory in dealing with people and identified himself with his minister to an extent unusual for a private secretary, he came to be respected in the Department for his ability, intelli-gence, and sharp wit. (To look briefly ahead, I took him back into the Home Office later on in a senior post, but he died, much too soon.) John Harris had been adviser to a number of ministers, and, to start with, Roy and the Foreign Secretary, Michael Stewart, shared his services. But it was not long before he devoted himself full-time to Roy, to whom he was of crucial importance. He had particular skills in dealing with the press and questions of publicity, but in effect he functioned as a special adviser over the whole field, before such appointments became common. He was always at Roy's side. Roy trusted him, liked to chew problems over with him, and depended greatly on his advice. He was not much liked in the Department to begin with, but as time went on I think that opinion about him became more favourable (and, to look ahead again, his later contribution as a Home Office minister was well regarded both in the Office and in the House of Lords).

By contrast to Roy having a circle of friends he liked, there were some people he always found it difficult to get on with and he did not always try as hard as I thought he might to get over his feelings. I have already mentioned the Commissioner of Police, and I thought it desirable to transfer one or two officials to other posts although, as I recall, Roy made only one specific request that an individual official should be moved. I do not want to leave the impression that there was a favoured inner circle and that others were in outer darkness—he had dealings with, and was very ready to listen to, many members of staff, nearly all of whom were liberal-minded people who welcomed Roy's refreshing approach and reforming zeal. It was certainly welcome that in the Secretary of State, for the first time since Rab Butler, we had a real Cabinet heavyweight.

We knew that Roy led a pretty active social life, but he normally disposed of the business put to him quickly and efficiently. There were just occasional hesitations. He found it difficult to decide who should be asked to be Chairman of the new Parole Board, and in the end, with time running out, I had to chivvy him into making a decision. He then and there plumped for John Hunt, spoke to him later that day in some remote mountainous area of South America, and told me that evening that it was all fixed. (It was some time later that John Hunt called on me to find out just what was the public appointment he had accepted. Anyway, it was a job he did very well.) On another occasion Roy said that he wanted to put a paper to the Cabinet about race relations, and that he would write it himself. He wrote about half of it, and then it lay on his desk for quite some time. Eventually I took it away and finished it, and Roy then circulated it

But these were trifling matters. Overall, this was an exhilarating and exciting time.

Roy was a man of many parts, and many accomplishments, but I think that he would have rated this first period as Home Secretary as one of the most rewarding of his life. He certainly attained a very high place in that long list of holders of the office of Home Secretary.

Dick Taverne

Dick Taverne QC was educated at Balliol College, Oxford. He became Labour MP for Lincoln in 1962 and was apppointed Parliamentary Secretary at the Home Office in 1966, soon after Roy Jenkins became Home Secretary, and in 1968, after Roy Jenkins had become Chancellor, moved to the Treasury, where he was Minister of State and then Financial Secretary. He left the Labour Party in 1972 and was elected as an independent social democrat for Lincoln at a by-election in 1973. He held his seat until the second general election in 1974. He was made a life peer in 1996 and sits as a Liberal Democrat. His books include *The March of Unreason* (2004).

Chapter 7

Chancellor of
the Exchequer

Dick Taverne

As Chancellor of the Exchequer, Roy Jenkins achieved his most powerful position in his career in British politics. His reforms at the Home Office may have had more lasting effect on the social and cultural life in Britain, his defiant stand against the rest of his party over Britain's entry into the European Community may have won him most public respect and by founding the SDP he may have made his most influential contribution to the shape of British party politics, but it was during his time at the Treasury that he exercised the levers of power most directly. He was the dominant force in the Cabinet, the master of the House of Commons, a Chancellor who transformed the economy from weakness to strength; and, had he been more ruthless, he could probably have forced Harold Wilson from office to become Prime Minister himself.

When he was appointed Chancellor at the end of November 1967, the state of the British economy and the fortunes of the Labour government could hardly have been more dire. Harold Wilson and James Callaghan, the previous Chancellor, had fought a long and ultimately hopeless battle to save the parity of the pound. It ended in humiliation. The reputation of both had been shattered. In Wilson's case his loss of standing was confirmed by an ill-judged broadcast after devaluation, in which he reassured the public (correctly) that devaluation did not mean 'that the pound in the pocket is worth 14 per cent less than it was', but the tone of the broadcast was so complacent, it was as if he was announcing victory at El Alamein instead of defeat at Dunkirk.[1] Not only was the balance of payments in deep deficit, but the Bank of England's reserves were so low that there was every possibility that the government might be forced into a disastrous further devaluation or into floating the pound, which in the circumstances would probably have been even more calamitous. By contrast, after his outstanding success as Home Secretary, Roy's own reputation was as high as that of any minister in the government. Indeed it was so high that his appointment was greeted by general acclaim in the press and by what Roy himself described as 'hyperbolic editorial comment' in the *Sunday Times*, which stated that the whole future of the British economy and of the Labour Party, and even of parliamentary democracy, depended on his success at the Treasury.

That dramatic prognosis was not entirely unjustified, since the economic situation was probably as threatening as it has been at any time since the end of the Second World War. When the Labour government was elected in 1964 after thirteen

---

[1] Ben Pimlott, *Harold Wilson* (1992), 481.

years in the wilderness, it was committed to an ambitious programme for the transformation of Britain and, on the assumption that it could achieve a higher rate of growth than its Conservative predecessor, the programme included plans for a large expansion of public spending. The spending plans were so ambitious that despite ferocious cuts subsequently introduced by Roy, public spending still rose from 44 per cent of GDP in 1964 to 50 per cent in 1970. It was the classic triumph of hope over realism. Nemesis, however, made her entry early, within weeks of the formation of the new government. The balance of payments was strongly negative. Early devaluation, which might have eased the problem, was ruled out by Wilson on political grounds, and the mixture of other measures which were relied upon instead—an import surcharge, higher interest rates, higher taxes (mainly in the form of a new selective employment tax on services), and the introduction of a statutory incomes policy—destroyed the promise of economic growth yet could not prevent a growing loss of confidence in sterling, leading to eventual devaluation in November 1967.

From today's viewpoint it is hard to envisage how completely the balance of payments then dominated economic policy. Those were the days of the Bretton Woods Agreement, which required maintenance of currencies within narrow bands round a fixed exchange rate, unless consent was obtained from the International Monetary Fund (the IMF) to a formal devaluation. To devalue was a major step, particularly for Britain, which was the home of the so-called sterling balances held by Commonwealth countries as a result of money lent to us during the war. Devaluation reduced their value and the prospect of further devaluations was therefore likely to result in withdrawals, which in turn were likely to cause a further run on sterling. And so on. Even without this incubus, our apparent inability to pay our way made it doubtful whether a further devaluation would be final. Indeed, since devaluation is followed by the so-called J-curve effect—the lower value of the pound raises the cost of imports and lowers the value of exports and therefore starts by making the trade deficit worse before it recovers—sterling might have collapsed completely, leading to the fall of the government. The first year or more of Roy's chancellorship was a long struggle to prevent a further devaluation, during which monthly trade figures were watched as closely as a patient's heartbeat after a severe heart attack. And for most of those months the beat was irregular, giving rise to profound worries about the patient's health. Roy once described the differences between his time at the Home Office and the Treasury in one of his favourite meteorological metaphors: at the Home Office sudden storms blew up out of a clear sky and vanished almost as suddenly as they arose; by contrast the Treasury was a long Arctic winter slowly lightening into spring.

Roy soon established a good relationship with the civil servants at the Treasury. The very able Permanent Secretary at the time, Sir Douglas Allen, now Lord Croham, said he was 'the finest Chancellor I worked with'. They had not felt at ease with his predecessor. In the words of Sir Douglas Wass, who was a relatively junior official at the time, there was a change from 'a Byzantine, unpredictable system to an open and logical one'. Roy was a good listener and although he liked to keep meetings small, he listened to the views of more junior civil servants as well as to those of the top mandarins and would positively invite dissent. Indeed he accepted briefings direct from civil servants at any level above assistant secretary, as long as a copy was always sent to Douglas Allen. He was not particularly interested in the way the Treasury was run, which he was happy to leave to the Permanent Secretary, just as he left the hard task of implementing cuts in public spending to the Chief Secretary, Jack Diamond. The mutual respect between ministers and mandarins was demonstrated when unusually, after the change of government in 1970, the four top mandarins, Sir Douglas Allen, Sir Frank Figgures, Sir Donald MacDougall (chief economist), and Sam Goldman gave a farewell dinner for Roy and Jack Diamond in the Cabinet Room of the Reform Club.

I was one of his junior ministers, from April 1968 until the 1970 election, first as Minister of State, then as Financial Secretary, and I found the Treasury a happy place to work in. Roy's team was hand-picked, people he trusted and respected and whose company he enjoyed. Indeed Iain Macleod, one of the leading lights of the Conservative opposition, described the Treasury team as 'the most formidable team in the government', adding, for good measure: 'the only formidable team in the government'. As Chief Secretary, Jack Diamond was a charming but relentless, dedicated scourge of spending departments and an almost miserly guardian of the public revenues. By contrast, Harold Lever, the Financial Secretary, was an unusual socialist who had made millions by speculating on the Stock Exchange, a brilliant dilettante with exactly opposite instincts to Jack's. It was almost true to say that he opposed every cut in spending and every rise in taxes and favoured giving everybody every pay increase they asked for. He also argued that the more we borrowed, the stronger our international position would be, because big debtors caused everyone big problems. He was exceptionally imaginative and effective in dealing with the IMF and the moguls of international finance, which more than made up for his domestic heterodoxies.

He was also the wittiest speaker in Parliament.[2] He left to become Paymaster-General in November 1969 and Bill Rodgers then joined the team.

One choice memory I have is of an occasion when Jack Diamond turned the tables on Harold Lever. A proposal was mooted to disallow interest relief against tax on overdrafts. Roy's formidable private secretary, David Dowler, was against it, for personal reasons. So was Harold, because it would increase tax burdens. So were some civil servants on economic grounds. Jack and I and some other civil servants were in favour, but the meeting to discuss it with Roy was arranged by David Dowler for a time when we were both committed elsewhere, and in the absence of any of its advocates, the proposal was rejected. We protested and Roy was persuaded to allow a rerun. Harold led the opposition and started an argument about the hardship it would cause: 'Take poor Charlie, a man of modest means' (Harold's examples were always about 'the average man on an income of £10,000 a year'—now equivalent to over £100,000 a year), 'Charlie, who has invested in a row of back-to-back houses in Manchester . . .' Jack interrupted: 'Correction, Harold: not poor Charlie, proper Charlie.' Harold did not recover and we won.

However, the big decisions were very much Roy's own, taken after close consultation, not only with his top professional advisers but also with two people who were as influential

---

[2] For instance, at 6 a.m., after an all-night sitting of the committee stage of the Finance Bill, when Harold and I were the ministers in charge and had both nodded off, a Conservative, John Hall, the MP for High Wycombe, asked, 'Could we know which of the two ministers is in charge of this clause so that at least one of them could wake up?' Harold (whose clause it was), waking instantly from deep sleep, answered, 'The Honourable Gentleman is no more justified in inferring from the fact that our eyes are closed that we are asleep than we would be in inferring from the fact that his eyes are open that he is awake.'

in terms of policy and politics with Roy as Alastair Campbell and Peter Mandelson have been with Tony Blair: they were David Dowler, already mentioned, a very political civil servant who had followed Roy from Civil Aviation to the Home Office and then to the Treasury, and John Harris, later Lord Harris of Greenwich, his political adviser. Both were extremely astute interpreters of the political mood and of likely reactions to budget changes or other public announcements. John Harris was the ideal go-between in Roy's dealings with the press, as he had excellent relations with the most important journalists, and Roy, justifiably, placed great trust in his judgement. David and John travelled with Roy almost wherever he went and must share some of the credit for the political wisdom he displayed that was an essential element in his successful chancellorship.

Although Roy had gained a first-class degree in politics and economics at Balliol College, Oxford, he was by no means a professional economist. Yet in retrospect it was a combination of economic numeracy and good judgement that was most needed at the time. The overall strategy was essentially simple. Public expenditure had to be reduced and taxes had to be raised, in order to reduce consumption and direct more resources into exports. Furthermore, action was needed to neutralize the potential threat from a mass withdrawal of the sterling balances. Decisions about how large the reduction in spending was to be, in which areas, which taxes should be raised, by how much, what assurances should be given to the holders of the sterling balances, and assessing how the markets would react, were essentially matters of judgement rather than economic expertise. Could he win sufficient support from his Cabinet colleagues and in the end from the parliamentary party? That depended on political skill and his standing in the party and the country.

Nearly all financial commentators have praised his management of the economy and in retrospect declared him the most successful Chancellor since the war—certainly before 1997. The one exception is Edmund Dell, a minister in both of Wilson's administrations, who ended up as Secretary of State for Trade in the Labour government of 1974–9. In his book *The Chancellors* (1996) he agrees that Roy did what he had to do and that no one else could have done it with such élan. But in his view, Roy acted too late when he was first appointed and then consistently did too little. Further, according to Dell, he mishandled the sterling balances by paying too high a price for securing stability; and finally, he was wrong to desert Barbara Castle and Harold Wilson over the trade union reforms mooted in *In Place of Strife*. These criticisms should be considered on their merit, but it should be borne in mind that in stark, and in some ways refreshing, contrast to most Labour ministers of the period, Dell always outhawked all other hawks. He was inclined to believe at all times, in total contrast to Harold Lever, that any course prescribed was too soft and that either spending should be cut back further or taxes should be raised even higher.

The first charge, that Roy wrongly delayed action too long, is one to which he himself pleads guilty. Within a few days of assuming office he had to answer a short debate initiated by Michael Foot (not a man noted for economic realism) urging him not to cut demand. Roy assured the House, 'We do not want to dig a hole and leave it empty', that is, before exports were ready to fill it. This, he acknowledged later, was nonsense. Demand should have been cut as soon as possible. He also recognized that he should have brought his first budget forward to February 1968, to coincide with his announcement of expenditure cuts: 'To present one half of the measures and to threaten a tough budget in two months' time was not wise, either materially or psychologically.' The result of procrastination may well have been that the surgery had to be more drastic than it need have been. However, in the event, the fact that the budget was as tough as it was had a big and salutary impact on market opinion, as well as on Parliament. More reserves were lost as a result of delay, but as they were eventually recovered, this did no permanent damage.

Because the J–curve effect delayed improvement in the balance of payments and because of frequent turmoil in currency markets, occasioned by uncertainties surrounding the dollar, the mark, and the franc, the buffeting of the pound continued throughout the rest of 1968 and caused Roy to take further measures that November: a further increase in indirect taxes, new hire purchase controls, a lower ceiling on bank lending, and a requirement that importers had to pay a deposit of one-third on their purchases. While it could be argued, following Dell, that these measures showed that the budget measures had been too lax, no one thought this at the time of the budget[3] and Dell's judgement benefited greatly from hindsight. However, during November, when a conference in Bonn failed to produce any assistance or cooperation from Germany, France, or the United States to stabilize the markets, there was a moment when we thought Armageddon had arrived. I remember having to address a city audience at the time and raising loud and prolonged laughter by comparing the task of making an amusing after-dinner speech in such circumstances to giving a lecture about the funnier side of the bubonic plague.

The criticism of Roy's handling of the sterling balances also seems misplaced. Dell argues that Roy was too generous in guaranteeing holders of these balances their value in dollars

---

[3] Except the Tory maverick John Biffen.

while continuing to pay them the higher interest rates due on sterling, as a result of which some increased their sterling holdings. But it was both vital and difficult to persuade them not to withdraw their money. The only way was through a generous deal. And it succeeded.

Somehow sterling survived, the trade figures started to improve, and the sun climbed slowly, but, as Roy observed, oh how slowly! It was discovered that as a result of a technical hitch, throughout this fraught period the figures of exports had been under-recorded by a small but significant amount, which would have saved much angst. By mid-1969 the monthly balance was mainly favourable. By the end of Roy's chancellorship the dollar and gold reserves had been dramatically strengthened, the balance of payments was in steady surplus, there was a solid budget surplus as well, we had enjoyed two and a half years of economic growth at 3–4 per cent annually, and while inflation was high by modern standards, it was not appreciably higher than that of countries such as the United States, which had not devalued, or France, which had devalued by less. This formidable success had been won at a price. There was some tax relief in the last of Roy's three budgets, which was well received and popular, but the relief was extremely modest compared with the extra tax burdens and expenditure cuts imposed by earlier measures. Seldom can a Chancellor have inflicted greater pain during his tenure. But as Dell wrote, 'Never has pain been inflicted with greater elegance.'

That brings me to one of the reasons for Roy's success: his political skills and his standing at the time. Tony Crosland had seemed to many the obvious choice to succeed Callaghan as Chancellor—he was a professional economist and Jim Callaghan's candidate. But Wilson chose Roy, partly because he found him personally more congenial, mainly because he had greater confidence in his ability to control the House of Commons. This was in fact a compelling reason. As Home Secretary, Roy had twice turned apparent disasters (first over the Blake escape and then over accusations of mishandling disciplinary matters at Court Lees, an approved school) into parliamentary triumphs, and as Chancellor part of the success of his first budget speech (which, as he recorded, lasted two hours and twenty-seven minutes—Roy was devoted to numerical exactitude) was due to the compelling nature of the argument and the felicity of its phrasing. He was undoubtedly the outstanding parliamentary performer of the time, despite a voice that lacked resonance and a rather poor delivery. Like Churchill, he took immense pains over his speeches, which were meticulously argued and elegantly expressed, but he also had a gift like Churchill's for impromptu adaptation and repartee, possibly less witty but immensely effective.

In the House the Shadow Chancellor, Iain Macleod, had a formidable reputation as a debater and was probably the ablest member of the Conservative front bench. Yet time after time Roy worsted him, so that *The Spectator* (which Macleod had once edited) described their confrontations as a contest between Macleod's cobra and Roy's Rikki-Tikki-Tavi. Part of the reason was that after the autumn of 1968 the Conservatives found it increasingly difficult to deny that the government's central policy was working, and found it more and more difficult to explain away its success. One of the most memorable parliamentary occasions was a debate in November 1969, after the Conservative Chairman Anthony Barber, perhaps in desperation, had accused the government of cooking the books and presenting the trade figures in a more favourable light than was justified. He mentioned a particular sum of £22 million, which he said had been concealed. Unwisely Macleod repeated the

"*We thought it had gone out!*"

Fig. 7.1 Garland, *Daily Telegraph*, 5 November 1969

point in the debate on the Queen's speech. Roy roasted both
Macleod and Barber. When Barber interrupted, Roy asked him
five times where he had obtained the figure of £22 million.
Each time Barber answered evasively and Roy pursued him
remorselessly. (The only comparable recent occasion was when
Jeremy Paxman asked Michael Howard seventeen times
whether he had played any part in the sacking of a civil servant.)
Finally, with a great flourish, Roy revealed that it could only
have come from a publication issued by the government itself.
A contemporary *Daily Telegraph* cartoon showed a beaming
Roy as a firework exploding and reducing Barber's and
Macleod's clothes to rags.

Roy's parliamentary successes were often based on reflection as much as rhetoric. I remember one speech when Enoch

Fig. 7.2 Mahood, *The Times*, 26 March 1968

Powell interrupted him with what appeared to be a telling point. Roy paused and thought and looked at the ceiling. He delayed his reply so long that there was an uncomfortable feeling among his supporters that for once he had been put off his stride. Then he said: 'The Right Honourable Gentleman's logic, as always, is impeccable. But since he always starts from false premises, he is bound to come to the wrong conclusion.' In an off-the-cuff remark he had summed up Enoch Powell's whole career.

There were other reasons for his high reputation and standing. Despite being a so-called 'right-winger' in the Labour Party, he had won left-wing admiration by his social reforms at the Home Office. As Chancellor, he maintained his high standing and increased his influence in Cabinet. According to Dick Crossman in 1968, he was 'the dominant force in Cabinet' (on a later occasion, in 1970, he described him as 'omnipotent'!),

97

and John Campbell, Roy's biographer, wrote that, after Roy became Chancellor, 'the Prime Minister was effectively in his power'. There was a cartoon at the time of a tiny Wilson, dragged behind a huge dog with Roy's face, vainly crying 'Heel!'. His power was also illustrated when Michael Stewart left the Department of Economic Affairs (DEA) in April 1968 to replace George Brown as Foreign Secretary and Wilson planned to appoint Barbara Castle in his place. Roy wanted to wind up the DEA, which had been a failure and which had made life more difficult for the Treasury. He was therefore strongly opposed to Castle, who was an effective minister and a powerful personality, becoming its head and reviving its influence. When Wilson told him of his plan, Roy said, 'Prime Minister it is for you to appoint whom you like. I will leave my resignation with your secretary on the way out.' Peter Shore was appointed instead, who was at that time so ineffective that Roy could ignore him as well as the DEA. (He even avoided being photographed with him.) Macleod in a subsequent debate suggested that there was no point in keeping the DEA simply 'as a mink-lined basket for the Prime Minister's pet poodle'. It duly disappeared. There was no doubt that once he became Chancellor, at least until the turmoil caused by *In Place of Strife*, Roy was the only possible alternative to Wilson as Prime Minister.

With Wilson's reputation so low and his own so high, could Roy have become Prime Minister? Wilson and his kitchen cabinet at Number Ten seemed to be obsessed by plots, indeed at times almost paranoid about them.[4] While he often suspected plotters who did not exist, there were plots to replace him on

---

[4] Possibly with the exception of Marcia Williams, Harold Wilson's closest adviser. John Harris had a great regard for her good sense and independent-mindedness and she once told me the feeling was mutual.

at least two, and possibly three, occasions. The first rumblings of rebellion, hardly a conspiracy, much less of a plot than Wilson believed, was in the summer of 1966, while he was in Moscow and when devaluation first seemed a serious possibility. Callaghan was then seen as Wilson's challenger, although Roy's name came up. The next occasion was in May 1968, when a large group of Jenkinsites wanted a move against Wilson after a public call for Wilson's head from Cecil King, the powerful Chairman of the *Daily Mirror*, then the most influential news-paper in Britain. Roy was the obvious and only heir apparent. The third threat to Wilson came in 1969, when the party was in uproar against Barbara Castle's proposals to curb trade union power (*In Place of Strife*). By then Callaghan had restored his reputation and was a possible alternative challenger to Roy. One historian reported that Roy encouraged the plotters: Ben Pimlott, by and large a defender of Wilson and a critic of Roy, wrote in his life of Wilson that while Roy 'owed his ascent into the Government's stratosphere entirely to Wilson's patronage', he 'dabbled in the blackest treachery'. Was this true?

Before turning to the plots, it is worth revisiting Roy's rela-tions with Harold Wilson, other leading members of the Cab-inet, and his own supporters. Roy on the whole got on well with Wilson, whom he found, as most people did, amiable and personally considerate. Apparently on at least two occasions they had pleasurable conversations about railways. As an under-graduate Wilson had won the Gladstone Memorial Prize with a long dissertation entitled 'The State and the Railways in Vic-torian Britain', and Roy, with his eclectic tastes, his passion for numerical detail, and his own fascination with the railway sys-tem, was quite happy discussing timetables. (They must have been fascinating conversations.) Wilson also supported him in the many difficult battles in Cabinet, not always strongly or vocally, but he was the only person in Cabinet who voted with him throughout. Indeed Roy once told me that his only solid allies in Cabinet for his economic policy were Wilson, Denis Healey, and Barbara Castle.

On the other hand, from time to time their relations were strained. While Wilson rather admired Roy, admiration was not mutual, or at best, in Roy's case, spasmodic. Relations became very bad about the time of the Cecil King affair, when Wilson accused Roy at a Cabinet meeting of leaking to the press: 'I know where a great part of the leaking and backbiting comes from. It arises from the ambitions of one member of this Cabinet to sit in my place.' In fact the original source of the leak came from Crossman, and when Wilson found this out, he was duly apologetic and withdrew his accusation at the next meeting of the Cabinet. Furthermore, Wilson was not an effective Prime Minister and his poor management, his opportunism, lack of strategy, and whole style of government had contributed substantially to the economic crisis. His low public standing, both at home and abroad, was a drag on recovery, and while he did not say so explicitly in his memoirs, Roy must have been acutely aware, indeed many people kept telling him, that he would do the job much better. He must have felt tempted to lead a rebellion during Wilson's bad patches.

I had recently joined the Treasury team when the storm caused by Cecil King broke. There were frantic messages from Number Ten urging Roy to disown King and declare his confidence in Wilson. An emergency meeting was held in Roy's office with David Dowler, John Harris, and myself. Both David's and John's views were clear: Roy should declare his loyalty to Wilson and confidence in his leadership, just as Churchill declared his confidence in Chamberlain in May 1940. Roy thought for a long time and then said, in a rather bad–tempered manner, which he sometimes showed when turning a proposal down, 'No, I won't. There has been too much double talk in this government. I don't have confidence in Harold's leadership and I'm not going to say that I have.' That was that. The turmoil and Wilson's anxieties subsided. No one commented that Roy had not issued a statement. I gave no advice, as a new member of the Treasury team, but went away with my admiration for Roy's integrity and judgement enhanced.

Roy was surrounded by devoted followers who were much more eager to launch a revolt than he was: many of them were 'plus royalist que le Roy', or as he put it in *A Life at the Centre*, 'There was a dedicated group of commandos, waiting as it were with their faces blackened to launch a Dieppe raid against the forces of opportunism.' In fact the Dieppe analogy was false. Many of them were dying to launch a full–scale invasion. Roy's supporters did not always help his cause. The Treasury Twins, David Dowler and John Harris, while generally outstandingly good advisers on policy and tactics, were sometimes counter-productive because of their partisanship. The world was strictly divided into two classes: you were either for Roy and good, or against him and bad.

During the negotiations about the sterling balances we found that one of the obstacles to agreement was a young brigadier from Ghana who had been appointed their Finance Minister and who, I discovered, had a great admiration for Jim Callaghan after the latter's skilled chairmanship of a Common-wealth finance ministers' conference. I suggested that I should enlist Jim Callaghan's help in persuading the young brigadier. (I had been a junior minister at the Home Office under Jim Callaghan for four months after he had succeeded Roy as Home Secretary and before I went to the Treasury.) David and

John were appalled. 'You *must* not talk to Jim. He's a *bad* man. He's trying to screw us. And anyway he doesn't understand and would cock it all up.' Their reaction seemed to me outrageous and, I still think, completely unjustified. I should have taken the issue to Roy. But in fact relations between Roy and Callaghan were not good. According to Pimlott, in early November, just before Callaghan left the Treasury, Wilson had suggested that Roy should become part of an inner Cabinet and was surprised at the venom of Callaghan's reaction, who launched into a bitter attack on the then Home Secretary as 'an ambitious, conspiring opportunist'. Roy was not impressed with Callaghan's stewardship at the Treasury and, as mentioned, Callaghan had lobbied hard for Tony Crosland to succeed him instead of Roy.

To the best of my recollection, Roy's parliamentary commandos were neither encouraged nor discouraged by him. Bill Rodgers shares my view that Roy took a very cautious, if not passive, line. Philip Ziegler in his biography of Wilson has recorded that they compiled an impressive array of names, but that at the beginning of July 1968 Roy aborted the conspiracy. I believe that the first half of 1968 was the time when he might well have become Prime Minister, if he had been sufficiently ruthless and had been single-mindedly dedicated to the pursuit of power. Wilson was at his weakest. He himself was at his strongest. And the country's position looked and was pretty desperate. In *A Life at the Centre* Roy likens his actions, or rather inaction, at that time to Butler's failure to seize the main chance in 1953 (when both Churchill and Eden were incapacitated by illness). He says at the end of the book that 'I may have avoided doing too much stooping, but I also missed conquering.' This was eminently the moment to conquer. But Roy felt, with some reason, that to challenge Wilson would also have meant some stooping. After all, however inadequate Wilson's leadership was in many ways, he had appointed Roy, although he realized that Roy was the main threat to his leadership and that he was strengthening the position of the only heir apparent. Furthermore, Wilson supported Roy in Cabinet throughout a very difficult time, particularly when battling for painful cuts in expenditure, such as the cancellation of the F111 aircraft, which the Ministry of Defence regarded as vital to the future of the RAF. Indeed during the period of Wilson's government Roy's view of Wilson fluctuated, from exasperation and occasional contempt to liking and a degree of admiration. I believe the main reason why he did not let his commandos loose was because he thought it would be a somewhat dishonourable act. Also in his mind was the risk that a challenge would split the party and endanger economic recovery.

The second opportunity to strike came during the tumult in the party over *In Place of Strife*. When Barbara Castle presented her proposals for curbing strikes, both Wilson and Roy strongly supported them. In 1969 strikes were one of the main threats to future prosperity and in retrospect the proposals seem even more sensible than they did at the time. Roy strongly urged both of them to get the proposals through quickly in a short bill. There seems little doubt that if this had been done the reforms would have gone through relatively easily. Instead momentum was lost, negotiations were started with the trade unions, which gave them time to mobilize opposition, and a coalition was formed in the Labour Party between right-wing trade unionists and the Left. Inside the Cabinet, Callaghan defied the Prime Minister and blatantly voted with the unions when the matter was raised at the National Executive of the Labour Party. As Roy took the view that the position had become hopeless, he finally told Castle he was deserting the cause, news which 'she accepted like St Sebastian receiving another arrow'.

First, was his desertion a blemish on his record, as Dell argued? It seemed a case of bowing to the inevitable, whereas Wilson and Castle were apparently ready to emulate Davy Crockett at the Alamo.[5] Nevertheless, Roy admitted that Wilson and Barbara Castle emerged 'with more credit than the rest of us'. Secondly, was this another lost chance to become Prime Minister? Several of his supporters, such as his parliamentary private secretary, Tom Bradley, were urging him to abandon his support for the bill long before he did so, because they said its cause was hopeless and the bill was the only thing standing between him and the premiership. But it is clear that on this occasion Roy was much more loath to act than in 1968. Although anti-Wilson feeling was stronger in the parliamentary party than ever before, it would have been an act of sheer opportunism, which was one of the main complaints he had against Wilson's leadership. In fact the main threat to Wilson this time came from Callaghan, whose reputation had been restored at the Home Office and whose opposition to trade union reform had made him the obvious focus for discontent. But he felt unable to move without Roy's support and realized this would not be forthcoming. Wilson survived again.

One final charge is made against Roy's record as Chancellor: that he lost Labour the election by refusing to produce a giveaway budget in 1970. His budget was a responsible one, with modest tax reliefs. Despite the urgings of several Cabinet colleagues, notably Crossman, he was determined not to throw away the economic gains of so much toil and sweat by cheap election bribery. If his budget lost the election, ironically it was

---

[5] After a heroic fight against overwhelming odds, Crockett blew himself and the citadel up rather than surrender.

not because it was too responsible but because it proved unexpectedly popular and its popularity persuaded Wilson to plump for an early election, which he lost, when a later one might have been victorious. Polls conducted after the budget showed that it won strong support, with 66 per cent considering it fair, an exceptionally high approval rate. For the first time in many years one opinion poll showed the government ahead of the Conservatives. A responsible refusal to bribe the public had, in the event, won the plaudits of the multitude.

However, the election was lost and Wilson's wish that Roy should succeed him, declared when it looked as if Labour was heading for an easy win, was never realized. 'What if?' is always a question that fascinates historians. Had *In Place of Strife* been pushed through quickly, had the balance of trade figures not been distorted on the pre-election Monday by the fortuitous timing of the imports of expensive Jumbo jets, had England not lost to Germany in the last ten minutes of the World Cup on the previous Sunday night, had the election been postponed, possibly any of these events might have turned defeat into victory. The history of the Labour Party would have been very different and Roy would probably have succeeded Wilson as Prime Minister. Another might-have-been that could have enabled him to achieve that ambition was success for the SDP and the Alliance in 1983, which seemed possible for one brief flickering moment after its launch; but Roy's chancellorship gave him his best chance.

In my view, Roy was always most likely to capture supreme power through succession from within government rather than by assault from outside. He was never a populist politician, the natural leader of a barnstorming campaign, inspiring his troops to raise ladders against castle walls and to brave the burning oil. He was more likely to gain popular respect than arouse mass enthusiasm. As Prime Minister he would have impressed through the wisdom of his strategy, the regard of his colleagues, and the eloquent and dignified defence of well-judged measures, but he was less likely to win an election for the leadership of the Labour Party conducted under today's rules, even if the Labour Party had become a modern social democratic party in pre-Blair days. For his place in history perhaps it did not matter. Through his outstanding success in the two great offices of state in the first Wilson government, he achieved much more than most who successfully climbed to the very top of the greasy pole.

David Marquand

David Marquand started his career as a leader writer on *The Guardian*. After teaching and research posts at Oxford and Sussex universities, in 1966 he was elected Labour MP for Ashfield. In 1977 he became chief adviser in the Secretariat-General of the European Commission, and political adviser to Roy Jenkins as Commission President. Subsequently, he held chairs of politics at the universities of Salford (1978–91) and Sheffield (1991–6) and was Principal of Mansfield College, Oxford (1996–2002). His books include *Ramsay MacDonald* (1977), *The Unprincipled Society* (1988), *The Progressive Dilemma* (1991), *The New Reckoning* (1997), and *Decline of the Public* (2004).

Chapter 8

'The Welsh Wrecker'

DAVID MARQUAND

The 1970 election was a watershed in British history. It was also a watershed in the hitherto smoothly ascending career path of Roy Jenkins. It ushered in a period of economic crisis and political polarization, unprecedented since the end of the Second World War. Jenkins faced testing challenges and agonizing choices, which were to sweep him from the political moorings he had occupied for a quarter of a century. To remain true to himself and his beliefs, he had to slough off his old political skin, and grow a new one. He had to unlearn many of the habits and assumptions he had taken for granted for nearly a quarter of a century. Not least, he had to break away from the Labour Party, into which he had been born and in which he had spent his political life. It was a difficult, often painful task, and it is not surprising that he made false starts and sometimes seemed bogged down in uncertainty. The remarkable thing is that, by the end of the decade, he had changed sufficiently to launch the most dramatic and successful challenge to the existing party system since the 1920s. For most of that time I was an increasingly disaffected, firmly Jenkinsite, Labour MP. I then became a rather implausible Brussels bureaucrat; by the end I had returned happily to academia. From these varied vantage points, I watched him slowly reinvent himself—occasionally with exasperation, more often with admiration, and always with affection.

When Parliament was dissolved in May 1970, all this was in the future. At 49, Jenkins went into the election campaign expecting to become Foreign Secretary in the third Wilson government to which the opinion polls pointed. He also expected that he would be the front-runner to succeed Wilson as party leader and probably as Prime Minister when the latter retired in the not-too-distant future. He had good reasons for both expectations. Wilson had already told him that he planned to send him to the Foreign Office in the next government, and that his own prime ministership would not last long. Quite apart from that, Jenkins's achievements in the governments of 1964–70 were unequalled by any of his possible rivals. As a backbencher, he had been a man of obvious promise, but no one could have called him a parliamentary star. As a minister, his reputation had soared, easily outdistancing those of his older Oxford contemporaries and rivals Denis Healey and Tony Crosland.

In part this was due to his laboriously acquired, but seemingly effortless, mastery of the House of Commons. He had made himself the most deadly parliamentary gladiator on the Labour front bench, and one of the two or three most deadly in the House of Commons. There was more to his rise than skill at the dispatch box. His courageous and buoyant liberalism as Home Secretary from 1965 to 1967 shone like a candle in a naughty world, partially redeeming the government's dismal

1. Roy Jenkins and his mother, c.1923

2. Oxford Union Standing Committee, November 1940 (Aneurin Bevan, seated in the front row next to Roy Jenkins, came from Tredegar, twelve miles from Abersychan)

3. With Denis Healey at the Labour Party Conference, June 1945

4. Southwark Central by-election, 1948

6. With Hilary and Anthony Crosland, July 1953

5. Jennifer Jenkins, Charles Jenkins, and his godfather Clement Attlee, 1949

7. Minister of Aviation,
October 1964

8. The Home Secretary and
the Birmingham Ambulance
Service, 1967

9. Chancellor Jenkins prepares his budget speech, April 1969

10. At East Hendred, 1970

11. Singing Auld-Lang-Syne with James Callaghan and Jenny Lee at the Labour Party Conference, October 1971

12. Keeping Britain in Europe, April 1975, with Jo Grimond, Cledwyn Hughes, Willie Whitelaw, Reginald Maudling, and Sir Con O'Neill

13. Twenty-five years as MP for Stechford, 1975. Left to right: Sir Frank Price, former Lord Mayor; Denis Howell, MP for Small Heath; unknown; RJ; Jennifer Jenkins; Clive Wilkinson, leader of the City Council; Mrs Elsie Smith; Roy Hattersley, MP for Sparkbrook; George Canning, previously RJ's agent, then his chairman; Brian Walden, MP for Ladywood; and Julius Silverman, MP for Aston

and justly unpopular handling of the economy. The dogged determination and ultimately victory-crowned 'two years' hard slog' of his chancellorship set the seal on his reputation as the single most successful minister in the outgoing government. Labour candidates had pathetically little to crow about when the election came. The government's only undoubted achievements—civilizing Home Office legislation at the beginning, and success in turning around the balance of payments at the end—were both due to Jenkins. His only serious rival on the Labour front bench was James Callaghan, but Callaghan's stock had fallen in government while Jenkins's had risen.

Yet Jenkins had handicaps as well as assets. He was often mocked for his posh accent and allegedly grand manner. (*Private Eye* called him 'Smoothiechops'.) However, these mattered less than an imbalance in his Labour Party support. In the parliamentary party he had a hard core of enthusiastic followers and an outer circle of respectful admirers, but he had no real base in the party outside Parliament. Unlike his hero and mentor, Hugh Gaitskell, who had been elected Treasurer before contesting the leadership, he had never been elected to the party's National Executive. He was a quintessential insider in a party founded by and for outsiders; a man of power, not of protest. (Significantly, he chose 'Nine Men of Power' as the title for a collection of biographical essays published in 1973.) He was steeped in the high politics of the late nineteenth and early twentieth centuries, and wrote about them with insight and elegance; too often he gave the impression that he thought the ghosts of Balfour and Asquith still haunted the Palace of Westminster. Like the grandees of the turn of the century, he owed his reputation to glittering performances in the introverted villages of Westminster and Whitehall, but status there did not automatically translate into status in trade union branches or constituency general management committees. When the 1970 election was called, Jenkins was the front-runner in the succession stakes, but even then no one who knew the labour movement would have thought him a likely shoe-in. The handicaps which would have told against him loomed ever larger as events drove on.

The first such event was Heath's election victory. After six years as a minister, Jenkins found himself unexpectedly in opposition. According to his memoirs, he found the experience disorientating, but if so he was not disorientated for long. In August 1970 my wife, two children, and I visited the Jenkinses on a Tuscan holiday. He was at his best: vinous, relaxed, happy, gossipy, and funny. His mind, he wrote in his memoirs, was in tune with the 'Tuscan peace'.[1] A harsh critic might have thought him a little complacent, but in the circumstances complacency seemed forgivable. In the general election George Brown, Labour's Deputy Leader, had lost his seat. A meeting of Jenkins supporters in Dick Taverne's London flat agreed that he should stand for the vacancy. He duly did so, and was triumphantly elected on the first ballot, with 133 votes to Michael Foot's 67 and Fred Peart's 48. Though his crushing victory was partly due to Callaghan's decision not to stand, it seemed to confirm his position as Wilson's heir presumptive. It was buttressed by the shadow chancellorship, which gave him ample opportunities to win debating victories—particularly after Iain Macleod's death in July 1970 and the unimpressive Anthony Barber's appointment as his successor. Only Callaghan, lurking 'like a big pike in the shadows', as Jenkins put it in his

[1] Roy Jenkins, *A Life at the Centre* (1991), 311.

memoirs,[2] could challenge his pre-eminence, and for the moment, Callaghan was virtually invisible.

More ominous creatures were all too visible. In the party outside Parliament, a swirling leftward current, reflecting deep (and understandable) disillusionment with the disappointing record of the Wilson government, was already beginning to run. Dick Taverne held his seat at Lincoln with a reduced majority, but at the count his far-left agent, Leo Beckett, turned angrily to him when it became clear that the general election had been lost, and declared bitterly, 'This is all the fault of prescription charges and the attack on the unions. I knew it would happen. The people won't stand for it.'[3] There were plenty of Leo Becketts in constituency Labour parties and trade union executives. It is not difficult to see why. On the issues on which it had been returned to power in 1964 and 1966, the Wilson government *had* failed. It had promised to raise the rate of economic growth, but no such rise had materialized. It had nailed its colours to the mast of economic planning, but the deflationary package with which it had tried to fend off an inevitable devaluation had made nonsense of its plan. Thanks largely to Jenkins's stubborn resolution, the forced devaluation of 1967 had worked, but only after a long delay and at the cost of further spending cuts. Many hitherto moderate party members, as well as long-standing left-wingers, felt cheated. Before the election they had stifled their doubts. Now they began to suspect that the Left's explanation for what had gone wrong— that Wilson's ministers had whored after the false gods of the mixed economy and betrayed their own people in the process—might have something in it.

[2] Ibid. 310.
[3] Dick Taverne, *The Future of the Left: Lincoln and After* (1974), 49.

Had the social democratic Right offered a convincing alternative explanation, the leftward current might have been halted. Unfortunately, we found it extraordinarily difficult to do so. One reason was that most leading social democrats had been members of the government, and were implicated in its failures. A more serious one was that the most obvious manifestation of Labour's lurch to the left was an increasingly strident hostility to the European Community, which the outgoing Labour government had applied to join, and with which the Heath government soon started to negotiate entry terms. Over Europe, the Labour Right was split. Though most social democrats were in favour of entry, some were not. The apolitical, trade union Right (the 'tearoom vote', as it used to be called) were mostly indifferent, and in some cases hostile; on the whole, they took their cue from the party leadership, and to a lesser extent from their unions. The more salient the European question became, the more beleaguered were the pro-European social democrats, and the more isolated from their old allies. Partly for reasons of principle, and partly because our political survival was at stake, Europe became an all-consuming preoccupation for almost two years. All this applied with special force to Jenkins. He was not just an enthusiast for Community entry; he was irrevocably committed. He had been the chief Labour champion of the European cause for more than a decade. When Gaitskell was leader, he had resigned from the opposition front bench to campaign for it. One of his most memorable speeches as Chancellor of the Exchequer was a commanding exposition of the political case for membership. For him to wobble now was unthinkable. And not wobbling meant giving primacy to the European issue over all others.

Like a subsidence-induced crack in the wall of an old building, Labour's European schism developed gradually. As late as

January 1971 Jenkins made a hardline pro-European speech from the Opposition front bench, without recriminations from his colleagues. Outside Parliament, however, the anti-European tide was running strongly; and the mood of the parliamentary party was beginning to shift accordingly. In January 132 Labour MPs signed an unofficial anti-European Commons motion. By March it was becoming clear that, even with a strong pro-European lead from the top, it would be difficult to hold the parliamentary party to the pro-European line which Labour had taken in government, and that the party conference in October would almost certainly vote against entry.

Jenkinsite pro-Europeans did their best to stem the tide. Thanks largely to David Owen's flair and energy, and with Jenkins's avuncular support in the background, some of us managed to persuade 100 Labour MPs to sign a pro-European declaration, also signed by a number of continental social democratic leaders, with Willy Brandt at their head. It was published as an advertisement in *The Guardian* on 10 May. This did wonders for Jenkinsite morale, and proved to the rest of the party that Jenkins was still a political force to be reckoned with, but with hindsight it also carried a less obvious message. Jenkins and his pro-European followers were no longer party insiders. Insensibly, and without fully realizing it, we—and he—had shifted to the outside track. We were a minority, a party within a party like the Bevanites of yore. Jenkins himself had become the Bevan of the Labour Right—an eloquent, passionate, mercurial, and vulnerable Celt, torn between loyalty to the party which had helped to make him what he was, and a visceral unwillingness to bow the knee to a machine which seemed bent on forcing him to betray his beliefs.

After the *Guardian* advertisement, the pace hotted up. On

25 May 1971 Callaghan abandoned the shadows. In the unlikely location of a Southampton primary school he launched a fierce attack on the government's stance in the entry negotiations, in language which implied that no acceptable terms would ever be arrived at. Most damaging to the European cause was his populist appeal to latent British Francophobia on the non-issue of whether French should be the language of Europe, foolishly raised in a passing comment by Pompidou in a *Panorama* television programme. After evoking the sacred names of Chaucer, Shakespeare, and Milton, Callaghan ended with the immortal words 'Non, merci beaucoup'.[4]

The 'non merci' speech was a bombshell. Wilson saw it as a threat to his leadership, from the only potential successor with a realistic chance of using the European issue as a lever for supplanting him. Even before Callaghan's démarche he had shifted his position slightly, but perceptibly, towards the anti-European camp. Thereafter his shift steadily gathered momentum. As it did so, others shifted too. In late June Geoffrey Rippon, the ministerial leader of the British negotiating team, returned in triumph from Luxembourg with agreed terms for British entry. In July Denis Healey, who had announced his conversion to EEC entry in a *Daily Mirror* article at the end of May, underwent a sudden reconversion to rejectionism. Tony Crosland, once almost as outspoken a pro-European as Jenkins himself, told his constituency party that Europe was a low priority for him, and that although he was still in favour of entry he would not vote to keep Heath in power. On 17 July the Labour Party held a one-day special conference on EEC entry. Thanks largely to a magnificent debating speech by the most talented of the younger social democrats, John Mackintosh, pro-Europeans left the hall in

[4] Kenneth O. Morgan, *Callaghan: A Life* (1997), 395.

good spirits. But Jenkins himself was unable to speak; as Deputy Leader, he was bound by the collective responsibility of the National Executive. The conference ended with a tortuous and lacklustre speech by Wilson, denying that the terms agreed by the government would have been accepted by the Labour Party, and making it clear that he was now against entry. In his memoirs Jenkins recalled that listening to Wilson 'was like watching someone being sold down the river into slavery, drifting away, depressed but unprotesting'.[5] At the time, most Jenkinsites reacted with riper language.

It was now clear that Labour faced one of the most bruising internal battles in its history. Both sides flexed their muscles and counted heads. The chief head-counter on the pro-market side was William (Bill) Rodgers, whose deft, sympathetic, but insistent unofficial whipping generated a mood of mutual loyalty and moral commitment in the pro-market camp, without which Jenkins would have had few followers. Jenkins himself did not do much counting, but he did a lot of flexing. Without histrionics of any sort, and without bringing pressure on anyone else, he made it utterly clear in private meetings with his supporters that, come what may, he would be in the pro-entry lobby when the time came. Others could backslide, or abstain, if they wished. He would not. After more than thirty years I can still hear the steel in his voice. I trembled a little, but I exulted; and I am sure others did the same. Some pro-Europeans did abstain in the end, but a substantial majority of us followed Jenkins into the pro-entry lobby. We did so because he had set the standard by which the rest of us felt bound to judge ourselves.

That was not all. At the special conference, Jenkins had been muzzled. He must have been bursting with suppressed emotion.

[5] Jenkins, *A Life at the Centre*, 320.

At a meeting of the parliamentary party two days later, it flowed out like lava from a hitherto quiescent volcano. In a speech of blistering passion, which no one who heard it will ever forget, Jenkins tore apart the tormented convolutions with which Wilson had justified his change of front and the breezy little Englandism with which Callaghan had justified his. He was interrupted every two or three sentences by violent applause; when he sat down there was an eruption of enthusiasm which lasted for several minutes. (According to Jenkins's memoirs, an elderly Scottish MP contrived to bang the table in front of him with his feet.[6]) There was a price to be paid. The anti-European Left were furious. 'I used to respect you a great deal,' Barbara Castle told Jenkins, 'but I will never do so again as long as I live.' Dick Crossman told him (with some justice), 'the trouble with you is that you think you are a Gaitskell and you are nothing of the sort. You are much more a Bevan than you are a Gaitskell. You have all the Welsh capacity for wrecking.'[7] Always prone to bouts of paranoia, Wilson thought the demonstration had been deliberately orchestrated to undermine him, and probably became marginally more inclined to the anti-market camp as a result. But the benefits far outweighed these costs. Thanks to Rodgers, the Labour marketeers were becoming a cohesive group. Thanks to Jenkins's speech at the party meeting, we were a group with a leader whom we were proud to follow.

The moment of truth came on 28 October, when the House voted on the principle of Community entry. By now, the Labour Party Conference had voted against by a crushing 5 to 1 majority. The parliamentary party had followed suit, by 159 to 89. By 140 to 111 it had also voted to impose a three-line whip. Despite these formidable pressures, 69 Labour MPs

---

[6] Jenkins, *A Life at the Centre*, 323.   [7] Ibid. 323–4.

voted for entry, Jenkins and Douglas Houghton, the chairman of the parliamentary party, at their head. Another 20 abstained. The majority for entry was 112. This was not the end of the story. The enabling legislation to make a reality of Community membership was still to be passed; and Jenkins was to face many agonizing dilemmas during and after its passage. All the same, the 28 October vote was the great climacteric of his career. For him, nothing would be the same again.

What drove him on? Why did he spurn abstention—the classic way for a minority to indicate dissent from a majority decision? Why did he become the Welsh wrecker who so disconcerted that specialist in wrecking, Dick Crossman? Where did the passionate commitment that lay behind his parliamentary party speech come from? Part of the answer is that if the vote on entry had gone the other way, Britain would have been self-excluded from the Community, and that Jenkins thought self-exclusion would be a national disaster. But the roots of his commitment went deeper than that. He was a European of the head, but he was much more a European of the heart. He had not always been one. Unlike Heath, whose Europeanism stemmed from travels in a Nazi-haunted continent on the eve of the Second World War, Jenkins was a Euro-sceptic in his early days as a backbencher. He loyally supported the Attlee government's European policy and voted against the Schuman Plan. But, by the time I came to know him in the early 1960s, his imagination and sense of history had been gripped by the audacious grandeur of the European project. It retained its grip on them for the rest of his life.

That was only part of the story. For him the European question was not only about Europe. It was also about Britain—about the kind of country Britain was to be, about the quality of her political and social life, about the identity that would take the place of her old imperial identity. Though I never heard him say this, I believe that Jenkins saw the battle over European entry as part of an even more momentous battle for the soul of post-imperial Britain—a battle between outward-looking tolerance and generosity of spirit on the one hand, and mean-minded, Pecksniffian narrowness on the other. He knew, of course, that some (though far from all) Labour anti-Europeans shared the liberal values that had inspired his civilizing reforms as Home Secretary. But he feared that, if the 'antis' won, their victory would let loose a Franken-stein's monster of illiberalism, xenophobia, and resentment. Finally, the European question—at any rate as posed in 1971—was about the responsibilities of political leadership. For Jenkins, the sight of a stampede by former Cabinet ministers retreating from the commitment to Community membership they had made in office was shocking as well as offensive. In one of his favourite condemnatory phrases, their behaviour was below the level of events. He was not a fastidious political dandy, unwilling ever to dirty his hands. He knew as well as anyone else that politics sometimes involves trimming. But it was one thing to trim on the everyday questions that make up the small change of politics, another to do so on a great, historic question that might determine the future of the country for generations. For Jenkins, the vote on Community entry was comparable in significance to 'the first Reform Bill, the repeal of the Corn Laws, Gladstone's Home Rule Bills, the Lloyd George Budget and the Parliament Bill, the Munich Agree-ment and the May 1940 vote'.[8] To trim on such a vote was to devalue the currency of democratic politics.

[8] Jenkins, *A Life at the Centre*, 329.

By a terrible irony, the aftermath of the 28 October vote saw him mired in political confusion and personal misery. No sooner was the vote on entry over than Michael Foot and Tony Benn announced that they would stand for the deputy leadership. Jenkins had to decide whether or not to stand as well. Overhanging that question was the more painful question of what to do when the enabling legislation on Community membership came before the House. It would be a logical absurdity to vote against the enabling legislation having voted for the principle of entry; it would also be demeaning. Yet if the pro-Europeans abstained or voted with the government they would have to leave the front bench and abandon their positions in the party hierarchy. Most of Jenkins's supporters still thought in conventional Labour Party terms. They were desperately anxious to return to the party fold, and persuaded themselves that he would still have a chance of inheriting the leadership at some stage in the future if he returned as well, and retained the deputy leadership as a symbol of his return. The corollary was, of course, to vote with the party on the enabling legislation. Not for the last time, Jenkins paid too much heed to the more cautious of his friends. And so he stood—in effect announcing that he still hankered for the inside track and did not really want to be a wrecker after all.

Then came a further turn of the screw. All three candidates for the deputy leadership were required to announce their voting intentions on the enabling legislation. Jenkins made a tortuous and, as he thought in retrospect, 'sophistical' statement, explaining that he would have no difficulty in voting with the party, providing he was not called upon to undo his 28 October vote; and promising that he would resign if he found it necessary not to vote with the party in future. On that basis he was re-elected as Deputy Leader on the second ballot, with

140 votes to Michael Foot's 126. It was an agonizing affair; and in retrospect I have no doubt that he made the wrong choice. But I can hardly blame him. I made a similarly tortuous and sophistical statement to my own constituency party.

He soon discovered that he had locked himself into a prison of inconsistency and humiliation. The second reading debate on the European Communities Bill, giving effect to the vote of principle, took place on 17 February 1972. Had Jenkins abstained or voted with the government, he could plausibly have claimed that he was acting in accordance with his statement to the parliamentary party. He had undertaken to vote with the party unless he was called upon to undo his vote of 28 October; and a vote against the second reading would do precisely that. Unfortunately, the logic of his statement ran counter to the logic of his decision to stand again for the deputy leadership. He had stood in the knowledge that enabling legislation would have to be tabled sooner or later, and that that legislation would have to have a second reading. He had not said that if the Labour Party voted against the second reading he would defy the whip; had he done so, he would not have been elected. He could hardly announce that his conscience would not allow him to vote with the party after all, and then resign from the post to which he had been elected only a few months before. Even if he insisted that his statement to the party logically implied a refusal to vote against the second reading, such a course would seem both casuistical and frivolous—not only to the increasingly rampant anti-Europeans, but to many of his pro-European supporters as well. Accordingly, Jenkins voted with the party. I remember sitting in the Smoking Room with him and a hangdog group of pro-Europeans, waiting for the Division. We could not bear to go into the Chamber to listen to the wind-up speeches. When the Division was called, we slunk off to the Labour lobby, lacerated by guilt. I suspect, though he never said so in my hearing, that this must have been the worst moment in Jenkins's political life.

He soon faced the prospect of further humiliation. For some time, Tony Benn had advocated a referendum on Community entry. He had had little support. But as the European Communities Bill journeyed through the Commons, Conservative anti-marketeers seized on the idea, and put down an amendment requiring a referendum before the legislation could take effect. In mid-March Benn tried to persuade Labour's Shadow Cabinet to support the referendum amendment, and failed by 8 votes to 4. Then the Labour Party National Executive decided to stir the pot, and 'invited' the parliamentary party to consider voting for a referendum. On 29 March, on the eve of the Easter recess, the Shadow Cabinet reversed its previous decision, and voted for a referendum by 8 to 6, Wilson and Callaghan both voting with the majority. For Jenkins and his closest supporters in the Shadow Cabinet, this was the last straw. They were opposed in principle to referendums (no nationwide referendum had ever taken place in Britain). They also feared that, if the Labour Party voted with the Conservative anti-marketeers, the referendum amendment might be carried and that the referendum itself might be lost.

Their reaction to the Shadow Cabinet vote had deeper roots as well. With appalled despair, they had watched the party leadership turn a somersault on the principle of Community entry. Now it had turned another one. To appease the anti-marketeers, they had forced themselves, sick at heart, to vote with the party on the second reading of the European Communities Bill; and they were ashamed of having done so. Now the anti-marketeers were trying to make them vote against their convictions again. If they submitted, further humiliations would almost certainly be inflicted on them. Having tasted blood twice, the anti-European Left would be thirsting for more. Jenkins, in particular, was convinced that, with Wilson in tow, the antis were determined to do everything they could to harass and demean the Labour Europeans. His greatest asset was his extraordinary standing with the non-political public, who saw him as a man of principle with the courage to stick by his beliefs. He feared that a second act of appeasement would undermine his public reputation and encourage the Left to try to force him into a third. He felt bound to stand and fight. And that entailed resignation from the deputy leadership.

David Owen, Robert Maclennan, and I made a forlorn pilgrimage to East Hendred to dissuade him, but it was clear from the moment we got there that his mind was made up. When the House returned after the recess, he duly resigned. George Thomson and Harold Lever resigned from the Shadow Cabinet with him. On the ostensible issue, I still think Owen, Maclennan, and I were right and Jenkins wrong. The referendum is now part of Britain's unwritten constitution, and the heavens have not fallen. Of course, a referendum on EEC entry might have been lost, but general elections are sometimes lost by the governments that hold them, and no one would consider that a justification for suspending them. Democracy is a risky business. Benn's vision of proletarian socialism was hopelessly flawed, but he was right in thinking that Community membership was too momentous a question to be settled by the ordinary processes of Britain's parliamentary system. However, the ostensible issue was not the real one. In truth, Jenkins's resignation was not about the referendum. It was the only way he could see to lance a swelling boil of misery and guilt, caused by the fundamental falsity of his position as part of the collective leadership of a party with which he passionately disagreed on the central issue of the moment. He resigned on the wrong issue. It would have been better not to have stood again for the deputy leadership, or to have resigned over the 28 October vote on the principle of Community membership. But resignations are often wrongly timed, as Aneurin Bevan showed in 1951 and Michael Heseltine in 1986. Like them, Jenkins resigned because he would not have been able to live with himself otherwise: because he had to have space in which to be his own man again.

By yet another irony, he was unsure how to use the space once he got it. He was now firmly on the outside track. He had left the party hierarchy within which he had risen with astonishing ease and speed. He could not rationally expect to return to it as an insider: his only hope was to overwhelm it as an outsider. But that was easier said than done. He was, after all, an insider by instinct as well as habit. In any case, outsider politics bristled with hard questions. Should he break with the Labour Party altogether, and try to mobilize middle opinion behind a new grouping and a new political alignment? Or should he try to mobilize moderate opinion *inside* the Labour Party against the opportunistic tergiversations of the leadership and the dogmatic intolerance of the Left? Should he try to save the party system from the polarizing forces which were making it ever narrower and more rigid? Or should he try to replace it? It took him a long time to find answers to these questions. Until he had done so, he was bound to fumble; and most of his followers fumbled too.

Three examples stand out. Before his resignation, David Owen and I had persuaded him that he ought to broaden his appeal by making a series of speeches, unconnected with the

European question, which might later be published as a short book. We hoped he would emulate Joe Chamberlain's 'Unauthorised Programme' of 1885, and offer a radical alternative both to Bennite socialism and to Wilsonian pragmatism. Nine months after the election Judith Marquand, my wife, had left the Treasury to work for him; she, Owen, and I became a mini-Think Tank, commissioning papers, preparing briefs, and drafting speeches. On one level, the project was a success. *What Matters Now*, the paperback in which the speeches were published, has worn better than most such books do. Yet Jenkins himself seemed oddly ambivalent about the operation. The first speech, largely drafted by me, ended by calling for a new kind of politics and quoting Andrew Marvell's tribute to Cromwell for 'cast[ing] the kingdoms old into another mould'. It was interpreted as—and was, in fact, intended to be—an easily decoded critique of Wilson's whole style of leadership. But when Jenkins was asked in a radio interview if he was making a bid to oust Wilson, he insisted that his call for a new politics had nothing to do with personalities.

It would be wrong to make too much of this: Aneurin Bevan and even Winston Churchill executed comparable zigzags in their days in the wilderness. Much more significant was his approach to the later speeches. He titivated the drafts we gave him, and delivered the results with his customary skill, but I never felt that his heart was in it. When the series was over, he made no real attempt to develop the ideas he had set out or to campaign for them in Parliament or the party. At the time I was grievously disappointed. In retrospect, I can see that Owen and I—and in an odd way Jenkins himself—had failed to plumb the depths of his predicament or the agonizing uncertainties that went with it. The premiss of the whole exercise was that the Labour Party could be saved for the pluralistic, tolerant social democracy for which he had stood since his early days in politics. Deep down, and without fully realizing the implications himself, he was beginning to doubt that. He did not know how to act on his doubts. Indeed, he had not yet acknowledged their existence, either to himself or to others. Even so, they niggled in the background. The result was an uneasy stasis.

The second example was less public. Dick Taverne's defiance of the Labour whip on the 28 October vote had outraged the dominant far-left faction in his constituency party; and after a long and bitter battle he was deselected. With characteristic boldness, he resigned his seat and stood as an independent in the by-election that followed. It soon became clear that public opinion was with him. Early in 1973 he told Jenkins that he thought he would win. He added that if Jenkins broke from the Labour Party and campaigned for him, the victory would be overwhelming, and that the by-election could become the launching pad for a new party. Jenkins toyed with the idea. I remember his raising the subject with me, in an exploratory, almost wistful fashion; and I expect he did the same with others. But he told Taverne that the timing was wrong: potential Labour recruits to any new party would be preoccupied with the nationwide local elections which were due in May. No doubt, he also feared—almost certainly correctly—that none of the heavyweight Labour Europeans in the Commons would follow him. But the real reason, I believe, was that, when it came to the point, he was not yet ready to cut the cords of sentiment and memory that tied him to the Labour Party. In the end, Taverne won the by-election with 58 per cent of the vote and a majority of around 13,000. But it would be eight years before a Jenkins-inspired breakaway from the Labour Party finally took place.

The third example followed logically from the second.

After Lincoln, insider instincts increasingly prevailed over outsider doubts. A sadly depleted group of Jenkinsite MPs used to meet periodically in each other's houses, more for mutual support than for any significant political purpose. Again and again, we chewed over the great question: should Jenkins stand for the leadership against Wilson? When he resigned from the front bench, he had undertaken not to stand for any parliamentary party office in 1972, but he had said nothing about later years. Robert Maclennan, in particular, was a passionate and eloquent advocate of a leadership challenge in the autumn of 1973, but he was by no means alone. According to his memoirs, however, Jenkins himself was always sceptical. In retrospect, it is not difficult to see why. Insiders do not challenge incumbent leaders, not in the Labour Party at any rate. Standing against Wilson would have been a quintessentially outsider act, for which he was still unprepared, emotionally and intellectually. Instead he decided to stand again for the Shadow Cabinet, as most of his senior supporters predictably advised. With Britain's membership of the Community an accomplished fact, and the European question apparently settled, it was the obvious course for an insider. He came a respectable fifth in the election; and accepted the shadow home secretaryship. The Welsh wrecker, it seemed, had come in from the cold.

Or had he? By now a general election was beginning to loom. It was self-evident that Jenkins's chances of displacing Wilson would be much greater if Labour lost than if it won. More importantly, it was also clear that the causes he held dear would be much more likely to prevail after a second Labour defeat than after a victory. If Heath won a second term, Britain would be inextricably part of the European Community. The pendulum of Labour Party opinion would probably swing back towards the social democratic Right, as it had done after the 1955 defeat. On the other hand, victory for a Labour Party which had shifted far to the left would make the social democrats' position even more difficult than it was already. Ambition and principle pointed to the same conclusion: a Conservative victory was in Jenkins's interests. To judge by their memoirs, David Owen and Bill Rodgers were both reluctant to acknowledge this brute fact of political life,[9] but it was bound to lurk at the back of Jenkins's mind, and it haunted Jenkinsite confabulations like an unacknowledged spectre. It did not stop him from demolishing the hapless Anthony Barber in a savage, brilliant wind-up speech in a censure debate on the eve of the Christmas recess, or from enthusing the Labour benches as they had not been enthused for years, but it meant that a lingering question mark hung over his return to the parliamentary party's inner councils.

That question mark dominated the next two years. In February 1974, desperate to save his incomes policy from the depredations of the National Union of Mineworkers, Heath called a general election on the ticket of 'Who Governs?' Almost without exception, politicians and pundits thought he would win. A lunchtime Jenkinsite gathering at Robert Maclennan's house the day before the election was officially announced unanimously agreed that if Labour lost, as we all expected it to do, Jenkins should stand forthwith for the leadership. Though Jenkins himself seemed curiously unhappy about the idea, the rest of us all agreed that if Labour won, he should insist on becoming Chancellor of the Exchequer. I left the meeting feeling more cheerful about politics than I had felt

---

[9] Bill Rodgers, *Fourth Among Equals* (2000), 136; David Owen, *Time to Declare* (1991), 213.

since the entry vote in October 1971: at last, an end to our long months of confusion and hesitation seemed to be in sight.

As in 1970, the politicians and pundits turned out to be wrong. In the election, Labour won a smaller share of the vote than the Conservatives, but it emerged with slightly more seats. After trying and failing to make a deal with the Liberals, Heath grumpily resigned; and Wilson formed a minority Labour government. The question mark hanging over Jenkins's return to Labour's collective leadership was cruelly exposed. With a challenge to Wilson now ruled out, the choices before him were all distinctly unappetizing. His followers all thought he should insist on returning to the Treasury. However, he did not really want to become Chancellor of the Exchequer again, even if—as seemed possible for a fleeting moment over the post-election weekend—Wilson offered him the job. Another option was to stay out of the government altogether. But that would have meant outsiderdom with a vengeance; and having just fought the election on the party manifesto, it would have been difficult to turn around and claim that there were irreconcilable policy differences between him and his putative Cabinet colleagues. The only remaining option was to go to the Home Office, which he had been shadowing since his return to the front bench. That too was unappealing. Nine years before, appointment as Home Secretary had been a big step on an upward escalator. Now it would be a small, but unmistakable, step on a downward one.

With fatalistic inertia, he eventually accepted Wilson's offer of the Home Office. Then followed one of the most depressing gatherings of my life. The Jenkinsite group had agreed to meet on the Monday evening following the election. Jenkins was late. As soon as he arrived, he blurted out the news that he was to be Home Secretary, not Chancellor. Cruelly, but truthfully, Rodgers insisted that this was a defeat and asked if he had made it clear that he wanted the Treasury. Jenkins angrily replied that it had been difficult enough to succeed as Chancellor when Wilson wanted him in the post, and that it would be utterly impossible if he had forced himself on a reluctant Prime Minister and Cabinet. The meeting petered out on a note of sour dismay. Though few of us saw it then, it is clear now that Jenkins's career at the summit of Labour Party politics was effectively over. He had closed off the outside track, and the inside track had led him to the buffers. For the time being, at least, the Welsh wrecker had been out-manoeuvred by the English Artful Dodger.

But only for the time being. Wilson's overriding aim was to keep the Labour Party together, and his proudest boast, that he managed to do so, in spite of the schism over Europe. In the short run, shunting Jenkins into the remote pastures of the Home Office instead of appointing him to the politically central post of Chancellor was a smart move, from this point of view. At the Treasury he would have had to fight continual divisive battles with his colleagues and the Bennite Left, causing uproar in the party. At the Home Office he could be, as Wilson himself put it, 'semi-detached'. In the long run, however, semi-detachment made Jenkins more of an outsider and less of an insider, and helped to pave the way for his eventual breakaway. By August 1974 the doubts Jenkins had suppressed during the *What Matters Now* exercise were beginning to reach the surface. He wrote privately that the outlook was 'shrouded in darkness, danger and confusion'; and began to think that 'the only way through this miasma might be outside the mould of traditional two-party politics'.[10]

---

[10] Jenkins, *Life at the Centre*, 388.

The first public milestone on the road to a breakaway appeared in the following summer. In opposition, Labour had committed itself to 'renegotiate' the terms of EC entry which Heath had agreed, and to submit the results to the judgement of the people. In October 1974 Wilson called another general election and won it with a small majority. By now the party was firmly committed to a referendum when the renegotiation process was over. In March 1975 Wilson pronounced himself satisfied by the renegotiated terms. After much agitated coming and going, it was agreed that the referendum would be fought by cross-party 'umbrella' organizations, and that Jenkins would be president of the pro-European organization, Britain in Europe.

Against our expectations, the referendum was pure joy for Jenkins and the Jenkinsites. Jenkins threw himself into the Yes campaign with inspiriting enthusiasm and brio. He presided over the Britain in Europe executive, with the 'loyal, resourceful, comforting' Willie Whitelaw, whom Mrs Thatcher had recently defeated in the Conservatives' leadership election, as a genial, morale-boosting adjutant.[11] Accompanied by Conservative or Liberal allies, he addressed crowded, attentive halls all over the country, ending the campaign with a packed, 2,000-strong meeting in the Central Hall, Westminster. A couple of hours before the Central Hall meeting, he recorded a forty-five-minute television debate with Tony Benn, which was watched by an audience of 9 million. There was no doubt that he was the star of Britain in Europe. Throughout, he had the morale-enhancing scent of victory in his nostrils, but that was not the only source of the élan that put him centre-stage. He revelled in the chance to escape publicly from the narrow

---

[11] Jenkins, *Life at the Centre*, 416.

rigidities of party politics, to work cooperatively with like-minded Liberals and Conservatives in a great, national cause, and to appeal, across conventional party lines, to a public that seemed to hunger for serious, non-partisan argument. The final result—a crushing 2 to 1 majority for staying in the Community—was a personal triumph as well as a victory for the European cause. Less obviously, it also gave a powerful boost to his growing disdain for the constraints of party. Before the referendum he had been, in the parlance of Soviet dissidents, an 'internal émigré' from the Labour Party. Now he was well on the way to becoming an external one.

His referendum 'high' was followed by a deep six-month 'low'. He became increasingly ill at ease in a directionless, ineffective, and often illiberal Cabinet, and increasingly exasperated with the Labour Party shibboleths to which most of his colleagues paid obeisance, but he saw no escape from either. Then—as so often in his career—fate intervened. At a Boxing Day party in December 1975 Lord Goodman told him that Wilson had made up his mind to resign in March. Soon afterwards the prospect of a still more unexpected change of fortune appeared on the horizon. In late January 1976 Wilson told him that Community circles felt that the next President of the Commission should be British; and that Heath and Jenkins were the only *papabile* British possibilities. Jenkins, Wilson added, ought to have the first refusal. Jenkins's immediate response was to turn the offer down, but a few days later he changed his mind and wrote to Wilson to that effect. A month later he visited Paris, where President Giscard d'Estaing and Jean Monnet, the greatest of the Community's founding fathers, urged him to take the job. To all intents and purposes, he now had the offer of the Commission presidency in his pocket.

All this time Wilson's impending resignation had been a

closely guarded secret, but on 16 March it was publicly announced. The opportunity for which Jenkins had been waiting since the late 1960s had come at last—nearly five years too late. Even so, he threw his hat into the ring. His motives were mixed. According to his memoirs he realized that he had no chance of winning, and stood only because he did not want to disappoint the 'troops' behind him. I am not so sure. I suspect his position was more complicated than that. He did have troops, and he did have obligations to us, but I don't believe he would deliberately have embarked on a draining, hopeless election campaign solely for our sakes. I think he—and we—operated on two different levels at once. On the top level, he expected to lose. He knew he was now out of tune with large sections of the Labour Party and they with him. He also knew, none better, that for some time he had done virtually nothing to cultivate support among the marginal voters in the parliamentary party. And yet, on a much deeper level, an ember of hope still glowed. Sixty-nine Labour MPs had defied the whip with him in 1971; surely that was a worthwhile launching pad? In any case, what did he have to lose? It was worth a try. As far as I can remember, that was my own mood at the time. I suspect it was his as well.

Be that as it may, we fought a vigorous campaign. There were six candidates altogether—Callaghan, Foot, Healey, Benn, and Crosland, as well as Jenkins. The election was by exhaustive ballot, and we all took it for granted that no one would win on the first ballot. Everything would depend on the relative positions of the four right and centre candidates. The canvassing returns were hard to read: even more than in ordinary elections, the voters did not always tell the truth. This left ample room for self-deception; and we eagerly deceived ourselves. We were desperately anxious for Jenkins to win, not just because we liked and admired him, but because we saw him as the only unequivocal standard-bearer of a liberal, internationalist social democracy that none of the other candidates could be relied upon to fight for. If he came ahead of Callaghan on the first ballot, we told ourselves, or even if he were only a short distance behind, he could come through in the end, by picking up votes from Crosland and Healey.

These false hopes made the result almost unbearable. On the first ballot Foot was top with 90 votes, Callaghan second with 84, and Jenkins third with 56. Benn had 37, Healey 30, and Crosland 17. In retrospect, Jenkins's vote was more than respectable, but at the time it came as a bitter disappointment. He and his campaign team met in a state of shock to discuss what he should do. With characteristic belligerence Dickson Mabon urged him to fight on. The rest of us all agreed, without serious discussion, that he had no alternative but to withdraw. Victory, we decided, was now impossible, and there was no point in playing games. Jenkins closed the meeting with Robert E. Lee's adieu to the defeated Confederate Army: 'With an increasing admiration of your courtesy and devotion to your country and a grateful remembrance of your kind and generous consideration for myself, I bid you all an affectionate farewell.' In the end, Callaghan won on the third ballot, with 176 votes to Foot's 137.

The sequel was even harder to bear. Though there can be no certainty, it seems clear that before the leadership campaign began Jenkins had decided that, while his first preference was to be Prime Minister of Britain, his second was to be President of the European Commission. The foreign secretaryship was a good third in his list of preferences; staying on as Home Secretary was a bad fourth.[12] Perhaps in deference to his

---

[12] Jenkins, *European Diary* (1989), 6; *Life at the Centre*, 442.

friends, perhaps because he had changed his mind about his priorities, perhaps because the leadership campaign had temporarily reinvigorated his appetite for British politics, he now made a bid for the Foreign Office. However, Callaghan turned him down. Most of his closest friends urged him to stay, but after Callaghan's rebuff Brussels beckoned irresistibly. He stayed on as Home Secretary until September 1976. On 6 January 1977 he was installed as President of the European Commission. It felt like the end of an old song.

Once again, surprises were in store. When he left British politics, Jenkins was careful not to rule out a return. During his first, unhappy months in Brussels, he told me that, although he never thought about the House of Commons during the day, he dreamed about it every night. I assume (though I don't know) that Westminster hankerings became less acute as he settled in, but I never felt that the Commission was his *métier*. He was a successful President, but the presidency did not fulfil him. He was a politician of passion and force, not a diplomat, and still less a technocrat. In Brussels his greatest qualities—the political courage that led him to defy the party whip in the vote on Community entry, the Celtic fire that enabled him to inspire the Labour Europeans at the never-to-be-forgotten party meeting in the summer of 1971—were smothered. Beneath the Balliol carapace, he was a political romantic, as he showed in his great biographies of Gladstone and Churchill, and there was not much scope for romance in the corridors of the Berlaymont.

Yet the Commission presidency was an excellent vantage point from which to keep an unobtrusive eye on the British political scene, and Jenkins made full use of it. Half his weekends were spent at East Hendred; old political friends visited him in Brussels; and he retained his links with the Labour Committee for Europe. On one extraordinary occasion Harold Wilson lunched with him in Brussels and urged him not to cut himself off from British politics, since he would almost certainly be needed in a coalition government. (Jenkins told me what Wilson had said with a revealing mixture of surface scepticism and inner excitement. I am sorry to say I pooh-poohed the idea.) Meanwhile, he watched and brooded. He thought Callaghan a better Prime Minister than he had expected, but from his Brussels eyrie he could see, all too clearly, that the increasingly rickety Labour coalition was in deep, perhaps terminal, crisis, while a narrow, bitter ideological fundamentalism made the running in both the major parties. Then came the 1979 election, Labour's defeat, and Mrs Thatcher's arrival at 10 Downing Street. Suddenly, the politics of the Left and centre-left became fluid again. Like a veteran warhorse scenting battle, Jenkins began to hanker for action.

I saw him twice that summer. The first time was in Strasbourg, where I had gone to observe the first meeting of the first directly elected European Parliament. At a private dinner after the session we talked light-heartedly, but with a serious undertone, about the possibility of forming a new party, and about who among the parliamentary Jenkinsites would be likely to join it. We thought Bill Rodgers would do so, and probably Shirley Williams as well. David Owen, we thought, would stay in the Labour Party. On my second visit, this time to Brussels, Jenkins told me that he had been invited to give the Dimbleby Lecture that autumn, and showed me the start of a draft text. I thought it too academic, and told him so. My last encounter with him before the Dimbleby explosion was on a dank November evening at East Hendred. By now the lecture was almost ready for delivery. According to his memoirs, Jenkins thought me 'not noticeably enthusiastic' when I read it, but that says more about his own pre-lecture tension and need for reassurance than about my reaction. I did not foresee how far the Dimbleby ripples would spread, but I rejoiced at its call to arms. Only one small point worried me. Jenkins ended the draft with a call to strengthen the political 'centre'. I got in touch with Richard Holme, with whom I was then in close contact, and told him what Jenkins planned to say. 'For God's sake,' said Holme, 'he mustn't talk about the centre: Liberals hate being called a centre party; we see ourselves as radicals.' I gave Jenkins Holme's message. He insisted that he had to refer to the 'centre'; his peroration was built around Yeats's famous line 'The centre does not hold'. In the end we compromised on 'radical centre'; and to the great subsequent advantage of Tony Blair, the term entered the political language. So far as I know, Blair has never acknowledged his debt, either to the Dimbleby Lecture peroration or to the SDP which flowed from it. He owes it just the same.

Anthony Lester

Anthony Lester QC is a practising member of Blackstone Chambers and a Liberal Democrat Peer. He was Special Adviser to the Home Secretary (Roy Jenkins), from 1974 to 1976, with responsibility for policy advice on equality legislation and human rights. He introduced two Private Members' Bills in the Lords to incorporate the European Human Rights Convention into UK law and has argued many leading cases before English, European, and Commonwealth courts. He has published numerous books and articles on constitutional law and human rights. He was made a life peer in 1993.

Chapter 9

The Home Office Again

ANTHONY LESTER

My friendship with Roy Jenkins began in 1963, a few months after Hugh Gaitskell's tragically early death. We met through my friendship with Gaitskell's elder daughter, Julia. I was 27 and Roy was 43 years old. We were drawn together by our connections with the United States. Roy had visited the States a few months earlier and had spent a month in Washington writing for an *Observer* series, meeting President Kennedy, Robert Kennedy, and their advisers. I had recently returned from two years of graduate study at Harvard Law School, which led to my becoming involved with civil rights and the struggle for racial equality. Roy was impressed by the style and substance of the Kennedy administration. During the long hot summer of 1964, when I returned to the Deep South to report for Amnesty International, I was given an introduction by Roy to Bobby Kennedy, who was then the US Attorney General. On my return, I became legal strategist of a newly formed NGO, the

Campaign Against Racial Discrimination, whose main aim was the enactment of a comprehensive and effective law to tackle racial discrimination in Britain.

In December 1965 Roy became Home Secretary in the first of his two periods of enlightened leadership at the Home Office. That remarkable first period received much more attention in Roy's obituaries than did the second period, when I worked with Roy at the Home Office between 1974 and 1976, before he departed to become President of the European Commission and I returned to the Bar.

My only contribution to that first liberal interlude at the Home Office arose when Roy asked me, and his old Oxford friend and publisher Mark Bonham Carter, to help him to prepare a major speech about race relations in Britain, and to develop a strategy to secure effective legislation to combat racial discrimination. Roy was in a difficult position because his predecessor at the Home Office, Frank Soskice, in Roy's words, 'a remarkably bad Home Secretary', had earlier persuaded Parliament to enact a narrow and toothless Race Relations Bill, and the Wilson government had no appetite for further measures.

Roy wanted to pave the way for comprehensive and effective race relations legislation, and to move public opinion to support measures to promote equality and equal citizenship. His speech, written in his own words, is remembered for the phrase, 'I define integration, therefore, not as a flattening process of assimilation but as equal opportunity, accompanied by cultural diversity, in an atmosphere of mutual tolerance.' It remains the best ministerial statement on this complex subject, made at a time when there was no developed public philosophy on race relations in Britain. His speech also marked the beginning of a skilful campaign to persuade his colleagues to support a new Race Relations Act.

The campaign succeeded in enabling Roy to commit the government to new legislation before leaving the Home Office at the end of 1967 to replace Jim Callaghan as Chancellor of the Exchequer. The result was Callaghan's Race Relations Act of 1968, a measure wide in scope—applying to racial discrimination in employment, education, housing, and the provision of goods, services, and facilities, but weak and ineffective in enforcement.

During his time as Chancellor of the Exchequer and in opposition, Roy and I saw much less of each other. I had meanwhile become convinced of the need for legislation to tackle sex as well as race discrimination, and had given a Fabian lecture advocating a British Bill of Rights based upon the European Convention on Human Rights. Shortly before the February 1974 election I sent Roy a paper which I had written with my wife, Katya, under the auspices of the Runnymede Trust. Our paper criticized the narrowly restrictive proposals made by the Heath administration to legislate against sex discrimination, and made stronger and more far-reaching proposals for comprehensive legislation.

Roy returned reluctantly to office as what he described in his memoirs as a recidivist Home Secretary. He had expected Labour to lose an election which they did not deserve to win. He had hoped to be Chancellor of the Exchequer. He was depressed and dispirited, loath at first to take decisions. The government did not have a majority in the Commons and another election was inevitable in a matter of months.

Labour's manifesto had promised equal status for women and the creation of powerful legal machinery necessary to enforce anti-discrimination laws, as well as the elimination of discrimination on grounds of colour. Over lunch at East Hendred, Roy told us that he lacked confidence in the capacity of his Home Office advisers to develop an effective legislative policy to tackle sex and race discrimination. He suggested to a fairly obviously pregnant Katya that she might become his Special Adviser. When she declined, he asked me to come, observing that in that way he would have two for the price of one.

It took only a few minutes for me to decide to abandon my practice at the Bar to work with Roy as his Special Adviser, in theory for four days a week, in practice for seven. I have never regretted the decision. At the time it was almost unheard of for a member of the Bar to leave to work in government; special advisers were a recent innovation in British government. But it was an easy decision to make because it had Katya's complete and selfless support, and because I knew that I would be working closely with an outstandingly able and effective Home Secretary on issues about which he and I cared deeply.

Roy explained that my job would be to 'make a nuisance' of myself. He also explained that, in his experience, the best special advisers were those who 'argued to solutions', rather than those, like Tommy Balogh (his tutor at Balliol and economic adviser in the first Wilson government) who 'argued to conclusions'. I was unclear how I could at the same time make a nuisance of myself and argue to practical solutions, but I decided to do my best to develop policies that had a good chance of being accepted and of being translated into workable legislation. Roy also made it clear that, if I came to work with him, I should not expect any future patronage but would return to the Bar when he gave up office.

I arrived at the Home Office in early May, two months after the government had been formed. In his memoirs, Roy recalled that I found him in a 'half-bereft state', and that my main medium-term role was to encourage and give direction to his human rights commitment, keeping him up to the mark.

The two Ministers of State at the Home Office were Roy's close friend and former Special Adviser at the Home Office and the Treasury, John Harris, and Alex Lyon, MP for York, from whom Roy was much more detached. Alex had a puritanical streak and kept a bust of Oliver Cromwell on his desk. His private secretary was the tempestuous Clare Short. Roy was later to describe his disappointment with Alex, 'mainly because he entrenched himself with his private secretary . . . in a bunker of suspicion against almost everybody else'. Shirley Summerskill was the parliamentary under-secretary concerned with anti-discrimination policy. The Permanent Secretary was the affable and relaxed Sir Arthur Peterson.

The Home Office inhabited an elegant and rambling edifice in Whitehall that has since been annexed by the Foreign and Commonwealth Office.[1] Ministers and senior civil servants occupied half of a hollow square of adjoining rooms. George the Tea Man pushed a splendid wooden trolley down the Victorian corridors every afternoon, dispensing tea, biscuits, and newspapers. Most afternoons (except on Fridays), the deputy secretaries would gather in the corridor to chat, like a group of relaxed dons exchanging gossip in an Oxbridge senior common room. They were well educated and well mannered, but they were also deeply conservative and capable of being as devious as any fictitious Sir Humphrey.

---

[1] Once Roy knew of the plot he made a late manoeuvre to reverse the plan and make the FCO go to Queen Anne's Gate, on the excellent ground that the Home Office was the senior department in 1782 and therefore for all time. It was a good and true tease, and happily caused some brief consternation for officials in both departments.

It was agreed, as terms of my appointment at deputy secretary level, that I would have ready access to the Home Secretary; full access to all relevant documents; and a Special Adviser (Angela Byre, a discrimination lawyer) to assist me with the work on equality legislation. There was impressive departmental expertise in the area of the criminal law, but much less in the area of civil law, which was treated as the preserve of the Lord Chancellor's Department and other specialist departments. This meant that Roy did not have access to worthwhile legal advice on issues beyond criminal law.

Matthew Oakeshott briefed Roy on economic policy. I briefed him on other issues beyond the direct responsibility of the Home Office as they came up for discussion in Cabinet, such as Michael Foot's legislation to protect trade union closed shops, or the botched proposals for Scottish devolution. I was not meant to act as a legal adviser, and was once rebuked by the Senior Legal Adviser for having questioned official advice to pursue what I regarded as a potentially hopeless appeal to the House of Lords against a damning judgment by Lord Denning's Court of Appeal holding the Home Office to have abused its powers in relation to television licence fees. Happily Roy decided, against official advice, not to appeal. His decision was a good example of a Home Secretary who respected the rule of law and was a good judge of the public mood. Hayden Phillips, then Roy's assistant private secretary (and after the October 1974 election his principal private secretary), had to write his 'concession' statement to the Commons because officials could not bring themselves to give in.

Elwyn-Jones was a charming and genial but weak Lord Chancellor, keen above all to preserve his office, but reluctant to put his head above the parapet when the rule of law was threatened by left-wing militancy. Roy filled the gap as best he could, showing that one does not have to be a lawyer to be an effective minister of justice able to protect judicial independence.

Ministers in the second Wilson administration were encouraged to bring in special advisers, but there was no established practice as to how special advisers should conduct themselves, still less special advisers like me, who had been recruited for their technical expertise rather than for any wider political role. It was important that the civil servants with whom I was to work had confidence in my professionalism. I made it my practice not to see Roy on any matter of policy except in the presence of one of his private secretaries, so as to avoid any impression of backstairs politics or undue influence.

I was greatly helped by Hayden Phillips. He was on easy terms with Roy and was sympathetic to my role and to the policies we intended to pursue. We formed a working partnership. He played a key role in our dealings with Roy, linking me with ministers and civil servants, and reducing potential sources of conflict. He was a liberally minded innovating entrepreneur; and there were not many of them to be found in the Home Office in 1974.

Not even Hayden was able to apply sufficient oil to the Home Office machine to avoid the friction created during the first few months after my arrival. My immediate task was to develop legislative policy to tackle discrimination. Given that we had a minority in the Commons and faced a formidable Opposition, Roy decided that it was tactically sensible to introduce a Sex Discrimination Bill first, and then to introduce a Race Relations Bill that matched its provisions.

My radical ideas were unwelcome to the Home Office team dealing with anti-discrimination policy. The same team had advised the previous government to adopt a policy to which they were firmly wedded. They regarded me as an unwelcome and (as they hoped) temporary nuisance. To make matters worse, by the time of my arrival, some policy decisions had already been taken.

A couple of days after my arrival I studied what had been agreed at junior ministerial level and circulated a memorandum explaining why I thought that something more radical was called for. The official response was glacial, understandably, because I was seeking to undo decisions already made. At my first meeting with officials from another department (Education) to discuss sex discrimination policy, Home Office officials pointedly distanced themselves from my position.

During the next few weeks I did not trouble Roy with the sometimes heated arguments occurring within the team about my proposals. That was until out of the blue I was invited to lunch by a deputy secretary from the Department of Employment. He began by saying, 'As you know, my Department agree with your proposals, but if you want to achieve them you should advise the Home Secretary to transfer responsibility for the Bill to my Department.' I replied that it was surprising news to me that I had his Department's welcome support, and that I would not advise Roy as he proposed, since that would mean limiting the Sex Discrimination Bill narrowly to the employment field.

I went back and sent for the relevant Department of Employment papers. There was no explanation or apology as to why they had deliberately been kept from me. The papers did indeed support my approach, which is why they had been concealed. I told Roy that I could not do my work unless this kind of official obstruction was overcome. His solution was to send me home to write the first draft of what became the White Paper *Equality for Women*. He later recalled in his memoirs that there had been more departmental opposition at upper-middle level than he had ever previously encountered. It was difficult for me to deal with this aspect of the politics of the Home Office bureaucracy. I had been used at the Bar to open argument with cards face upwards on the table, and welcomed reasoned argument with the able civil servants around me. I was disappointed that they lacked the self-confidence to explore the options in open discussion.

The White Paper was published in September 1974. Thanks to Roy's ability to understand the complex issues and the policy choices to be made, and thanks to his commitment to comprehensive and effective equality legislation, detailed proposals had been worked out and agreed in a matter of only a few months. This work shaped both the Sex Discrimination Act 1975 and the Race Relations Act 1976. That summer we also published a scheme for the independent review of complaints against the police, prepared under the direction of John Harris.

While I was putting the finishing touches to the White Paper, Roy was preoccupied with the problem of how best to handle the hunger strike by Dolours and Marion Price in their efforts to be sent back to Northern Ireland to serve their sentences for causing explosions and major casualties at the Old Bailey and the Army Central Recruiting Depot. When they refused artificial feeding, there was a likelihood that they would die within a matter of a few weeks, and that there would be an outbreak of further Irish terrorist violence. Roy's instinct was that they should go back, but he did not want to be seen to be caving in to duress.

Katya and I went to East Hendred for a sunny weekend lunch at the moment when Roy was intending to draft a public statement explaining why he had decided to transfer the Price sisters to Northern Ireland. But the words would not come to justify his position. Fortified by one of Roy's dangerously potent dry Martinis, I argued that he should make it quite clear that he would not move under threat and that if the sisters were determined to kill themselves, we must allow events to take their course. After a half-hour discussion, Roy was persuaded to take a firmer line. He sent us off for a walk while he sat in his deckchair for two hours drafting his statement.

It was characteristic of Roy to have written it personally. It was a remarkable statement explaining the painful dilemma he faced and his thought processes. On the surface it gave a tough message, but to a politically perceptive reader there was more than a hint of scope for compromise. After several weeks of hectic behind-the-scene negotiations, the hunger strike ended, and the sisters were transferred to the women's wing at Durham Prison (and then to Northern Ireland in March 1975). We were able to breathe a sigh of relief before the next horrific waves of Irish terrorist violence in London, Birmingham, and Guildford led inevitably to the Prevention of Terrorism Act 1974.

Terrorism was an overwhelming concern, especially during the first half of the two years. Roy visited the injured children of the White Tower outrage and went to Hamley's to buy them presents. Birmingham was especially moving, and he said of dealing with terrorists and their demands, 'Give them patience, but nothing else.'

Even at times of greatest stress, Roy maintained a balance between his working time and time spent in the company of his friends, usually over a relaxing lunch or dinner, often at Brooks's. His immense curiosity about people and ideas and his need to keep in touch with the world beyond the Home Office were met by his vast range of social contacts—a need and a curiosity that he kept throughout his life. It made him a wiser politician and a better Home Secretary. He was also hugely sustained by Jennifer's loyal and unstinting support. She was in every way his intellectual equal, and her values are a mixture of radical principle and shrewd common sense. Theirs was a political as well as a personal partnership. Jennifer was also a great support to me behind the scenes.

Roy was always much aware of number, time, distance, and the brevity of life. During the October 1974 election campaign I toured the country with him, wondering at his command of physical and social geography. He was forever suggesting to his police driver how he might cut a few miles from the journey by taking a back road. Wherever we went, he knew about the place, its history and local politics, and made me aware of the narrowness of my London metropolitan vision of Britain. He loved measuring and counting. When canvassing he kept a counter in his pocket, which he clicked each time he shook hands with a constituent, to see whether he had reached whatever was his performance indicator. He loved the railways and was one of only two people I have known who enjoyed redesigning railway timetables—the other became a railway manager. He made his speeches to meetings of all kinds across the country, but never once did he patronize his audience by talking down to them.

When we reached Edinburgh, we had dinner with John Mackintosh, MP for East Lothian, professor of politics, and authority on Cabinet government. John was one of those rare politicians who never achieved ministerial office because he stuck to his principles and put his constituents before personal ambition. He was a champion for Britain in Europe, with a well-honed intellect and sharp sense of irony.

By this time Roy was ever more disillusioned with the Labour Party and its government. He was disheartened by

Denis Healey's inability to tackle galloping inflation, by Michael Foot's unilateralism and surrender to trade union pressure, by the fact that half of the Cabinet was in favour of leaving the Common Market, by Tony Benn's eccentric industrial projects, and by the lack of commitment to the rule of law, when even Tony Crosland was putting the Clay Cross councillors above the law. John spent much of the meal expressing his despair at what had become of the Labour Party and urging the case for a new form of politics. On our way to bed Roy remarked that 'John is absolutely right. The Labour Party would collapse like a house of cards if it were effectively challenged. The trouble is that I am too rooted in the party by family and tradition to make the attempt, and I lack sufficient courage.' It was only after Roy had distanced himself from British politics as President of the European Commission that his home thoughts from abroad decided him on the need to break the mould and create the SDP. But for the rest of his term at the Home Office he remained in a state of deep discontent with the government and the party. His state of mind in the aftermath of the election is revealed by his dedication in a copy of his *Nine Men of Power* in which he wrote, 'from Roy in memory of the election campaign of September/October 1974, which (thanks largely to you) was at least more agreeable than that of February'.

After the election the government had a majority of only four votes in the Commons, but at least it had a majority and we were there to stay. The manifesto promised to give real equality to women, including making Barbara Castle's Equal Pay Act of 1970 'fully effective throughout the land' by the end of 1975, to strengthen legislation protecting minorities, and to introduce an independent element into complaints against the police. The Equal Pay Act was fatally flawed from birth, but I was not allowed to improve it in making the Sex Discrimination Bill. We kept the rest of those promises.

Free speech and privacy were recurring issues initially because of unfair press attacks on Harold Wilson's secretary, Marcia Williams, and on Wilson himself. Wilson's hostility to the media and his concern to prevent leaks to the press became an obsession. He threatened to bring in a privacy bill to curb media malpractice, and a series of 'gagging writs' were issued by his lawyer, Arnold Goodman. A meeting was arranged between Wilson (flanked by his Press Secretary, Joe Haines, and his Senior Policy Adviser, Bernard Donoughue) and Harold Evans, the editor of the *Sunday Times*, about a possible package of measures that would involve the reform of libel and contempt law in return for a privacy law to tackle media intrusion and harassment. Evans rejected the proposal because of his fear that a privacy law would be applied by the courts to prevent publication of information and ideas of legitimate public interest. He may well have been influenced by the government's misguided attempt—then in its early stages—to stifle publication of Richard Crossman's *Diaries*. When the case came to trial before Lord Widgery a year later, Roy wanted to give evidence on behalf of the publishers but considered that he could not do so as a member of the government. The Crossman affair added to his doubts about the political judgement of the Attorney-General, Sam Silkin.

After the government's defeat in the Crossman diaries case, Wilson's fears about future publication of ministerial memoirs by Barbara Castle, Tony Benn, and others continued. He asked Lord Radcliffe to look at the existing conventions and fashion new rules. When the Radcliffe Report was eventually published (in January 1976), Wilson attempted to persuade Roy and others to sign binding undertakings not to breach confidence. They refused to do so, but the attempt was symptomatic of Wilson's narrow-minded and self-serving approach to freedom of political expression.

In May 1974 a Royal Commission on the press was set up at Wilson's instigation to consider the economic state of the press and its editorial standards. Most newspapers were lukewarm and suspicious of the government's motives in establishing the Commission. Also in May 1974 Michael Foot launched his Trade Union and Labour Relations Bill. Because of the increasingly militant activities of one wing of the National Union of Journalists, the protection given by the bill to closed shops was widely regarded as a serious threat to the freedom of national and provincial newspapers.

Within the Home Office the inherent tension between freedom of speech and personal privacy was reflected at ministerial level. John Harris, as a former newspaper man, was passionately in favour of free speech. Alex Lyon had been a member of Kenneth Younger's Royal Commission on intrusions into privacy, which reported in 1972. He had introduced a Private Member's Bill on privacy and had written a minority report disagreeing with Younger's rejection of an enforceable general right of privacy. Alex was passionately committed to preventing media intrusion into private lives, and apparently advised Wilson behind the scenes. Roy's instincts (like John Harris's and mine) were for the protection of free speech. His work as an author had led him to introduce the Obscene Publications Bill in 1959, and to give evidence for the defence at the *Lady Chatterley* trial in 1960.

Roy recognized that there was a pressing need, in the words of the election manifesto, to 'protect the citizen from unwarranted and mischievous intrusion into the citizen's private affairs', in the area of what has come to be known as data protection, as well as a need for greater freedom of information about the workings of government. Unlike most in Whitehall, he really did believe in the need for more open government, by replacing the Official Secrets Act (again in the manifesto's words, 'by a measure to put the burden on the public authorities to justify withholding information') while avoiding a situation in which the business of government had to be conducted in a goldfish bowl. The depth of Home Office hostility to freedom of information legislation was profound. The deputy secretary responsible for that area of policy told me with the utmost gravity that, were I to publish a book describing the colour of the wallpaper in the Cabinet Office, I would be guilty of criminal wrongdoing—and rightly so. I wrongly diagnosed him as needing psychotherapy, but came to realize that the real cause was more widespread and enduring—the desire to control information as the key to the enjoyment of power.

In December 1974 Roy and I, together with Arthur Peterson and Hayden, travelled to the United States to learn more about how to translate policy into practical reality. We went to specially arranged seminars at Harvard Law School (on privacy and freedom of information), and at the University of Pennsylvania (on anti-discrimination legislation). We discussed the newly enacted US Freedom of Information Act with the editorial staff of the *New York Times* and the *Washington Post*, and we visited criminal justice, bail, and diversion-from-custody projects run in Manhattan by the Vera Institute of Justice. Roy's spirits rose and he was equal to the formidable body of expertise to which he was subjected.

During our visit Arthur Peterson met some American officials to discuss the Freedom of Information Act. He came back with dire warnings, about its exorbitant costs. No one else we

met was enthusiastic about the legislation, including the journalists, who regarded it as a tool for large corporations rather
than for the benefit of the press or the people. Unfortunately,
it was too early in the life of the legislation for them to have
understood its value in promoting the free flow of information
about government activities. On our return, only four members of the Wilson Cabinet (Roy, Denis Healey, Shirley
Williams, and Tony Benn) were in favour even of our modest
suggestion to make the Ombudsman responsible for moni-
toring and enforcing openness (as John Major's government
eventually did); and the manifesto commitment was abandoned when Merlyn Rees became Home Secretary.

When we reached Boston, the British Consul gave a lunch
in Roy's honour to which the leading Irish American politicians were invited. Roy was apprehensive that they would ask
him hostile questions about the Prevention of Terrorism Act.
He was relieved when the questions concerned his Obscene
Publications Act and the need to curb pornographic material.
As we were leaving, I drew his attention to a Massachusetts senator who seemed sympathetic to the IRA. Roy approached
him on the sidewalk and warned him, in Churchillian style,
that if terrorist violence continued he would be unable to
answer for the safety of his Irish constituents in Birmingham
Stechford. The voluble senator was left speechless as Roy
strode away.

Our visit to the States was important in making me realize
that the concept of discrimination which I had described in my
White Paper was too narrow. During our return flight I confessed my error to Roy, who agreed to go back to his colleagues
seeking authority to widen the bill. The result was the introduction of the concept of indirect discrimination that covers
discriminatory effects as well as causes. Our American visit was

also valuable in demonstrating the success of projects to divert wrongdoers from prison, an area covered by John Harris, who was working with the Probation Service on various diversion schemes, and preparing what became the Bail Act 1976.

While we were putting the finishing touches to the Sex Discrimination Bill 1975, Roy was contacted by an old political friend from the Kennedy era, McGeorge Bundy, on behalf of the American trustees of the Rhodes Trust. Bundy asked whether the bill might be used to enable the trustees to open their scholarships to women. Roy was immediately attracted to the idea, but, when his views were communicated to officials, the chief Charity Commissioner, Fitzgerald, came to see him protesting that we would be violating a fundamental principle of charity law dating back to Queen Elizabeth I, namely, that trustees must give effect to the wishes of the donor, Cecil Rhodes, who wanted his scholars to be men.

Roy explained that he did not believe that it was right to be bound by a donor's wishes in all circumstances and for all time. He pointed out that the law already recognized that colour bar in a will or charitable bequest would be unenforceable as against public policy. What we proposed was to include a power in the legislation allowing single-sex charities to seek leave to open their awards to both sexes. This was done in 1976 in the case of the Rhodes Scholarships by an order declaring them to be tenable by women. Later it made it easier for traditionally male Oxbridge colleges to admit women. No one has ever criticized the reform (apart from Charity Commissioner Fitzgerald), but a more conventional Home Secretary would have succumbed.

To give another example of Roy's iconoclastic and libertarian instincts, he received a letter from Brian Inglis, the biographer of Roger Casement, asking to be shown the Home

Office papers relating to the events leading to Casement's trial and execution for treason. Inglis explained that his motive for seeing the material was 'mere curiosity'. The official Home Office response was that this was not a good enough reason, and that Inglis had no 'need to know'. Roy said that, on the contrary, as a biographer himself, he regarded mere curiosity as a sufficient reason. In the end the Home Office persuaded him not to do as Inglis wished, since the time needed to vet the records on grounds of national security would be disproportionate. It was only years later, when I read Inglis's biography, that I learnt about the Home Office legal adviser Ernely Blackwell, and of his malignant hatred of Casement, and the extraordinary actions he had taken, after Casement's conviction in 1916, to ensure that he was executed.

In early February 1975 Roy was plunged deep into the slough of despond when he heard that Margaret Thatcher had replaced Ted Heath as Tory leader. Even though few observers recognized it at the time, Roy understood immediately that one effect would be to polarize British politics, marginalizing the values in which he believed. Within the government the situation worsened throughout 1975, with roaring inflation and the collapse of sterling; doctrinaire measures to nationalize the ports and aerospace industry; and Michael Foot's misguided trade union legislation. Cabinet meetings throughout this period had a depressing effect on Roy. He came back from one disastrous meeting complaining that once again Crosland, Healey, and he had failed to make common cause. 'The trouble is', he lamented, 'that we have known each other for so long, and are eaten up with petty jealousy and rivalry.'

The event Roy most enjoyed during his second term as Home Secretary was his role in the 1975 European referendum campaign at the head of the pro-Europe campaign. It gave him new energy and, for several months, while I was working on what became the White Paper on Racial Discrimination (published in September 1975), Roy was devoting most of that great energy to the campaign. It proved a great success both for Roy's morale and in its result, but what Hayden and I most admired was the way Roy handled all the Home Office business that mattered, and his Cabinet responsibilities at the same time. It was an impressive combination of energy, discipline, and capacity.

We rarely disagreed, but we did disagree about what may seem a tedious argument about institutional architecture, namely, the nature of the Commission for Racial Equality, which was to replace the Race Relations Board as the authority responsible for promoting racial equality and combating discrimination. I wanted it to be like the Equal Opportunities Commission, concentrating on strategic law enforcement as well as assisting in individual cases. The problem was that there was another existing body alongside the Race Relations Board, the Community Relations Commission, that had been created to promote 'harmonious community relations' and to pay for local community relations officers in some eighty-five voluntary community relations councils, and for some local community projects. Since its birth, the CRC had been handicapped by the fuzziness of its aim and staff weaknesses. I was concerned that a merger of the two existing bodies would mean that the new CRE would inherit a lot of dead wood and be distracted by race politics from strategic law enforcement. On the other hand, Mark Bonham Carter argued for merger, and in the battle for Jenkins's ear, he won the argument. Roy described my proposal for the continued existence of a separate CRC as a 'floating kidney'. Almost thirty years on the CRE continues to suffer from its congenital defects.

In August 1975, at my suggestion and with Roy's support, an inter-departmental group was set up to consider the question of legislation on human rights, with particular reference to the European Convention on Human Rights. The group was chaired by Brian Cubbon, one of the ablest Home Office officials, who soon became Permanent Secretary of the Northern Ireland Office, and then of the Home Office. Cubbon chaired the group impressively even though he was deeply hostile to my proposal to make Convention rights enforceable in British courts. We produced a report which explained the arguments for and against the incorporation of the Convention rights into UK law. It was prepared for publication as a Green Paper.

At this point, the Permanent Secretary, Sir Arthur Peterson, asked me to see him. He explained that he and the permanent secretaries of the other departments were concerned that if the report were published it would distract the public's attention from what really mattered for the health of British democracy, namely, the introduction of proportional representation for Westminster elections. I was taken aback, but replied that *both* electoral reform and the protection of human rights raised important issues, and that there was every reason for the public to be able to have access to the careful study we had made of how to give domestic effect to the Convention rights.

At the Cabinet Committee meeting to discuss this, ministers decided, despite heavy official briefing, to authorize publication. Roy wrote a foreword stating that the report 'has an important contribution to make to public understanding of the issues involved'. What we did not anticipate was that, instead of the report being published through HMSO as a government Green Paper, it was sidelined; a few hundred copies were published by the Home Office in June 1976, without any publicity. Nor did we anticipate that incorporation would be resisted so strongly by senior officials within the Home Office and the Northern Ireland Office, and beyond, long after Roy and I had left the government.

In December 1975 we published a White Paper on computers and privacy in which we recognized the need to secure that all computer systems in which personal information is held, in both the private and public sectors, are operated with adequate safeguards for the privacy of the subject of the information. Six months later Roy set up a Home Office Committee on Data Protection, chaired by Sir Norman Lindop. The members of the Committee included Paul Sieghart and William Goodhart, both of whom had worked within Justice on ways of protecting personal privacy, and Hugo Young, the distinguished and independent-minded writer and journalist. The Lindop Committee was asked to advise the government on the objectives to be incorporated into legislation establishing permanent safeguards. Their report, and Paul Sieghart's wider work in the Council of Europe, influenced subsequent European and British data protection legislation.

One of my last significant pieces of work was to prepare a speech on Scottish devolution for Roy to deliver to the Inverclyde Junior Chamber of Commerce in Greenock. The government's proposals were deeply flawed. Instead of generous measures of devolution, based upon quasi-federal constitutional principles, to be interpreted and applied by the courts, the government preferred over-prescriptive legislation, in which ministers would police the boundaries between central and devolved government to ensure a large measure of Whitehall command and control. The proposals suffered both from fear of Scottish home rule and from a distrust of judicial review, and Roy had argued in vain for an alternative approach, based on my suggestions.

Roy's speech was markedly different from what the government had in mind, and attempts were made by the Cabinet Office to persuade him to water it down. The speech could not have been delivered to a less appropriate audience: the members of the Junior Chamber of Commerce were not naturally inclined—especially in their cups—to take seriously weighty matters of constitutional reform. Their hospitality was generous, but the occasion was more akin to a Cambridge Bumps Supper than to a political meeting. Fortunately, the speech was not entirely wasted; it was of some use during Roy's famous by-election campaign in Hillhead in 1982.

Looking back, Roy recalled that, once the decision to go to Brussels had been finally made, he felt both liberated and exhilarated. He wrote in his memoirs, 'I realised retrospectively how ill the shoe of British politics had been fitting me. I had felt neither at ease in, nor derived pride from my membership of that Government of 1974, and I ought to have got out before.'

His record as a great reforming Home Secretary, whether during the early and happier period or as a recidivist, has never been equalled by his successors, even when their governments had controlling majorities in the Commons and after much longer periods in office. What is remarkable about his second period as Home Secretary was that, given his low morale, his discontent with the government to which he belonged, and the distractions of the European referendum campaign, he managed to achieve so much.

He had a first-class and well-rounded intellect, and a wide knowledge of history and literature. More than that, he had shrewd judgement and a sense of proportion, striking a balance between liberty and order. He was not a liberal zealot nor was he wishy-washy in the values for which he fought. He had a unique capacity to translate his principles into practical reality, leading public opinion when a weaker minister would have chosen to defer to popular prejudice and follow the line of least resistance. He knew the importance of deciding on a defensible position and sticking to it, rather than being flushed out, digging in again, and then being on the run. He had a great capacity for hard work in sustained bursts, but he did not make the mistake of becoming a workaholic.

Because he was a sensitive man, aware always of his own vulnerability, it took great courage for him to act as he did. He was fun to work with and a marvellous companion and friend. He inspired fierce devotion and loyalty among those who worked with him, even when they disagreed with him. He was receptive to new ideas and not hidebound by tradition. He was a statesman who brought integrity into politics at a time when politicians were falling ever more into disrepute.

In an essay published a year after Hugh Gaitskell's death, Roy noted that what Gaitskell had left to British politics included 'a memory which is in standing contradiction to those who wish to believe that only men with cold hearts and twisted tongues can succeed in politics'. That is also a fitting tribute to Roy Jenkins as I knew him and worked with him during two unforgettable years.

Kenneth Baker

Kenneth Baker was a Conservative MP from 1968 to 1997. His Cabinet posts included Environment Secretary, Education Secretary, and Home Secretary. He was also Chairman of the Conservative Party. He was made a Companion of Honour in 1992 and a life peer in 1997. He has edited several anthologies of poetry and published his memoirs. His books on political cartoons include *The Kings and Queens: An Irreverent Cartoon History of the British Monarchy* (1996) and *The Prime Ministers: An Irreverent Political History in Cartoons* (1995). His latest anthology is *The Faber Book of Landscape Poetry* (1997).

Chapter 10

A Life in Caricature

KENNETH BAKER

It is entirely appropriate that there should be one chapter in this book on the cartoons of Roy Jenkins. Writing in 1992 in a collection of cartoons about Europe, Roy had written,

High quality political cartoons have an ability to summon up a mood or a situation with an economy and a vividness which very few paragraphs of prose can match. They also age well. Some jokes can make just as big an impact today as they did 30 or even 60 years ago. That is one reason why a leavening of cartoons, some photographs are necessary as well, makes much the best mixture in illustrated volumes of biography or autobiography.

When Roy Jenkins became Minister for Aviation following Labour's victory in October 1964, he was virtually unrecognized as a national political figure. No leading cartoonist had bothered to draw him. When Labour was in opposition they naturally focused upon Harold Wilson, George Brown, Denis Healey, Jim Callaghan, and Anthony Wedgwood Benn, and

"... and now Roy, we don't even need an Aviation Minister!

Fig. 10.1 Jak, *Evening Standard*, 11 February 1965

"ANYBODY IN ?"

Fig. 10.2 Emmwood, *Daily Mail*, 25 October 1966

even figures that have now slipped out of public recognition like Patrick Gordon Walker, Ray Gunter, Fred Willey, Michael Stewart, and Alf Robens.

There are very few cartoons of Jenkins in his first job—in fact I have found only one (Fig. 10.1). It is clear that the cartoonists did not quite know how to portray him. He was *un homme sérieux* with an earnest face, bland and going bald, the glasses were to come later—no gift for a caricaturist. They all like distinguishing marks which become their 'tabs'—for Chamberlain it was the wing collar and the umbrella; for Churchill the cigar; for Wilson the pipe; for Margaret Thatcher the handbag; and for Tony Blair the big ears and teeth. It took a long time for cartoonists to find a 'tab' for Jenkins, and one only emerged as his career developed and his lifestyle become known—it became first a champagne glass and then a bottle of claret.

On becoming Home Secretary in 1965 Jenkins emerged as a major political figure, but home secretaries seldom get favourable treatment. As far as the public was concerned, he was personally responsible for the spectacular escape of George Blake from Wormwood Scrubs—I experienced much the same when two IRA convicts escaped from Brixton. The Home Secretary is the helpless victim, and the cartoonists depicted Jenkins peering into an empty prison (Fig. 10.2). In the 1980s Jenkins was blamed for having created the permissive society while he was at the Home Office, but no contemporary cartoonist attacked him for that—that came later (Fig. 10.3).

Following Callaghan's resignation on the devaluation of the pound in 1967, Jenkins as Chancellor of the Exchequer became the second figure in the government (Fig. 10.4). It was a spectacular progress and, as Wilson was then massively

Fig. 10.3 Gary, *Daily Mail*, 1980s

Fig. 10.4 Mahood, *The Times*, 30 November 1967

LOCAL LAD MAKES BAD  *Emmwood*

1964   1966   1968

Fig. 10.5 Emmwood,
Daily Mail, 18 January 1968

POCKET CARTOON
by OSBERT LANCASTER

"Were I *a* non-smoking teetotaler, with a brand new car, mad on collecting savings certificates and living in an underdeveloped country, I'd say Mr. Jenkins has done a splendid job!"

Fig. 10.6 Lancaster, *Daily Express*,
20 March 1968

169

unpopular, losing by-election after by-election, it was not long before the cartoonists, such as Emmwood at the *Daily Mail*, depicted him as the next Prime Minister (Fig. 10.5).

Within six months Britain was facing a major financial crisis and Jenkins had to act to save the pound. His toughness in increasing taxation by over a £1 billion in his budget and in closing the banks for three days contrasted with Wilson's preference for devious accommodation. The cartoonists made Wilson the major butt of their attacks, but Jenkins was chided by Osbert Lancaster over his wide range of tax increases—he was another Cripps (Fig. 10.6).

As the economy improved, Jenkins was seen as the author of this success, which was capped by another magisterial budget in 1969. This was celebrated by Franklin in the *Daily Mirror*, who, for the first time, depicted Jenkins playing tennis, which was his favourite physical relaxation (Fig. 10.7). In this cartoon Iain Macleod and Ted Heath are both shown depressed about Jenkins's success while Wilson leads the compliments. Although being regularly depicted as the next Labour Prime Minister, many Labour MPs blamed him for the defeat in June 1970 and Gibbard at *The Guardian* foresaw that Callaghan was waiting in the wings (Fig. 10.8).

Jenkins and Callaghan were seen as the two contenders for the Labour leadership—Jenkins from the Euro Right and Callaghan from the trade unions. Jenkins's enthusiasm for Heath's successful negotiation of Britain's entry into the Common Market led some cartoonists to detect the beginning of the great detachment. When Jenkins won the Charlemagne Prize in 1972, Garland at the *Daily Telegraph* illustrated where his real interests lay (Fig. 10.9).

On Labour's somewhat unexpected victory in February 1974 Jenkins returned to his old office as Home Secretary—

'Yes, Pancho's now gaining the lead .. what determination .. what a come-back ..'

Fig. 10.7 Franklin, *Daily Mirror*, 27 June 1969

'Heir today, gone tomorrow—eh Roy?'

Fig. 10.8 Gibbard, *Guardian*, 9 July 1970

Fig. 10.9 Garland, *Daily Telegraph*, 8 March 1972

Fig. 10.10 Garland, *Daily Telegraph*, 1974

Fig. 10.11 Garland, *Daily Telegraph*, 20 December 1979

Fig. 10.12 Garland, *Spectator*, 10 July 1982

a post I suspect he enjoyed more than the Treasury. But Callaghan was busy cultivating Labour's grass roots, with which Jenkins felt little empathy, and he did not conceal his lordly disdain—'When did you last see the TUC?' (Fig. 10.10). His future now lay outside the Labour Party and domestic politics, and he grabbed at the chance of being the President of the European Commission.

For the next four years he dropped out of British politics, and the cartoonists abandoned him because they could not envisage him having any further impact on Britain's politics. He was never depicted as the king over the water, but after his Dimbleby Lecture, while he was still President of the European Commission, Jenkins set out his agenda for a new approach in British politics (Fig. 10.11). Following the election of Michael Foot as party Leader in 1980, Labour became unelectable and the party began to disintegrate. Three senior ex-Cabinet ministers led by Jenkins, who had weight and credibility, became the 'Gang of Four'. Jenkins had been

"By the very left, by the left, by the centre—quick march!"

Fig. 10.13 Cummings, *Daily Express*, 2 April 1982

Fig. 10.14 Bell, *Guardian*, 23 March 1982

largely forgotten by cartoonists, but when he emerged as the new party's leader he got a good press—the SDP turned the frog into a prince (Fig. 10.12). However, differences between the 'Gang' emerged, and Cummings at the *Daily Express* was quick to pick up on this (Fig. 10.13).

The cartoonists had much fun at the attempts of Jenkins to

"I ASSURE YOU THAT ROY IS STILL PLAYING A VITAL ROLE IN OUR CAMPAIGN!"

Fig. 10.15 Franklin, *Sun*, 31 May 1983

Fig. 10.16 Bell, *Guardian*, 23 June 2000

Fig. 10.17 Scarfe, *Scarfeface* (Sinclair-Stevenson, 1993)

return to the House of Commons—with his trouble pronouncing his 'r's' he couldn't quite say the name of one of the seats he fought, Warrington, and, as Steve Bell observed, in the seat he won, Hillhead, he had difficulty with 'Raith Rovers' (Fig. 10.14). His return to the House of Commons in 1982 was not successful: it had become a harder place and he was shown no respect. Franklin was quick to notice the splits in the Alliance as Jenkins was pushed by Steel and Owen into the kitchen (Fig. 10.15).

Jenkins seemed washed up, but hope for a major realignment of British politics returned when Blair became Leader of the Labour Party. It hadn't worked with the SDP or with the Steel–Owen Alliance, but there was a chance it might happen under New Labour. He welcomed the role of being Melbourne to Blair's Victoria, revelling in being the *éminence grise*: the tutor, guide, and friend (Fig. 10.16). He hoped that Blair would deliver proportional representation and the euro— his hopes were to be dashed again. The cartoonists became more benign as Jenkins was seen as a spent force in the hurly-burly of modern politics.

Over the whole of his career Jenkins was fairly lucky with the cartoonists. They always focus upon the Prime Minister and Leader of the Opposition, who appear hundreds of times. Even as a senior minister he had far fewer appearances, and for a crucial period he was out of domestic politics. The image that survives is of a civilized bon vivant, orotund, benign, respected, but not dangerous (Fig. 10.17). At no time do I sense that he was wounded or hurt by the cartoons. He took the only sensible approach that any leading politician should take to cartoonists when he said to Andrew Adonis, 'All first-rate politicians are figures of fun. Better to be a figure of fun than no personality at all.'

CRISPIN TICKELL

Crispin Tickell is Chancellor of the University of Kent and a veteran European. He was private secretary to the three ministers who successively negotiated British entry into the European Union (1970–2); Chef de Cabinet to Roy Jenkins as President of the European Commission (1977–81); Permanent Secretary of the Overseas Development Administration (1984–7); Ambassador to the United Nations (1987–90); and Warden of Green College, Oxford (1990–7). He was made a KCVO in 1983 and a GCMG in 1999. He is the author of *Climatic Change and World Affairs* (1977) and *Mary Anning of Lyme Regis* (1996); and has written extensively on international, European, and environmental affairs.

Chapter 11

President of the European Commission

CRISPIN TICKELL

For Roy Jenkins his presidency of the European Commission from January 1977 to January 1981 was at once the culmination of his European career, the end of his ambition to be a Labour Prime Minister, the opportunity for a major international success, and a time of frustration and eventual disappointment.

I was his Chef de Cabinet, or chief of staff, throughout. The role of the Cabinet in most European systems of administration is much more than that of any private office in Britain (as I found from previous experience as private secretary to three British ministers). In Brussels the Cabinet is the prime interface between politics and administration, and is accountable only to the President. It takes the broad view, gives advice on policy, writes many of its own briefs and speeches, often instructs the administration, works directly with the Cabinets of other Commissioners, and keeps its own papers. There is no inhibition about hiring political advisers and using them openly. But the system can only work effectively with good cooperation and understanding between Cabinets and the administration, and much of my time was spent with the Secretary-General and his officials as well as with the other Cabinets. Obviously the system has attractions, especially for presidents and prime ministers, but it carries risks (as the recent fuss in Britain over spin doctors and political advisers well shows). At the weekly meetings of the Commission, I sat behind the President and often represented him elsewhere. In a real sense I was his eyes and ears.

In such circumstances the composition of the Cabinet was crucial. From Britain, Jenkins brought Hayden Phillips, his private secretary from the Home Office, a lively and ever-resourceful friend. At the end of 1979 Phillips returned to the home Civil Service, and was replaced by Nick Stuart. Michael Emerson dealt mainly with economic affairs: he had a major part in the relaunch of economic and monetary union in 1977. He was replaced at the end of the first year by Michel Vanden Abeele from Belgium. Graham Avery, responsible for agriculture, came from the British Ministry of Agriculture, via the Cabinet of the previous Commission Vice-President Lord Soames. Roger Beetham from the British Diplomatic Service had had experience as press officer during the negotiations for British entry into the Community, and took the job of spokesman. More junior members at different times were Klaus Ebermann (Germany) and Étienne Reuter (Luxembourg).

Michael Jenkins (George Thomson's Chef de Cabinet in the previous Commission) greatly helped to ensure continuity as a Special Adviser during the first seven months, and was a valuable ally in the Secretariat-General in 1979 and 1980. As a kind of outlier, David Marquand gave advice on political matters. This was a formidably talented group. It was later criticized for being too British; but it is hard see how Jenkins could have chosen otherwise at the beginning.

Unfortunately I kept nothing more than an appointments diary during the ensuing four years, and the Jenkins *Diary* fills in some but not all the gaps. At the end I found that the Commission expected me to take the Cabinet archives with me, so I did so. It is daunting to look at them now, and appreciate the sheer scope of the Cabinet's activities, not only in the internal administration of the Commission but also between the Commission, the member governments, the Parliament, and even the Court of Justice.

The Commission is a curiously hybrid institution. It is not, I think, what Jenkins expected when he became its President. Certainly it is more than a civil service, and has powers to act in limited areas of competence defined by the treaties; but it is much less than a government. Its main job is to propose policy to the Council of Ministers in its various configurations, and then to carry that policy out. Where the line can be drawn in practical terms between the Commission and the member governments was a constant source of aggravation. Some, especially the smaller countries, wanted to push the line forward; others, especially France and Britain, wanted to hold it or even to push it back. The battle over the place of the Commission at the annual Western summit meetings at which areas of Community competence were on the agenda well illustrates this issue.

The first President of the Commission with political weight was the German Walter Hallstein. For many, particularly Helmut Schmidt, the German Chancellor at the time of

Jenkins's appointment, the choice of Jenkins as President meant a return to some of the ambitions and enthusiasm of the 1950s. He described the job to Jenkins as being 'Prime Minister of Europe'. The French President, Valéry Giscard d'Estaing, would not have gone so far, but he too recommended the Jenkins candidature as a means of boosting the European enterprise. For the British the motives were different: in the muddy maelstrom at the top of Labour politics at the time, the departure of Jenkins from the government was mostly welcome. James Callaghan made him a last-minute offer of the Treasury, but only when it was safely too late for Jenkins to accept. I doubt if many of Jenkins's colleagues saw the issue in European terms. For their part the smaller members of the Community were unreservedly keen on the return of a political heavyweight to the Commission. In the Commission itself there was some apprehension. It carried the implications of cultural as well as political change, and a certain wariness, tinged with optimism, was apparent.

I too was a bit apprehensive. In the course of a visit to an oil rig in the Gulf of Mexico, I had a startling message from the Foreign Office. Would I like my name to go forward as a candidate for the job of Chef de Cabinet to Jenkins? It seemed so unlikely that I would be chosen that I cheerfully said yes, encouraged by the blue sky above and the blue sea stretching in all directions. Later I reflected on my occasional tussles with the Commission during the negotiations for British entry between 1970 and 1972. Then I reflected on my equally trying tussles with the British negotiating team, and hoped, if I got the job, to try and regain the high ground between politics and administration which was then my responsibility.

The last four months of 1976 when Jenkins was President-in-waiting were difficult. Although Europe had been a central theme throughout his political career, he had had no direct experience of European institutions, and had never, for example, participated in a Council of Ministers. Operating from the Cabinet Office in London, he now travelled extensively within Europe, keeping away from the Commission offices in Brussels to avoid any embarrassment to his predecessor François-Xavier Ortoli. I usually accompanied him on these visits and took the records. He was given advice by the sage of Europe Jean Monnet, and came as intellectually prepared as anyone could be.

From the beginning he ran up against a major limitation on his powers. Although free to appoint his own Cabinet, he was far from free to appoint the other twelve Commissioners (two each from France, Germany, Italy, and Britain, and one each from the others). Nor was he free to sack any of them should need arise. Governments could—and did—take account of his views, but the decision was theirs. In the event some did listen to him, but most saw the choice in terms of domestic politics. Here Helmut Schmidt was a particular disappointment. Having supported Jenkins in all other particulars, he more or less confessed to him that his hands were tied when it came to the nomination of the German Commissioners. The two he chose were not those wanted by Jenkins, and soon they knew it. The same was so in one or two other cases. As for the French, Giscard wanted to reappoint Jenkins's predecessor, François-Xavier Ortoli, this time as a Vice-President. None of this made for easy relations at the beginning.

The problem was exacerbated by the distribution of portfolios or specific responsibilities within the Commission. Again Jenkins had no power of decision. It had to be a collective decision by the Commission as a whole. Juggling with the conflicting personal ambitions of the Commissioners, themselves encouraged by their governments to aim high, Jenkins had to use all the black arts of diplomacy to arrive at an arrangement which he knew some would never find satisfactory.

Things came to a head at a special meeting of Commissioners at Ditchley Park just before Christmas 1976. There were little meetings in corners, whispering in passages, walks around the lake, and some painful arm-twisting. Outside was a dank mistiness. The journalist David Watt brought it all together as a detective story in the *Financial Times* with one victim—the President—with a knife in his back in the library, and twelve suspects each with a motive. The twelve anxiously conferred, and eventually agreed to exculpate themselves with a distribution of portfolios. The corpse then briskly resurrected itself, and the job was done.

In fact not quite done. It took more strenuous negotiations, this time in Brussels, before the allocations were complete at 5.30 a.m. on 7 January 1977. Jenkins had done well. Previous Commissions had had an even harder and longer time of it. Inevitably some feelings were left pretty raw and they were exposed from time to time over the next four years. But by and large this team of different characters from different countries settled down to work together, under Jenkins's chairmanship, without major rows or confrontations or even irreconcilable differences over policy. Every week the Chefs de Cabinet met on Monday afternoon to prepare for the Commission meeting on Wednesday morning. Tuesday was often spent in reconciling any divergences and generally oiling the wheels of business. Jenkins had remarkable powers of sympathetic persuasion. He rarely forced issues, and unlike some of his predecessors avoided voting. Throughout he maintained good personal relationships with all his colleagues.

Nonetheless, the first half year of his presidency was not a happy time for him. He had moved from the busy politics and lively society of England to a somewhat provincial city where he knew few people, and none well, outside his job. His wife, Jennifer, was with him some of the time and gave him all support, but she had responsibilities in England. The broad pattern of his weekends became one in Brussels, one at his home at East Hendred in Oxfordshire, and one on his travels in Europe or beyond. There was no official house in Brussels, and the one he found in the rue de Praetère was nice but in no way grand, with only limited room for guests. There was also the language problem: although he worked hard at his French, it never came easily to him. Giscard usually chose to speak to him in French, no doubt to maintain the advantage. No wonder that Jenkins should have felt lonely and cut off from time to time.

His first priority was to master the Commission machine, and make it work for him. I found over the years that it contained a lot of first-class people, and a lot of third-class people. But it lacked the discipline and reliability of the British Civil Service, which can bring out the best even in second-class people. Speeches contained too much rhetoric. Briefs were often too abstract, and not directed to the practical needs of a meeting. They sometimes assumed too much, and, worst of all, missed deadlines. I spent many late nights rewriting briefs or speeches for the following morning. At the same time there was a high level of understanding of the immensely complex issues before the Commission, from trade policy and agriculture to the nuclear fuel cycle and the North–South dialogue, together with original and sometimes brilliant ideas about how to cope with them.

The hybrid character of the Commission was itself a challenge. I remember that when Jenkins visited China in February 1979, he was subjected to a penetrating interrogation by

Deng Xiaoping, the Chairman of the Chinese Communist Party and the most powerful man in China. Jenkins had previously seen other Chinese leaders who had made elegant little speeches and gone through a ritual of politenesses before coming, often in veiled fashion, to practical questions. Deng was forthright. His first question after we had sat down in the Great Hall of the People, each chair with its pot of tea and spittoon, was 'How much power have you got?' Jenkins gave the best answer he could: 'Some direct power in some areas but more indirect power as the proposer of policy and the executive agency of the Community.' Deng then switched to relations between the Commission and a directly elected European Parliament. Would they now be in conflict? Jenkins said that he thought the main target of any parliamentary frustration would be the member governments rather than the Commission, which would be a natural ally. The sophistication of these questions showed Deng's interest in developing special relations with Europe as a counterbalance to the power of the United States and the then Soviet Union.

The question of powers arose in acute form over Commission representation at the Western summit (or G7) meeting at 10 Downing Street in early May 1977. It was Jenkins's first real test. In November 1975 President Giscard d'Estaing had begun what were supposed to be informed and intimate personal meetings of Western leaders on the major economic issues of the day. Originally the cast was the heads of state or government of France, the United States, Germany, Britain, and Japan, with Italy added as an afterthought. Next year President Ford was host, and Canada was also invited. With the turn of Jim Callaghan, now British Prime Minister, in 1977, the character of the meetings changed. Inevitably the personal element diminished, preparations became more elaborate, the meetings looked more like a diplomatic circus, and those not invited became increasingly resentful. (As a personal footnote, when Margaret Thatcher held another G7 summit in London in 1984, she sent me off afterwards as her personal emissary to soothe the Australians and the Indonesians.)

Among those unhappy in 1977 were the smaller members of the Community, otherwise known as the Little Five, who believed, as did the Commission, that when matters of Community competence were discussed by the G7, as they inevitably were, the Community as such should be represented. So long as the six-monthly presidency of the Council was held by one of the Summit participants, it could be argued that the Community was at least present. But the presidency of the Council could not represent the Commission. So the obvious solution was for the President of the Commission to join the heads of state and government for a discussion on matters of Community competence, and for his representative to join the preparatory committee of personal representatives or sherpas (summiteers) for the same purpose.

From the moment this issue arose, Giscard made it clear that he was opposed to any Commission presence in the proceedings. He told Jenkins at a private meeting in Paris on 28 February 1977 that only sovereign governments should participate. Jenkins replied that he could not agree and spoke likewise to Raymond Barre, the French Prime Minister, the same afternoon. Over the following weeks support for Jenkins steadily grew, even among the non-European members of the G7. Giscard was unwise enough to write him a 4½-page letter setting out French objections, which he repeated privately during a meeting of the European Council (or heads of European states and governments) on 25 March. He had no real help from anyone, and Schmidt apparently nobbled him on the telephone. Eventually Giscard backed down grudgingly: the President of the European Commission could be present for any session or sessions on matters of Community competence. A somewhat comic postscript was the unsuccessful effort of the French to recover the original of the 4½-page letter.

I am sure that Giscard had expected his first word to be his last. The President of France was used to getting his own way, particularly on matters European. From this time onwards his relationship with Jenkins became cooler. By supporting a heavyweight politician for the Commission he had effectively changed its status. It is significant that four years later he tried to reverse the change. On 8 October 1980 he spoke severely to Jenkins's successor, Gaston Thorn, to the effect that the independence that the Commission had recently shown now had to stop.

The main battle was over, but the guerrilla war now began. The British were as sticky as the French. As G7 hosts, they failed to invite Jenkins's personal representative to join the group of sherpas in Washington to prepare the meeting. Jenkins complained to Callaghan. Callaghan was in touch with Giscard. I went to see the Cabinet Secretary in London. The result was that eventually I was invited to the Washington meeting on condition that I attended only certain sessions. When I arrived at the meeting, the French sherpa made a little show of protest but admitted to me privately that his instructions were ridiculous. When IMF matters came up, I pointedly left the room, and the others said afterwards that the position was indeed ridiculous.

At Jenkins's level the same sort of comedy was repeated. He was invited to the preliminary dinner at 10 Downing Street, which Giscard then declined to attend. He was seated among the finance ministers rather than at the top table, and thereby missed discussion of the agenda of the meeting. He was excluded from the meeting next day, but did attend the day afterwards. I was then allowed into the room and took the record. Jenkins did very well with measured interventions that were well received. But he was not invited to lunch at Downing Street that day and went instead with the foreign ministers to Carlton Gardens. Throughout Callaghan's attitude was one of barely suppressed hostility, while Jenkins remained calm, polite, and measured, and did not complain.

The complaining came from me, all the more so when I found that at the concluding press conference Jenkins would not be invited to sit at the table with the heads of state and government, but would instead be put in the background with the finance ministers. I pointed out that Jenkins was the head of a delegation, and should be treated as such. If the decision was maintained, I would advise Jenkins to hold an independent press conference elsewhere at the same time. The press might find this interesting. After this threat, things changed. I suggested a compromise. Jenkins would sit at the table but would not speak. Callaghan as current President of the Council would represent the Community and speak for it. Eventually this was accepted. Jenkins was the only one at the table without a microphone in front of him and did not intervene. Callaghan said a few words for the Community through gritted teeth. He privately refused to accept that the Commission should necessarily be present at the next summit or during the preparations for it.

I have described this incident in detail because it showed what Jenkins was up against, and how he reacted to it. In fact he had won a notable victory. I was invited to the next meeting of the sherpas a few months later, and took part in the preparations for following summits. No one tried to deprive me of meals, and everyone realized that the dividing line between matters of Community competence and other matters was blurred. I did not insist on Commission rights and responsibilities, and simply tried to be helpful, contributing papers (even one on climate change) from time to time.

Jenkins's experience was similar. Although he was not invited to all the lunches and dinners, he attended almost all the working sessions and made effective interventions. For the final press conference at Bonn in 1978 he sat at the top table and even had a microphone but chose not to use it. At Tokyo in 1979 and at Venice in 1980 he had microphones and actually used them. By then the precedents had been set and were carefully followed. The absurdity of the London experience in 1977 had been largely forgotten, except of course by Giscard.

The G7 summits were an important element on Jenkins's external agenda as President. But for the internal management of the Community, the three European Councils a year, when the heads of European states and governments came together in restricted session, were crucial. There were also meetings of the Council of Ministers (foreign ministers whether formal or informal), meetings of the Committee of Permanent Representatives, meetings of specialized ministers (for example, agriculture or the environment), which he occasionally attended, meetings with the Economic and Social Council, and meetings with the European Parliament and its committees, with occasional participation in its debates. Beyond Europe were endless private meetings with governments at the top level, in which his status as a senior political figure in his own country made all the difference. As I saw for myself many times, his presence was itself an asset and he enjoyed great respect as a wise and central figure who held the strings. By the end of his first year he had recovered his spirits, and felt that he had something of a grip on the people who in their different ways made the Community work.

I doubt if this would have happened if he had not decided to take a major initiative of his own. In the summer of 1977 he felt that the Community had become becalmed. He detected no sense of strategy, no movements towards objectives, no feelings of excitement as in the early days. Europe might describe itself as being in the course of construction, but the builders seemed content with what there was, or were absent on prolonged tea breaks. They reacted but hardly acted.

It was in these circumstances that Jenkins began work to relaunch European economic and monetary union. He had already made something of a mark in this area by suggesting the creation of a new loan facility to encourage industrial investment in the Community. But the ideas he put forward in Florence on 27 October 1977 were much more ambitious. They were the product of hard work, not least within the Cabinet, and of wide consultation elsewhere. In a way they began with Jean Monnet, and it was appropriate that they were expressed in the first Monnet Lecture. The Werner Report of 1971 on the same subject had had little effect. Since then there had been violent and divergent currency fluctuations, including a sharp fall in the value of the US dollar. Jenkins believed that the time had come for the Europeans to do more to look after themselves.

The sequence of events has been described by Jenkins in his *European Diary* (1989), and subjected to detailed analysis elsewhere: first, discussion in the Cabinet at an away-day meeting; then, among Commissioners at a similar meeting; and then, among European foreign ministers. So far it had only been one item on crowded agendas. When the lecture itself was given, it created something of a shock. As this was probably the most important event in Jenkins's presidency and had the greatest consequences, it is worth dwelling on his main arguments. Underlying them was his belief that lack of a central economic mechanism was the Community's most important weakness, and that the time had come to correct it.

His seven points were: monetary union favoured a more efficient rationalization of industry and commerce than was possible in a customs union alone; a major European currency would be a joint and alternative pillar to the US dollar in the world monetary system, and a source of European strength and stability; it would limit inflation and lead to a common rate of price movement; it would favour investment and employment; it would improve and rationalize the flow of public finance to weaker or poorer regions; it would require new institutions, not necessarily federal or confederal, but something responding to Europe's particular needs; and last, it would be a model for eventual European political integration. In moving towards a union of this kind, he used the metaphor of a long-jumper.

He starts with a rapid succession of steps, lengthens his stride, increases his momentum, and then makes his leap . . . We have to look before we leap, and know where we are to land. But leap we eventually must . . . Politics is not only the art of the possible . . . it is also the art of making possible tomorrow what may seem impossible today.

Surprise and scepticism were the first main public reactions. Most commentators thought Jenkins's ideas were unrealistic, and *The Economist*, while commending them in principle, thought that monetary union in the form he had suggested it was a bridge too far. The Brussels correspondents of *Le Monde* and the *Neue Zürcher Zeitung* were openly hostile. *The Times* touched on a more delicate point. It found it strange that

Jenkins should be 'in the blue corner, wearing psychedelic federalist trunks' while François-Xavier Ortoli, now Commission Vice-President for Economic and Monetary Affairs, wore 'the sombre colours of good old British pragmatism'.

Ortoli was indeed unhappy, and had his own more modest ideas on the subject. He was a gradualist all the way, and the thought of leaps in any direction seemed to give him pain. Although Ortoli was in a small minority in the Commission, Jenkins did not want an open dispute or confrontation with him, and I had to use some drafting ingenuity in amending a paper he had written for a meeting of economic and finance ministers on 20 November 1977. In fact Jenkins's eyes were on the European Council of 5 and 6 December. The mood there was good, with amiable encouragement for Jenkins in the form of an official statement, and friendly words even from Callaghan. The Commission's loan facility, now called the Ortoli Facility, was also agreed.

By himself Jenkins could not advance much further. But things changed dramatically when he saw Helmut Schmidt in Bonn on 28 February 1978. Schmidt told him in strictest confidence that in response to the gyrations of the US dollar, Germany was now aiming for a European monetary system, not all that Jenkins had argued for at Florence, but a big step towards it. A lot would depend upon the attitude of France. Giscard faced legislative elections in March, which it then seemed likely he would lose. But assuming he won, then Schmidt said 'my friend Valéry' would almost certainly lend his support. In the event Giscard did win. From that time onwards progress was surprisingly fast through the European Councils at Copenhagen in April and Bremen in July. Jenkins might have been the godfather, but Schmidt and Giscard became the parents. I was kept in touch by their representatives as technical work proceeded. There was a near crash at the European Council in Brussels, largely because of some ill-advised French manoeuvring, but the European Monetary System came into formal operation on 13 March 1979.

Jenkins can take a lot of credit for it. A large part of what had looked impractical, unrealistic, even idealist, some seventeen months before had actually happened. Over 1978 Jenkins focused most of his energies on it in the Commission, with member governments and in the Parliament. There was one serious weakness, which he tried hard to correct but in the end failed to do so. The position of Britain was an increasing embarrassment. It was not for lack of effort on his part. The Cabinet kept the British broadly informed about what was going on, and for a while a senior British representative joined the Germans and French in their technical discussions. The British had every opportunity not just to participate but also to help shape it to take account of British interests. Instead they made their usual half-in half-out equivocations. At least they did not obstruct the others. At home Callaghan's government was already on a downward path, and for many British politicians Europe seemed unattractive, irrelevant, and far away.

All this was evident at the Copenhagen European Council in April 1978. I remember that after detailed discussions over dinner with his colleagues, Callaghan asked Jenkins to call on him privately in his hotel room. I went too. Callaghan asked him to explain what on earth was going on. Jenkins did so. Clearly some of it was new to Callaghan. A Treasury mandarin said several times, 'But this is very bold, Prime Minister.' Indeed it was. That was what seemed to make it alarming. Callaghan was particularly concerned lest it should be construed as anti-American. He showed no signs of wanting to be directly involved. Once or twice he looked like a baffled bull uncertain whom to charge. It is a tribute to Jenkins that neither Schmidt nor Giscard, nor indeed the other Community heads of government, ever blamed him for British tergiversations. They knew he had done his best.

Unfortunately there was a bigger British problem on the horizon, which blighted the last eighteen months of the Jenkins presidency. It was the British contribution to the Community budget from its own resources, usually known as the BBQ (the British Budgetary Question, or in the vernacular within the Cabinet the Bloody British Question). As I remember vividly from the entry negotiations from 1970 to 1972, it was clear then that the Community budgetary system meant that Britain, a relatively poor country, would eventually contribute a good deal more than it received from the Community budget: Britain received more goods than others from overseas and so paid more import levies, and needed fewer subsidies for its agriculture.

This was a penalty like others (for example, the Common Fisheries Policy) that the British had paid for their failure to join the Community at the beginning and to participate in creating its institutions. They had then accepted reluctantly the budgetary system on condition of a transitional period, in the hope that by its end things would have changed, and that anyway it would be easier to change the system from inside rather than from outside. But with the end of the transitional period in 1979 and a continually increasing Community budget, the imbalance—or inequity—became more and more evident. This problem was also linked with efforts to correct regional imbalances in the new European Monetary System (from which the British had now excluded themselves).

After the problems of Commission participation in the G7 summits and the creation of the European Monetary System, this was the most important—and saddest—for the Jenkins presidency. He was in a difficult position. As President and as British, he had to take particular care not to favour, or to be seen to favour, British interests. At the same time it was hard not to sympathize with the British predicament. Unfortunately the British had not endeared themselves in other ways to their colleagues in the Community nor indeed to the Commission.

Margaret Thatcher succeeded Callaghan as Prime Minister on 8 May 1979. She had made friendly noises about Europe when in opposition, but she took up the British case on the budget with aggressive zeal, and made the issue one that cast a cloud over British relations with the rest of the Community for the next decade and beyond. As Jenkins wrote in *European Diary*, hopes of the British exercising any leadership in the Community ran into the sand.

No one doubted that the British had a case. Perhaps the best solution was the most radical: to look again at the whole budgetary system, work out a better one which would avoid big deficits and surpluses, and link it to the correction of regional imbalances. But there were already strong vested interests in the status quo. No one wanted to look very far ahead. The French linked any change to agreement on agricultural prices and fisheries, and others consulted their own national interests. The Commission itself was divided, with Ortoli sometimes playing an unhelpful role. The result was long, bitter, and sometimes bad-tempered negotiations within the European Councils, at meetings of ministers of foreign affairs and of finance, and in endless bilateral encounters. There were threats and counter-threats, and every kind of arm-twisting. At one point the French even considered reverting to national subsidies for agriculture, which might have involved creating tariff barriers between Member States, and thereby the gradual unwinding of the Community.

After an epic night on 29 May 1980, a compromise was finally reached between foreign ministers. Reading my own detailed account of what happened, there were obvious heroes and villains, but nothing could have been achieved without the successive initiatives and technical work of the Commission. The two main heroes were Jenkins himself and Emiliano Colombo, the Italian Foreign Minister and current President of the Council of Ministers. Throughout the night Jenkins and Colombo held a kind of confessional of private meetings. Ministers went back and forth, and paper succeeded paper. Finally the Secretary-General of the Commission devised a winning formula for the remaining most difficult issue. By 10 a.m. on 30 May only the French had not agreed, but that was because they feared that Margaret Thatcher might disavow what had been accepted by the British Foreign Secretary, Lord Carrington. Eventually there was a nod from Paris, and the deed was done.

The aftermath was sour. The French were right to be apprehensive about the attitude of Margaret Thatcher. She received Carrington and the Lord Privy Seal, Ian Gilmour, with discourtesy on their return, and declined to recommend the agreement to the British Cabinet and later to Parliament. Fortunately she was overridden by her colleagues, and the press was broadly in favour. For his part Schmidt was unhappy about the performance of Klaus von Dohnanyi, who had been one of the most helpful during the night. Giscard publicly accepted the agreement next morning, but the French Permanent Representative apparently regarded it almost as a personal defeat. As President of the Council, Colombo received the agreement of the other Community governments the following week.

For everyone it was more of a relief than a victory. Jenkins wearily remarked to me afterwards that it would be for the next Commission under a new President to give effect to the agreement and draw the right conclusions from it. He himself felt damaged by the whole affair and physically unwell.

Over his four years in Brussels, Jenkins exercised a superintending role over all the business of the Commission, but he left management to the Commission Vice-Presidents and Commissioners within their portfolios. Obviously he had to intervene from time to time, and there were disagreements, but it is a tribute to his powers of leadership that these never erupted into anything serious. Part of my job was to help smooth over any difficulties, and deal with problems before they became too big.

Jenkins's relationship with Ortoli required particularly careful handling, but each liked and respected the other. There were no practical difficulties between Jenkins and Finn-Olav Gundelach, in charge of agriculture. Both were agreed on the need—then as now—for reform of the Common Agricultural Policy, but the Commission was as ever frustrated by the member states. Vicomte Davignon, in charge of industry and technology, was a rapid and brilliant operator, full of original ideas and a source of strength. Lorenzo Natali for the current enlargement negotiations, Antonio Giolitti for regional affairs, Christopher Tugendhat for the budget and staff matters, were steady allies. Wilhelm Haferkamp may not have been Jenkins's original choice, and was certainly careless about his expenses (a cause of some scandal in 1979), but he was a warm and generous person who ran his portfolio of external affairs well enough. Hank Vredeling for social affairs was something of an eccentric, and could be truculent, but he has to his credit the Vredeling Directive on worker consultation (after a long negotiation with unions and employers' organizations). Guido

Brunner for energy, Richard Burke for relations with Parliament, and Raymond Vouel for competition policy were less conspicuous. Claude Cheysson, later French Foreign Minister, who was often away on development aid issues, was always a sympathetic colleague. In the Cabinet he was known as the electric mouse. There was a little inner group of the most influential Commissioners—Ortoli, Davignon, Gundelach—which met from time to time, usually over dinner to clear the way on difficult issues.

I have recently checked Jenkins's travel diary, and wonder how he stood the wear and tear. There were not only constant little trips, usually by air taxi within the Community and other parts of Europe, but also excursions worldwide to represent and in some sense sell the European enterprise. As the biggest trading block in the world the Community had worldwide interests. He was in Washington almost every year to see President Carter, whose term of office coincided with his own. In 1977 he also visited Japan; in 1978 Sudan, Egypt, Canada, Greenland, and again the United States; in 1979 West Africa (Senegal, Mali, and Ghana), China, Japan, and Egypt; and 1980 the United States and India.

These visits may have been exhausting, but most were also fun. I remember riding with him on camels into Timbuktu, where enormous Arab and African crowds were assembled. Then came a feast at which the main course was a whole roasted camel, inside which was a sheep, inside which a chicken, inside which a pigeon, inside which an egg. We were given knives to hack bits off the camel's flank, which tasted greasily negative. In China we contrived on an evening walk in Chengdu to block the main street with a curious crowd, to discuss the current Chinese invasion of Vietnam with Deng Xiaoping (he said it was valuable training experience for his fat and useless generals), and to have an ideological argument with Chairman Hua about whether China was an underdeveloped, developing, or developed country. In India I persuaded Jenkins to descend into the jungle by helicopter to look (unsuccessfully) for tigers, and to take a ride on an elephant. I will not forget his sparkling conversation with the elegant President Sadat of Egypt at the Barrage at the point where the Nile divides.

In all his time as President, perhaps Jenkins's closest friend among the European heads of state and government was the mercurial Helmut Schmidt. In their numerous conversations Schmidt was amazingly indiscreet, at times buoyant, at times depressed, always warm, and greatly attached to 'his friend Valéry' even when Giscard made mistakes. Jenkins noticed that when this happened Schmidt switched off 'rather like a husband who pretends not to notice if his wife gets drunk'. Giscard could be disdainful, painfully conscious of his status, and sometimes self-defeating in his manoeuvres (too clever by half, as was often said). Only once did I detect signs of vulnerability, and that was before the French legislative elections which he feared he might lose. But he was always intelligent and constructive, and had more ideas and knowledge about Europe than anyone else.

Jenkins's relationship with Callaghan went back a long way, and after some rough moments in 1977 became noticeably warmer. Margaret Thatcher was something special. In their private discussions Jenkins used to play her like a matador. She would charge, and at the last moment he would step aside. It needed time and patience for him to register his points. But he usually did in the end, and she remained friendly and accessible, avoiding the shrill tones she adopted so often at European Councils. Jenkins had particularly good relations with Francesco Cossiga and Emiliano Colombo. Indeed I do not remember him having difficulties with any of the European leaders or their respective ministers. Any exasperation he may have felt he kept for me afterwards.

His relationship with Carter was also good, and I think they enjoyed their meetings. There were many complaints at the time, particularly from Schmidt, about Carter's lack of leadership. As Henry Kissinger remarked to me at a New York dinner party long afterwards, Carter never really saw the connection between things. This was more true at formal meetings, when he would solemnly change from one file to another, than at the private ones. I remember one particularly useful private meeting which went on longer than expected. The reason was that his adviser Henry Owen had, out of excessive respect for the President, backed into the grandfather clock in his office, and thereby stopped it. Not until an emissary from those waiting outside came to remind Carter did he realize what had happened and then led Jenkins into the formal meeting.

By 1979 there were moves afoot to ask Jenkins to serve a second term as President. I do not think he ever wanted to do so, but for the time being he was non-committal. He had become increasingly interested in British politics and the fate of the Labour Party following the elections of May that year. When he was asked to give the Dimbleby Lecture in London in November, the assumption was that it would be on a European theme. Instead he chose to go for what he later called 'a new anti-party approach to British politics'. This was the eloquent preliminary to his return to Britain. By mid-1980 he anyway felt bruised by the British budgetary question and somewhat exhausted. He did not want to announce his intentions too soon for fear of diminishing his authority, but by the autumn they were pretty clear. The Jenkins presidency ended on 4 January 1981.

It was a remarkable four years, and will stand out in the history of Europe. The choice of Gaston Thorn to succeed him itself tells a tale. Giscard had already made it clear that he thought that Jenkins had got too big for his boots. Giscard had his own ideas about the future of Europe, which only became public more than twenty years later. Even during the Jenkins presidency he had pressed a proposal for three wise men to look at the European institutions. Unfortunately the three chosen did not turn out to be all that wise, and their report was virtually ignored.

Thorn could never occupy Jenkins's boots and never attempted to do so. I tried to help his new Chef de Cabinet, but he retired after a month with a nervous breakdown. His successor was the admirable Fernand Spaak, former Commission representative in Washington, but he was shot dead by his wife a couple of months later.

Roy Jenkins was a true friend, and remained so until his death. After Brussels he returned to British politics, and I briefly to academia and then to diplomacy. During our time together we had no quarrels and only minor disagreements (for example, he liked to arrive at airports with only minutes to spare before take-off while I preferred to stick to the rules). Our judgements of people and their motives were very similar. We talked together on everything and nothing, from gossip and meteorology to the future of the world, and I learnt immensely from him. Throughout, his most conspicuous qualities were wide-ranging intelligence, tolerance, a sense of history, sympathetic understanding of others, and loyalty to his friends. I was lucky to be among them.

CHRISTOPHER TUGENDHAT

Christopher Tugendhat was a member of the Jenkins Commission from 1977 to 1981. He stayed on after Roy Jenkins's departure as a Vice-President under Gaston Thorn. Before going to Brussels he was a Conservative MP for the Cities of London and Westminster. Since his return in 1985 he has pursued a career in business and is currently Chairman–Europe of the US investment bank Lehman Brothers. He was made a life peer in 1993. He is also Chancellor of the University of Bath and has been Chairman of the Royal Institute of International Affairs (Chatham House). He is the author of *Making Sense of Europe* (1986).

Chapter 12

The European Achievement

CHRISTOPHER TUGENDHAT

'How many divisions has the Pope?', Stalin once famously asked. The President of the European Commission's position in relation to heads of state and government is somewhat analogous to that of the Pontiff *vis-à-vis* the great powers in the past, but much weaker as he lacks their 2,000 years of history and the mantle of the Almighty. He is entirely dependent in his dealings with them on his own strength of personality and intellectual fire-power.

Only three presidents have overcome this handicap: Walter Hallstein, Roy Jenkins, and Jacques Delors. There is, however, a great difference between them. Hallstein and Delors were operating within the framework of a set of objectives agreed by heads of state and government. In an important sense they were the instruments of the Member States' collective will and the architects of their design. They also each came from a country deeply committed to the European project. Roy had no such advantages. He became President at a time when the Community, as it was then, had no agreed programme, and was from a country as much at odds with European aspirations as it was with its partners.

Yet Roy succeeded in outfacing the formidable President Giscard d'Estaing, backed on this occasion by Prime Minister Callaghan, over the role of the presidency of the Commission at Western Economic Summits, or G7 meetings. He was sneered at for being overly concerned with his own personal prestige, but in fact there was a major issue of principle at stake. Fundamentally, it was about whether at these meetings the Commission should speak for the European Community as a whole or whether the smaller states should delegate that role to the larger ones who were there in their own right.

If he had lost the battle, the Commission would have been relegated to being a Secretariat like that of the OECD. By winning, Roy secured for himself and his successors the right to speak as practically an equal of prime ministers and presidents both at the G7 and within the Community itself. This made the Commission a political force in its own right, which in turn gave it the self-confidence and clout to relaunch the idea of European Monetary Union and later, under Delors, the Single Market programme.

When Roy arrived in Brussels, the idea of monetary union was to all intents and purposes dead. To revive it as he did in his Florence speech on 27 October 1977 required immense courage. Not only were the most important governments at best sceptical and at worst opposed; several of his Commission colleagues were quite frankly frightened. 'Soyez prudent,' urged more than one from countries now members of the euro zone. They were afraid as much of attracting ridicule for their utopianism as of incurring opposition from powerful governments.

But Roy persevered and, thanks to his persuasiveness and vision, Chancellor Schmidt and President Giscard were convinced. For a man who was not himself, and never had been, a head of government, to grip their imaginations and convince them that, despite what their own officials were advising, it was in their national interest to proceed down this road, was an astonishing achievement. When Delors pressed for the Single Market project nearly ten years later, it was an idea whose time had come, with Margaret Thatcher, as well as other heads of governments, ready to be convinced. When Roy spoke at Florence, his position was as lonely as that of Churchill when he first began to warn of the Nazi menace. Unlike Delors, Roy had to settle for at best half a loaf in the form of the European Monetary System rather than full monetary union. But with the benefit of hindsight we can now see that it was he who set in motion the process that led eventually to the creation of the euro zone.

When Roy left Brussels, his achievement there was widely underrated, including by me. The significance and long-term implications of retaining the Commission's seat at the 'top table' were not appreciated. The evolution of the EMS into full monetary union looked wildly improbable. We had also come to take for granted that heads of state and government within Europe and beyond treated him as an equal. It was mistakenly thought that this was because the Commission was so important rather than that its President was worth listening to, as some of his successors learned to their cost.

The Commission itself, like many bureaucracies, is an inward-looking body. Roy's habitual weakness of surrounding himself and working through a praetorian guard of devoted officials was resented. His reluctance to engage in bruising personal confrontation was mistaken for weakness. He was also, as I was, damaged by the bitterness left by the hard-fought but fundamentally justified struggles over the British budget contribution.

With the passage of time judgements have matured and, like a good claret, the quality of Roy's presidency is now more widely appreciated. In addition to his enduring achievements it can be seen that he was exceptionally skilful in getting his team of fellow Commissioners to work together. This is no easy matter, as his successors have found. Not only does the President not choose them; they come from different countries and, unlike colleagues within the same political party in a national environment, their fate and future are not bound together. Roy was able to get us to work as a team. Intimate personal lunches and dinners, even with those he found boring, played a part. But the real wellsprings of his authority were twofold. One was his statesman's grasp of the big issues and his eloquence in expressing his ideas on them. The other was his willingness to risk odium and even ridicule in the cause of what he believed to be right. It was these characteristics that inspired his colleagues to follow him.

Some also came to enjoy his foibles, and nowhere more than at the weekly formal meetings of the Commission, at which each of us spoke in our own language. Roy's love of metaphor, simile, and allusion caused the interpreters constant anxiety while providing amusement for those colleagues who could compare the English original with the rendering into their own language. Sometimes this proved impossible, as on one occasion when the interpreters were completely stymied by the pronouncement that our debate was 'thrashing about in the abstract', a phrase that will forever remain for me quintessentially Roy. However, my abiding memory of these occasions is of his presiding at our round table, wreathed in cigar smoke with Crispin behind him, gently guiding the debate and building on earlier conversations with colleagues until we reached the decision he wanted—or at least something not too far removed from it—without it being apparent quite how.

BILL RODGERS

Bill Rodgers was born and brought up in Liverpool. He was MP for Stockton-on-Tees (1962–83) and a minister through the Wilson and Callaghan governments. One of the SDP 'Gang of Four', he became a life peer in 1992 and succeeded Roy Jenkins as Leader of the Liberal Democrat peers (1998–2001). He has been Director-General of the Royal Institute of British Architects (1987–94) and Chairman of the Advertising Standards Authority (1995–2000). His books include *The Politics of Change* (1982) and *Fourth Among Equals* (2000).

Chapter 13

SDP

Bill Rodgers

In 1976, in the late afternoon of an April day, I was summoned across Whitehall from my office in the Ministry of Defence to the Home Secretary. Roy Jenkins rose from his chair and said, 'Well, it's all over, Callaghan is appointing Crosland.' He nodded towards a hand-written envelope addressed to Giscard d'Estaing, the President of the French Republic. I knew that it contained a letter declaring Roy's readiness to become President of the European Commission. We talked for a while and I sadly conceded that my resistance to his departure from British politics was at an end. A little before six o'clock we watched the television news for confirmation of events. There it was. Tony Crosland had become Foreign Secretary—the only job that might have kept Roy away from the Commission.

I would greatly miss him in the House of Commons, and not just for sharing the excitement of great occasions. I would miss congenial dinners when we were joined by other friends and cleared the cellars of Château Gloria before going benign into the Chamber for an important vote at 10 p.m.; and the occasional breakfast on the terrace by the Thames on a soft summer morning after an all-night sitting. The House is a place of deep affections and strong loyalties, as well as cruel moments. For fourteen years Roy's presence had been part of my pleasure at being there.

Roy was installed as President of the Commission at the beginning of 1977, and shortly after I visited him in his new home on the rue de Praetère. He glanced ruefully at the half-empty red dispatch box—a memento of his years as Chancellor of the Exchequer. There were no manuscript notes lying on the table, and the telephone did not ring. We talked about domestic politics and the consequences of the IMF crisis, but in a desultory way. Few of his former parliamentary colleagues expected him to return from exile to British politics.

I did not see Roy in his Brussels home again for another two years, but every three or four months we met at East Hendred. On one occasion I was involved in lengthy telephone conversations from Roy's study about negotiations between David Steel and Jim Callaghan, the Prime Minister, over the Lib–Lab pact—high politics at that time. But when I reported these exchanges to Roy, he was detached. In his *European Diary*, published ten years later, he mentioned the event in a single sentence. We talked for a long time in the autumn of 1978 about the state of the country and the possibility of the Labour government's survival, and my own experience in the Cabinet. But he seemed to be no more than an interested observer, 'networking'—to use contemporary jargon that Roy would have abhorred—keeping in touch with political events and personalities rather than contemplating any initiative or move of his own.

Then in May 1979 Margaret Thatcher won a convincing electoral victory and the Labour Party suffered its worst election result for half a century. On the eve of polling day there was a rumour that Roy was about to make a statement in support of the Conservatives. This was false, but later I discovered that he had broken his long record of Labour voting—by not voting at all.

It was this change of government that provoked Roy's change of mood. In what he later described as a couple of decisive weeks, he felt 'a resurgence of my political sap'. For the first time in some years he believed that he had a general message to deliver outside the framework of traditional politics. This, initially 'in inchoate terms', eventually became the Dimbleby Lecture of November 1979.

During the 1970s the two-party system which had dominated for a quarter of a century began to fracture. When Roy had been first elected at Stechford in 1950, 84 per cent of the electorate had voted at a general election and nine out of ten voters had chosen to vote either Labour or Conservative. But in the second 1974 election, Roy's last election before he left for Brussels, fewer than 73 per cent of the electorate had voted and only seven out of ten voters had chosen either Labour or Conservative. Given economic and social change, class-based party loyalties were diminishing and voters had become politically footloose.

Over the years Roy had seldom shown much enthusiasm for the broad sweep of political philosophy either in his speeches or in his writing. He had not competed with Tony Crosland in 'rethinking' democratic socialism in the 1950s, contributing towards the emerging revisionism of the Left only a short book, *Pursuit of Progress* (1953), and a New Fabian essay. He had also shown a certain reserve over the nuts and bolts of current controversy within the Labour Party, preferring to take a longer perspective and a more generous view of the contenders.

So neither I nor most of the remaining parliamentary Jenkinsites—those fifty-six MPs who had voted for Roy in his Labour 1976 leadership contest—anticipated any new message from him. We were preoccupied with the tough, messy battle against the rising tide of militancy within the Labour Party, and some felt that Roy had abandoned them. In August 1979 I raised with him in passing, and without expectation, the possibility that he might return to the House of Commons as a Labour MP. He was unresponsive and gave no hint of how his mind was moving or the significance of the Dimbleby Lecture he was planning.

Then, on the evening of 1 November, he showed me the draft. With only three weeks to the event he had worked all day to put it into shape and to spell out his firm proposals, and he was now reasonably satisfied. But I was not particularly excited by the outcome. Perhaps because I was full of (his) claret and sleep, and perhaps because I thought that Roy was too immersed in Europe to be saying anything of urgent relevance to domestic politics, I failed to recognize the importance of the forthcoming event. Nor did I realize that, despite leaving Parliament and choosing Brussels, Roy's voice would make news.

When, on the afternoon of 22 November, the gist of the forthcoming lecture passed from the Commons Press Gallery to the lobbies, there was excitement but some scepticism among many of his old parliamentary friends. There was tentative approval about the sentiments but concern about the timing. David Owen, more critical than most, thought that the lecture was a diversion from the main task in hand, of saving the

Labour Party, 'a foolish course . . . tempted by siren voices'. Shirley Williams saw it as 'a mildly interesting academic lecture, not much more'.

When I had heard the lecture that evening at the Royal Society of Arts, I told Roy that I could envisage sitting in the headquarters, actively organizing a new party. But even I was not convinced that this was a major event. I followed Roy's historical analysis in the lecture—Britain's last imperial adventure at Suez, its economic decline and adversarial industrial relations, its excessive political partisanship—but proportional representation loomed too large as a solution to all contemporary problems. I liked Roy's liberal programme— instinctive rather than didactic—but was electoral reform the only way? On the face of it, as the Labour Party was falling to pieces and the Tory 'Wets' were increasingly restless under Mrs Thatcher, 'a strengthening of the radical centre' was not really an inspiring call to arms.

The following morning the Dimbleby Lecture, *Home Thoughts from Abroad*, was published almost in full in *The Times*, with a leading article suggesting that a coalition of the centre-right might provide an alternative to the new Thatcher government. Well-disposed correspondents then contributed to the *Times* letters page. *The Guardian* said that 'as a contribution to practical politics, the lecture was intriguing but marginal', although it might be relevant in the future. Roy said that the mail was not enormous, perhaps 300 to 400 letters, but the quality was high. In fact, 'Dimbleby'—the lecture acquired its one-word status—steadily became deeply persuasive, catching the worried mood of the times. Its impact was less on the political activists than on the 'political virgins', as they came to be called. When the SDP was reaching its membership peak, over seven out of ten members had never before joined a party. It was precisely such a new party that Roy envisaged, appealing across a broad spectrum of disillusioned moderates.

David Owen remained hostile to the idea of any new party until he suffered from being shouted down at a Labour conference. Shirley Williams, at much the same time, said that a centre party would have 'no roots, no principles, no philosophy and no values'. As for me, my voyage out of the Labour Party was a slow, hesitant affair, not finally accomplished until the end of 1980. All three of us were preoccupied with difficult personal decisions about whether, how, and when we should change direction. Even Roy, six months after Dimbleby, was unsure whether—in the simile of his Press Gallery speech of 9 June 1980—his experimental aeroplane would finish up 'a few fields from the end of the runway' or 'soar into the sky'. Despite that, he remained steadfast, conveying his periods of despondency only to Jennifer and his diary.

Among Roy's political friends we called him 'Grand Roy', with teasing—and sometimes irritated—affection. But grand he was with the weight of an elder statesman. Without Roy, the argument behind Dimbleby—'a strengthening of the radical centre'—would have been welcomed but without excitement; and without Dimbleby, a new party would have lacked a prospectus.

Throughout 1980, in his fourth year in Brussels, the king over the water was building among a number of his colleagues a body of support for a break. But, as on other occasions in the past when I had to make a difficult choice, Roy put no pressure on me. He left me to reach my own decision at my own pace. He constantly made clear that he would join Shirley and me—and David Owen when the Gang of Three emerged in our open letter to *The Guardian* in August—on our terms if we reached the point of launching a new party. David Owen saw

Roy as yesterday's man, a sybaritic and whiggish figure, not obviously the stuff of which new parties were made. My assumption was that collective leadership should last as long as possible, but that Roy would eventually become leader once he had been elected to Parliament.

Roy described the road from Dimbleby as 'fairly stony' until the end of 1980; and some patient coaxing was required to remove 'small boulders' that were still blocking the way until much of January. But on 25 January we drafted *The Declaration for Social Democracy*—the Limehouse Declaration—and two months later the SDP was launched, with brilliant success. Within ten days we could claim 43,566 paid-up members and more than half a million pounds in the bank. Public meetings were arranged and they were packed. But the real test for the buoyant SDP was in the parliamentary arena. There was strong pressure on the existing MPs to resign their seats and fight a by-election. This was an attractive and defiant solution, but they would be picked off one by one, and few would survive. Far better if we could fight a by-election—and win—when a seat became vacant. It would give the SDP credibility and accelerate our momentum.

The opportunity arose at the end of May when the sitting Labour MP for Warrington left to become a judge. But Warrington—half-way between Liverpool and Manchester and dominated by the chemical industry and the distillery of Vladimir vodka—was not good political territory for us. Nearly half of the households lived in council houses and only one in ten were professionals. This was not the obvious economic and social profile of most social democrats. The Labour majority was over 10,000 (in a small electorate) and there was no local Liberal tradition. Shirley Williams was the favoured candidate, currently out of Parliament, popular with the public, and a Catholic in a strong Catholic constituency. But Shirley was unwilling to go ahead, and Roy might have been justified in ducking the responsibility given that, as David Steel put it, Warrington was not 'a Roy-type' of seat—a view that others shared. However, he believed that an effective by-election, with maximum publicity and a respectable result, was essential. When he was faced by the choice, and Shirley had declined, he telephoned me, saying, 'Now I suppose I'll have to do it,' with less than enthusiasm. But within a few days he announced his decision to go ahead, installed himself with Jennifer in the Fir Tree Motel, and set out upon an event as important as his Dimbleby Lecture—high risk for him and crucial to the future of the party.

As it turned out, the outcome was a personal triumph. Throughout most of June the campaign was quiet. The SDP made most of the running, but there was little change in the opinion polls, giving Roy about 30 per cent compared with 9 per cent for the Liberals in 1979. But Frank Johnson, the sketch-writer, said that 'the surprising news' was that 'people rather like Mr Jenkins'. Far from being a remote grandee, he was energetic, relaxed, and sociable in campaigning through the streets and never talked down to his voters. His visibility caught the imagination and he attracted an audience of over 300, the biggest meeting seen in town for many years.

With ten days to go, SDP supporters poured into Warrington, and the presence of both Jo Grimond, rather diffidently accompanying Roy around the shopping centre, and David Steel, attracting attention in the local funfair, raised morale further. We never expected Roy to win, but by the last Saturday of the campaign the feeling was of a festival, with Roy enjoying the role of the star performer. Losing on the Thursday was no anticlimax when he captured a spectacular 42.5 per cent of the vote.

When the returning officer announced the result, there was a wave of excitement. The Labour candidate, squeezing through to a majority of only 1,759 votes, claimed that his election victory had been in spite of a concerted press campaign. But after the formalities, and throwing away his prepared notes, Roy described the result as 'my first defeat in thirty years in politics', adding, 'and it is far the greatest victory in which I have ever participated'. This brought the house down.

The following day and during that weekend Warrington continued to be described as an astonishing result, echoing what Bob McKenzie of the BBC had said was 'the most sensational by-election result of the century'. *The Times* wrote about 'The Jenkins Effect', adding that Roy deserved 'immense credit for his courage in fighting the election, and for the intelligent, uncondescending and vigorous way in which he fought it'. It assumed that the Social Democrats would now work together with the Liberals as 'a third force to challenge both the Conservatives and Labour'. Other commentators called the by-election 'a watershed', the first real national test of the SDP and killing dead the thought that Roy might be out of touch with real politics.

Roy's own assessment of the by-election was that it was a success far beyond his expectation: 'It had underpinned the nascent SDP, created an experience and a climate which were highly favourable to the fostering of the Alliance, and increased both my own sense of confidence with the electorate (after nearly five years of separation) and my authority within the party.' The emerging role of the Alliance—a partnership of the SDP and the Liberals—was put on the official record when Roy was described on the ballot paper as 'Jenkins, R. H. (SDP with Liberal support)', and the Liberals played an enthusiastic part in the campaign. *A Fresh Start for Britain*, a joint statement of principles agreed between the two parties, had been published soon after Roy's adoption as the candidate. This was in keeping with Roy's view, from the time of Dimbleby until merger in 1988, that the SDP and Liberals should work together and avoid confrontation.

Before the launch of the party the Gang of Four had decided to cooperate with the Liberals and consider an electoral arrangement. But David Owen was hostile towards getting closer and believed that I had made a serious error at the time of the launch in agreeing on the equal division of parliamentary seats for the next general election. I too was cautious about the development of our relationship, believing that the SDP's identity should be firmly established and convergence then could follow at its natural pace. When provoked, Roy did not disown the description that he was more of an Asquithian liberal than a contemporary social democrat, and he might have reluctantly settled for the Liberal Party if Shirley, David Owen, and myself had not left the Labour Party. But he believed that a new party with a wider vision, rather than the Liberals, was more likely to break the mould of established two-party politics.

Roy said that David Steel was steady under fire from his own party—a critical test of leadership—and he always delivered what he promised. However, on this occasion there was one exception: he was unable to dislodge the sitting Liberal prospective candidate for Croydon North-West in favour of Shirley Williams at the first by-election after Warrington. But the hiccup was forgotten when Roy, Shirley, David Steel, and Jo Grimond spoke at the Liberal Assembly at Llandudno. A modest fringe meeting turned into a mass rally, described even in the broadsheets as 'remarkable', 'rapturous', and 'tumultuous'. 'Be in no doubt,' Roy said, 'there is now a perfectly feasible prospect of a Liberal–Social Democrat government after the next election, breaking the stultifying monopoly of power which the two big parties have too long enjoyed.' Then two months later Shirley fought and won Crosby, a sleepy and comfortably-off outer suburb of Liverpool, turning a Tory majority of nearly 20,000 into an SDP and Alliance majority of 5,289. This victory topped six months of political transformation from the summer of 1981, showing the Alliance overtaking in the polls both the Labour Party and the Conservatives and reaching a peak of 51 per cent.

Meanwhile, it was essential for Roy to fight another by-election and get into Parliament, and at the beginning of January 1982 another chance occurred. Glasgow Hillhead was very different from Warrington, and a Conservative majority of only 2,000 looked attractive. But Labour was in second place and the Liberals had previously won only a modest 14.4 per cent share of the vote. The dangers of an Anglicized Welshman fighting a Scottish seat, given the fluid state of Scottish politics, were very real. I had no view of my own about whether it was a gamble worth taking, except that anything short of winning would now be regarded as a major setback for the SDP and an end to Roy's prospect of leading the party.

My initial contribution to success was almost a disaster. I had been negotiating with David Steel about the division of parliamentary seats for the next general election and we had reached an impasse. On the last day of the year I wrote to Steel complaining that the Liberals were being impossibly difficult and thought that a public exchange through *The Observer* might clear the air. But the prominence on the front page of the newspaper on 3 January was more than I had planned, and I certainly had not anticipated the news of the Hillhead vacancy the previous day. Roy telephoned me early on Sunday morning, and his first words were ominous: 'You have just lost me Hillhead.' It was an untypically harsh reprimand and he was angry. However, over the next two or three weeks the tension was eased, the Liberal Hillhead candidate stood down in Roy's favour, and his campaign began to take shape towards the end of January.

In the last book he completed before his death, *Twelve Cities* (2002), Roy described Glasgow as 'a strange and in some ways slightly sinister city'. But at that time he wisely kept his counsel and otherwise found Hillhead studded with cultural and higher educational institutions. By contrast with Warrington, and despite the deprived working-class areas near the factories alongside the Clyde, the constituency had the third-highest proportion of professional qualified workers in the United Kingdom, and twice as many private owners as council tenants. It was potentially a thoroughly attractive parliamentary seat, which he might enjoy.

The campaign was much less demonstrative than Warrington, but appropriate to the genteel and middle-class districts of the constituency like Kelvinside, with its fine Victorian villas. Roy set the pattern of coffee mornings by appointment in comfortable drawing rooms, which made it quiet—perhaps too quiet—in a critical by-election. He drew on his reputation and personal standing in meetings with influential opinion-formers—the heads of significant organizations—so that his message and personality would seep through to his potential constituents. Later there was a lot of dogged door-to-door canvassing in the council blocks and the gloomy sandstone tenements.

Roy had ten public meetings in the last two and a half weeks, all of them packed; and he calculated that at the end he had addressed a quarter of the electorate—an unprecedented achievement in a by-election. A major event was the coming together of the Gang of Four, a week before polling day, to address a local school packed to the doors and overflowing with 1,000 more waiting outside. My two abiding memories were of an elderly couple, warmly dressed against a frosty night, sitting patiently on a wooden bench outside the school and waiting for the speeches to begin; and Donald Dewar, the Labour MP for Garscadden (who would have been welcome in our SDP ranks and later became the First Minister of Scotland), reconnoitring the meeting and marvelling at its size and vibrance. Roy's main policy initiative was unveiling home rule for Scotland with an elected Scottish assembly by proportional representation and transferring legislative powers from Westminster over health, education, housing, and transport. The following day the Labour, Conservative, and SNP candidates were scornful about his proposals, but they were not far removed from the agreement reached between the Labour Party and the Liberal Democrats in the 1990s which led to permanent constitutional change after the 1997 election.

The course of the by-election was far from predictable. On 'Black Sunday'—ten days ahead of polling day—an NOP poll in *The Observer* put Roy at 23 per cent of the vote, with the Conservatives at 30 per cent and Labour at 33 per cent (the Scottish Nationalists were, and remained, in fourth place). In four further polls Roy's share fluctuated as low as 26 per cent and his best forecast was 31 per cent. On the front page on 14 March there was the story 'Jenkins Faces Defeat', and on 24 March it was 'Jenkins Trails'. The nerves of the headquarters' staff became seriously frayed, Roy was increasingly tense and irritable, and Jennifer took over their exhausted supporters and drove them to redouble their efforts. For a while it was touch and go until, in the last couple of days, the feeling grew that the tide had turned.

In the circumstances a majority of 2,038 and a third of the total vote was seen to be a handsome victory, and Roy was widely and warmly praised. 'Triumphant Jenkins Boosts Claim to SDP Leadership', said the newspaper headlines. It added that he had presented the SDP 'with an ebullient first birthday present' and that he would invigorate Parliament and create a welcome stimulus of the political debate. David Steel urged the SDP to speed up the choice of its Leader, and Julian Havilland, the political editor of *The Times*, said that 'on all the evidence, [Roy was] the popular favourite ... which would make him the putative Prime Minister of an Alliance government'.

However, it was not quite as simple as that. From the peak of early December 1981 the opinion polls changed course, showing a steady fall in Alliance support, lifting only briefly after Roy's Hillhead victory, as the Conservative government recovered and the economy improved. This trend was ahead of the Falklands War, which began at the beginning of April, pushing up the Conservatives to 45 per cent in July, with the Alliance falling, even once below Labour. Apart from the arithmetic of public opinion, the Falklands War also changed the balance of standing between Roy, trying to find his feet again in the House of Commons, and David Owen, demonstrating himself to be an effective spokesman for the SDP and making his parliamentary reputation.

Roy was uncomfortable about the war, and stood back from its involvement. In the summer of 1981 Shirley told me that she would support Roy for the leadership, but as the election approached in May she chose to nominate David Owen. Immediately after Hillhead I assumed that Roy would win by about two to one. David Owen was the incumbent, as

Chairman of the parliamentary party, agreed by the Gang of Four a year earlier, but Roy, as a journalist put it, 'simply looked, sounded and behaved more like an experienced statesman and political heavyweight' than any other member of the Gang of Four. During a decorous campaign, Roy—who was initially rather too complacent—set out his familiar emollient approach to the Liberals, while David Owen softened his prickly views about them. It was a choice between the statesman and the young radical (they were almost twenty years apart) and although the statesman won, it was by the comparatively narrow margin of 26,256 votes to 20,864.

Roy's election as Leader marked the end of the SDP's heroic phase. We were now fully armed for the general election which would probably come within twelve months. There were recent disappointments—such as losing a by-election in Mitcham and Morden when the SDP MP decided to resign and stand again—but the division of Alliance parliamentary seats was virtually agreed, the party was now run professionally by a Chief Executive at the Cowley Street headquarters, and we had raised sufficient money to keep afloat. It was time to regain the party's momentum and push towards victory— or at least (scaling down from last December) to a number of new MPs.

But Roy, as he put it, 'was suffering battle fatigue' after Warrington and Hillhead; and the debilitating illness that was soon to trouble him may have been casting its shadow. He found difficulty in adjusting to a House of Commons different from the one he had known before his departure to Brussels, and to a different role and status within it. For most of a dozen years he had spoken with gravitas to an increasingly respectful House, resting on the dispatch box that was the symbol of authority, a reassuring object to grip during a tough speech.

Now the House was a rowdier, less disciplined place, with Labour and Tory MPs determined to make Roy's life as hard as possible, exposed on the SDP front bench and facing disruptive heckling.

Roy also found it difficult to handle David Owen, to whose abilities he gave generous recognition but whose black moods made working together unrelaxed. In my own diary at the end of 1981, I said that David Owen had been a pretty effective parliamentary Leader but what would happen if he lost the top job? 'David is proud and ambitious and not very tolerant. He won't take kindly to it.' And so it was. Once Roy had been elected, David Owen resented his defeat and fell into a prolonged deep sulk, unable or unwilling to play a constructive part.

In July, before the recess, Roy said that he would nominate a Campaign Committee at which he would normally take the chair, but which I would chair in his absence—entirely compatible with my responsibilities in the Gang of Four. But David Owen wanted to be the alternative chairman himself. Roy found this wearisome and he postponed a decision, hoping that the matter would be resolved by the autumn. As a result, the party became dangerously becalmed, suffering from the afterglow of the Falklands War with, at best, unspectacular progress marked by disappointing parliamentary by-elections.

In February 1983 the Liberal candidate Simon Hughes won a dramatic by-election in Bermondsey, a bleak inner-city constituency in poor Alliance political territory, and this lifted the opinion polls and raised morale. But a month later a by-election at Darlington, in which we started as favourites, slipped into disaster when the SDP candidate proved to be completely out of his depth. The SDP collapsed into third place and national polls fell back again. These problems were not of Roy's making, but inevitably some of the poor result washed off on him.

The general election, which began six weeks later, in early May 1983, was not a happy time. Roy was Leader of both the SDP and the Alliance, dubbed 'Prime Minister Designate'. A year earlier David Owen had argued that the two roles should be kept separate, by implication with Roy as the Alliance leader and Owen as SDP leader; and he regarded 'Prime Minister Designate' as a convenience agreed only by Roy and David Steel. When the campaign opened on 9 May, the opinion polls were showing the Alliance at below 20 per cent, and it stayed stubbornly low, on one occasion as low as 15 per cent, despite meetings that were large and sympathetic. Half-way through, depressed and frustrated, David Steel came to believe that dropping 'Prime Minister Designate' and switching the leadership of the Alliance from Roy to himself might break the logjam of potential support.

Eight years earlier, at the time of the European referendum, Roy had described David Steel as 'a most admirable Liberal', a man of sensitivity, reliability, and imagination. Steel was, he said, 'worth a major Cabinet place if he belonged to a major party'. Later, after Dimbleby, he showed both strategic judgement in encouraging the launch of a new, separate party—the SDP—and tactical skills in steering alongside his own Liberals. Roy found him 'very agreeable'—an epithet he often enjoyed—and a pleasure to work with, a dependable ally and (in contrast to David Owen) 'a prop rather than a sour critic'.

David Steel's qualities were, however, tested by the sluggish Alliance campaign and, by inference, Roy's disappointing performance, and he called for a 'summit' of the two parties at his home, Ettrick Bridge, on the Scottish borders. When Steel telephoned about the venue, I welcomed such a well-publicized meeting because I too recognized that our campaign had not caught fire. But I was surprised at Steel's suggestion that he should change places with Roy to become effectively Leader of the Alliance. Despite my earlier hopes, the campaign had not brought out the best in Roy but I was very doubtful that changing horses would result in a sudden rise of support rather than ridicule.

When we met at Ettrick Bridge on the morning of Sunday 19 May, I assumed that Steel's suggestion had been dropped, but the Liberals—with John Pardoe the front-runner—suddenly raised the matter and Steel produced what I called a draft abdication for Roy by which he would hand over the leadership of the campaign. Roy looked bruised and embarrassed, but after a brisk exchange we turned to other matters, until Pardoe raised it yet again. This time Shirley was outspoken about the attempted coup and I was outraged about their behaviour. In the end David Steel and Pardoe gave up the struggle and Steel and Roy eventually summoned a successful press conference, which made the Ettrick Bridge summit a good newspaper story, with not a breath about the tense and unpleasant coup which had failed. Roy later said that the Ettrick Bridge crisis was the result of an uncharacteristic error of judgement by Steel and he felt no permanent resentment towards him. But Roy suffered some damage, and a residue of unease remained.

As it happened, on the day of the Ettrick Bridge summit, the opinion polls at last moved the Alliance to over 20 per cent and climbed steadily in the final ten days of the campaign, overtaking Labour (the main target) on several occasions. It was hoped that a few further days would push the Alliance ahead, but this was not to be. When the votes were counted following polling day, the Alliance had won 25.4 per cent of the votes, with Labour 27.6 per cent and the Conservatives over 42 per cent.

Our joint share of the vote was above the previous high-water mark for post-war Liberals in 1974, representing nearly 2 million more voters, and the Alliance had come first or second in 332 parliamentary seats; and the six SDP MPs were part of a larger Alliance group of twenty-three, not equalled in size for a third party since the 1930s. It was a considerable achievement.

But that was not how it felt. The unfairness of the result, comparing our share of the vote with seats won, was plain, and the case for proportional representation was demonstrated as never before. But as long as the first-past-the-post system endured, we would be judged by its rules, and twenty-three MPs (Labour had 209) was just too few. We were also victim to comparisons with the drama and size of earlier SDP triumphs, the victories at Crosby and Hillhead, and with opinion polls that showed us enjoying the support of over half the country at the end of 1981. Even those of us who were strong supporters of the Alliance took little comfort from the election of six more Liberals than in 1979, while the SDP had been decimated.

That was the mood when Silvia and I sat in our cottage on the Sunday afternoon and Roy came over from East Hendred. The immediate issue was whether he should resign as Leader. David Owen had already been on the telephone to Roy, saying he should go without delay, and Roy said that when was now the only question. He may have hoped I would challenge this assumption, but I reluctantly agreed, saying it would be better to resign at once than carry on with Owen snapping at his heels. The following day Shirley, David Owen, Jack Diamond, John Roper, and I joined Roy at East Hendred. Roy indicated his intention to resign, which came as a shock to Shirley and Jack, who argued vigorously against it. David Owen grudgingly conceded a delay of a few weeks, but said that the principle of resignation was not negotiable. That effectively decided the matter, and Roy's resignation followed within hours.

Several of Roy's closest supporters who had seen him as their undisputed Leader since the days of Dimbleby were appalled. They believed that his stature—an accomplished man of government—would enable him to see off any challenge from David Owen when the post-election spasm of disappointment had passed and the need to work closely with the Liberals had been positively reassessed. I thought that they were wrong and Roy would have lost in any contest by a clear margin. His personal standing had not diminished, but he was seen to have failed to sparkle as a campaigning Leader and to show clever footwork in the House of Commons, and there was a long haul ahead through another Thatcher Parliament. SDP members would have sadly voted for change.

That weekend's work effectively ended the Gang of Four. Owen moved quickly to establish his own authority, style, and personal team. This was to be his own show. Three months later, at the SDP Salford Conference, he blocked any discussion of merger with the Liberals. Owen's antithesis of 'tough' and 'tender' encapsulated his social market approach, with 'tough' the dominant mood in keeping with his own temperament. Roy called Owen's policies 'sub-Thatcherite', but he had no wish to rock the boat once the leadership had passed from him. During the conference he opened a debate on electoral reform and made a farewell speech. He then resumed his familiar round of Alliance and SDP meetings and dinners, twenty-seven of them within less than three months in early 1984. He took on the leadership of the all-party Fair Votes Campaign; and among his busy schedule there was his 'passion for Hillhead', as he put it. He had become deeply attached to Hillhead, playing his full part as a constituency MP.

Despite recurring illness in the middle of 1984 and then during much of 1985 and early 1986, he attended the House of Commons whenever he could. He spoke in the budget debate every year and was in fine form in exchanges with the government over the Westland affair. Leon Brittan, the Trade Secretary, he said, had been 'pathetic' and the Prime Minister's behaviour 'more and more extraordinary'. As a result, Mrs Thatcher and her government were sinking 'deeper into the bog of deceit and chicanery'. Otherwise, he spoke about the European Community and Home Office issues and frequently put down Scottish questions. In his last speech in the Commons, Roy spoke against the restoration of the death penalty—defeated by 342 votes to 230—praising Ted Heath and the Home Secretary, Douglas Hurd, for 'a speech of notable courage and clarity'. In November 1986 *The Spectator* nominated Roy as the backbencher of the Year, a remarkable parliamentary recovery from his unhappy time four years earlier.

Roy remained a member of the SDP National Committee, although never an enthusiastic committee man; and attended the annual conferences and interim meetings of the Council for Social Democracy. Later he briefly became the Alliance Treasury spokesman. Even if he was rather less active in the day-to-day affairs of the party, his mature influence was not diminished. He kept close to David Steel and the Liberals, trying to soften the dividing line that David Owen had maintained between the two parties. He tried to avoid any public row, but he was outspoken in supporting the members of the Alliance Commission on Defence and Disarmament when Owen wrecked its agreed conclusions as insufficiently pro-nuclear.

The defence row was damaging to the Alliance, but in February 1987 the SDP won a by-election from Labour at

Greenwich and in March, in another by-election, the Liberals held on to Truro. On the eve of the forthcoming general election, opinion polls were showing the Alliance as much as ten points higher than four years earlier. If this followed the pattern of 1983, the 1987 result could be spectacular, but once the campaign was launched, the polls began to fall. On polling day the Alliance won 22.6 per cent, 3 per cent lower than four years earlier. Worse still, the Alliance vote in Scotland was 5.3 per cent down and, in the eleven constituencies of Glasgow, 6.3 per cent down. That was enough to end Roy's parliamentary career in Hillhead. He was, he said, not greatly hurt by his defeat; and retained his flat for several months. But before the end of the year he moved to the House of Lords.

Meanwhile, the controversial issue of merger between the SDP and the Liberals had to be resolved. In the early hours of the day, when the election results were nearly complete, I took part in a television programme, and when Robin Day asked me the obvious question, I said without hesitation that a merger was now the only course. That night, through the following Friday and over the weekend, the merger debate continued, with Shirley Williams and David Steel calling to settle the matter. In a measured interview in *The World This Weekend*, Roy said that he was in favour of a single party if the Alliance was to have a serious future. He had heard this message 'in a thousand Alliance Committee rooms and on tens of thousands of doorsteps'. Roy had no fixed view about the timetable, although the merger should take place as quickly and smoothly as possible.

But it was not quick and it was not smooth. The formalities of merger were not completed until the end of January 1988. After that a rump of Owenites remained in 'the continuing SDP' for two more years, carried on Owen's own shoulders.

At the time of Limehouse, David Owen had accepted the practical need to work with the Liberals but believed that it should be at arm's length and competitive; and when he became the SDP leader he hardened his view, accusing Roy of treating the SDP as 'merely a transit vehicle' to merger with the Liberals. Shortly after the election both Shirley and I, separately and privately, urged Owen to vote for a merger, however reluctantly, believing that he might be chosen as Leader of the merged party (a view that Roy would not have shared). Owen made no response, although we took it for granted that even if he campaigned against a merger he would accept the verdict, whichever way it went. The merger was agreed by a postal ballot, by three to two in a poll of 77 per cent, but he decided to fight on.

Roy strongly supported 'Yes to Unity' but he found immensely distasteful what he called 'these squalid quarrels'. The argument within the SDP, he said, was 'a classic example of civil wars being the most vicious'. He tried to conciliate and to encourage a pause for reflection, and later he referred to 'a nagging feeling' that he should have done more to 'transcend the mood of destructive bitterness which seized the party'. But there was now a simple choice: to keep the SDP a separate party or merge, and some blood was bound to be spilled. The tragic error was not Roy's—or Shirley's or mine, or the majority who voted yes—but Owen's unwillingness to accept the decision and then to find cohesion and common purpose with the Liberals.

Roy attended the meeting of the Council for Social Democracy at the Sheffield Conference in January and spoke before the final vote when the 'tedious' negotiations between the SDP and the Liberals had been completed. That summer he voted for Paddy Ashdown as the first Leader of the Social and Liberal Democrats, and shortly afterwards became Leader of the new party in the House of Lords.

He served for almost ten years and then five more on the backbenches. He attended most days and, when he spoke, members of the House would make a point of coming into the Chamber to listen. Characteristically, Roy's speeches drew on historical analogies, sharpened by dry wit and paradox, and marked by the precision of words, with usually a few unexpected ones. Some speeches were magisterial and others baroque but, above all, they were carried forward by the force of argument. Roy made his last speech—about his fears over war with Iraq—on 24 September 2002, but he followed the pages of *Hansard* until the Christmas recess—a fortnight before his death.

Within months of merger in 1988, Patricia Lee Sykes, a young American professor, published an extended obituary of the SDP under the title *Losing from the Inside*; rather later Ivor Crewe and Anthony King completed their scholarly but ultimately dismissive book *SDP: The Birth, Life and Death of the Social Democratic Party* (1995). But writing from the still short perspective of 1991, Roy did not 'in the least regret the adventure of the SDP and the Alliance'. He had always envisaged three possible levels of success: a complete breakthrough; a settled 'triangular shape of politics' with a significant third party; and, 'without achieving any rewards for ourselves', a Labour recovery.

Twelve years later, at the time of his death, two of Roy's levels of success had been reached. The Gang of Four underestimated the extent to which loyalty and sentiment, institutional ties, inertia, and luck would hold the Labour Party together until such a time, at the nadir of its fortunes and facing death, it would eventually rally. But in the 1980s the

SDP, in partnership with the Liberals, mounted the most serious challenge to the two-party system for more than half a century; and the Liberal Democrats, who are the product of the chequered merger, now have fifty Members of Parliament and are an integral part of the political geography of Britain. As for the Labour Party, by 1994 Roy was able to describe the new Labour Leader, Tony Blair, as 'the most exciting choice since the election of Gaitskell'; and three years later he could welcome, without contradiction, both a Labour government again and a confident surge of Liberal Democrat MPs. The SDP did not break the mould, but changed its shape beyond all recognition.

Donald McFarlane

Donald McFarlane was born in Glasgow, the son of a doctor. He was educated at Jordanhill College School and Glasgow University, graduating in medicine. Following a short-service commission in the Royal Air Force, he became a principal in a large general practice in the Anniesland area of Glasgow. He and his wife continue to live in the old Hillhead constituency.

Chapter 14

Glasgow

Donald McFarlane

R oy Jenkins came to the Glasgow of Auden's 'Night Mail' in the spring of 1982, seeking to be elected the Member of Parliament for Hillhead, where I was a senior partner in a large west-end general medical practice. My father had been a co-founder of the practice; thus I had been born, brought up, and educated in the constituency. I knew every street and lane, and particularly I knew the people who lived there.

My wife, Elsa, and I had first heard him speak at a packed public meeting in the McLellan Galleries in September 1981. He was billed as 'Joint Leader of the Social Democrats' and he stated that 'People want to hear a soundly based argument. They want positive proposals which combine responsibility with foresight.' He was seeking to break the mould, and this struck a positive chord in Glasgow.

Shortly after, the long-serving MP for Hillhead died and Roy was adopted as the SDP–Liberal Alliance candidate. He immediately held unofficial 'surgeries', to which the response was large and encouraging. These lasted for several hours, and after one of them I was introduced to Roy. I was immediately struck by his warmth and charm, his genuine interest in Glasgow, and also his sense of humour.

When the campaign officially opened, Elsa organized a St David's Day party at our house in Kirklee, inviting over 100 guests to meet the candidate. All accepted. Roy met and spoke to every one, keeping a careful note of the total by a 'clicker' concealed in his pocket. This was the first time I became aware of his fascination with numbers, time, and the weather. Jennifer was also present, despite a feverish cold, and we saw how well they complemented each other. The evening was an undoubted success. Now Roy had engaged Hillhead; soon he would embrace it.

The press tried to portray him as a carpetbagger, but the Hillhead electorate were too sophisticated and were used to viewing the political postures of editors with a very clear eye. Roy was the ideal candidate for a constituency which yearned for their Member to reflect their educated political opinions, and to make an impact on the national stage.

The warm welcome at the St David's Day party was repeated many times at packed public meetings and on walkabouts, but especially at the 'tea parties'. These were an unique innovation, being organized by sympathetic hostesses and largely attended by ladies whose differing views reflected the local political spectrum. They had a very positive impact, which surfaced in conversations at local social gatherings, and which intrigued the national press.

The public meetings were equally successful, and could be dramatic. They probably reached their zenith a week before polling day, when the Gang of Four (with Shirley Williams

14. President of the Commission (1977–81)
a) With fellow–Commissioner, Claude Cheysson

b) With Chancellor Helmut Schmidt at Bonn

c) With Pope John Paul II

d) With President Jimmy Carter

15. The Social Democratic Party
a) Bright Confident Morning, 1981 (David Owen, David Steel, RJ, and Shirley Williams)

b) The Warrington by-election, June 1981

c) Campaigning in Cheltenham with Richard Holme, 1983 general election

d) Disillusion, June 1985, with Bill Rodgers and David Owen

16. Oxford's Chancellor
a) Preparing to lead the Encaenia procession from Balliol hall

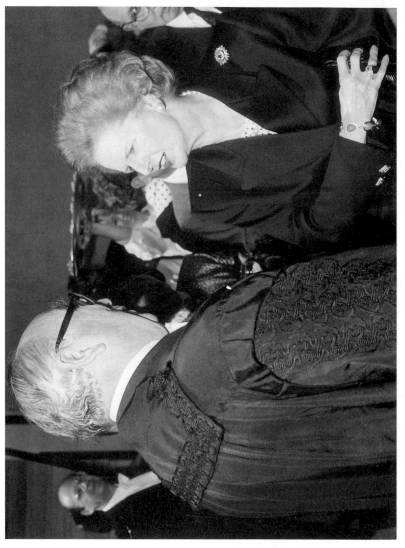

b) At the opening of the Margaret Thatcher Centre, Somerville College

c) With President Bill and Hillary Clinton

17. Winning the Whitbread Biography Award for *Gladstone*, 1996. The even more successful *Churchill* was still to come

hobbling in a plaster cast) addressed hundreds one evening at Hyndland School. The number was so large that it confused the Labour candidate, who mistakenly tried to attend. There was an overflow, which included my 80-year-old aunt, gathered in the playground in the clear, cold, moonlight. It had the atmosphere of a conventicle, and the whole added impressive momentum to the campaign. In contrast, Roy spoke to over forty clerics of all denominations at a private meeting. With one exception (concerning abortion) the ministers and priests attending were openly supportive.

And he won convincingly. For months after, wherever he went people would cross the road to shake his hand and wish him well, a stroll down Byres Road resembling a progress. A large group from Glasgow travelled to Westminster to witness him take his seat. After lunch at the Reform Club they saw the simple ceremony delayed by a debate on the threat to South Georgia by Argentina—surely a portent of more difficult days for the SDP.

During the campaign I had been able to introduce him to many academic and medical institutions. We were together most days, and from this grew our friendship, which flourished until the day he died.

Roy used to describe his fascination with Glasgow as a 'senile love affair'. But a love affair requires two, the object of his affections responding with youthful enthusiasm. He fulfilled his election promise and bought a flat in one of the most handsome terraces lining Great Western Road. I remember a Palmerstonian desk occupying prime position in the public room where he entertained a host of guests from within and without the city. Visiting friends included Aline Berlin and Marietta Tree, to whom he showed off his new charge with loving pride. He feared he was in danger of becoming a

Glasgow bore, but his adopted city loved it. Letters from constituents poured in, including invitations to attend and address events across the social calendar. He made a memorable speech at the prizegiving of Glasgow Academy, which, despite having Donald Dewar and Robert Maclennan as former pupils, is not a recognized seedbed of left-of-centre political views. Lady Marion Fraser, the wife of Sir William Fraser, the former Principal and present Chancellor of Glasgow University, still tells of his strong, steady support of that institution, of which he was an honorary graduate. He loved to compare it to a great grey eagle on its eyrie overlooking the Kelvin, in contrast to his Alma Mater, as a peacock on the banks of the Thames.

Being Roy, he was totally interested in his surroundings, their geography, their history, their place in the framework of Glasgow. He read a history of Hillhead, which I gave him, probably at one sitting, which drew his attention to the close ties between Glasgow and North America (Churchill's 'Saltwater Highway'). He was intrigued to learn of the philanthropy of the Smiths of Jordanhill, who also owned large estates in Virginia, and that Jefferson Davis, once President of the Confederacy, had visited Dowanhill after the Civil War.

The pace of his and Jennifer's regular visits left many exhausted. Entertaining at the flat included an annual Sunday claret (what else?) party, with guests coming from throughout the city, many meeting each other for the first time. He repeatedly visited all Glasgow's famous museums and galleries. He attended Sunday morning services at the constituency's churches—'sermon-tasting', my father would have called it. He attended Scottish Opera and met Sir Alexander Gibson frequently, who was then at the peak of his career. He became a patron of the infant Scottish Piano Competition, giving it invaluable support in its early days. Although he was viewed somewhat suspiciously by the Labour rulers of Glasgow, he effectively promoted its welfare at every opportunity—even in Edinburgh.

Nor were his and Jennifer's interests curbed by any boundaries. Picnics in the Trossachs, on Loch Lomondside, or the Firth of Clyde were hugely enjoyed. He loved the Queen's View on the Stockiemuir Road, visiting it especially during campaigns, 'to remind myself what is important in life'. His early morning walks from his flat in Kirklee, always at a brisk pace, and always carrying a stick, made him a familiar sight and led to him becoming an authority on the local architecture, although I never heard him particularly admire Glasgow's favourite son, Charles Rennie Mackintosh.

The 1983 election was very different from 1982. His national commitments made it necessarily so; thus he could only pay a limited number of visits. It was left to Jennifer to run the campaign for him with his local supporters, aided by visits from the Grimonds, the Bonham Carters, and rather uniquely, Richard Attenborough.

The year 1987 was always going to be more difficult. In 1983 the local Labour Party had planned their revenge on Roy, whom they had branded a 'traitor'. This attitude towards him was obvious in 1982, when, among others, Robin Cook and Neil Kinnock campaigned vigorously in the by-election. It followed that in 1983 they would mount a major effort to defeat Roy. Their failure, despite fielding a moderate and likeable candidate, culminated in disgraceful scenes at the declaration of the result, when the heirs to Red Clydeside vented their frustration with noisy and prolonged verbal abuse. John Harris, who always accompanied Roy on these occasions, described their behaviour as 'threatening' and a 'wall of hate'. This appeared a moderate description to Elsa and myself.

When Elsa protested to Donald Dewar, who was a witness, he replied, 'What can you expect?', then he turned away. This tribal dislike was more channelled and less public in 1987, although stones and eggs were thrown at houses of Roy's supporters from Anderston to Kirklee.

Initially in 1987 all seemed to be going well, with good public meetings and a positive response both on the doorstep and in the streets. But Roy knew better. On the day, Labour herded its vote to the polls and the Conservative core did not crumble. He fought to the very end. Cavalcades, with Roy standing up through the sunroof of the car, toured supportive areas of Hillhead until the evening of polling day, which, paradoxically, was clear and beautiful after a miserably wet morning. I dropped him off at Kirklee in order that he might shower and change. 'If you are about to be hanged,' he quoted, 'wear a silk suit.'

The winner was George Galloway. Roy was no longer the MP, but he remained tied to his love. He mused that he had found Hillhead 'more interesting, more intellectually and aesthetically stimulating, more complex, and most of all, more fun' than he had expected. The flat was sold, but his new duties at Oxford and the House of Lords did not lead to prolonged absences, as he remained in demand, being, with Jennifer, always welcome guests. Hillhead was delighted when his title was gazetted. Roy commented that the choice had not been a difficult decision, and, that 'they were the only ones who asked'.

ARTHUR SCHLESINGER, JR.

Arthur Schlesinger, Jr., was born in Columbus, Ohio, in 1917. A graduate of Harvard and a Henry Fellow at Peterhouse, Cambridge, he served in the war in the Office of War Information, the Office of Strategic Services, and the US Army. His historical writing covers the presidencies of Andrew Jackson, Franklin Roosevelt, and John Kennedy. He was on Adlai Stevenson's campaign staff in 1952 and 1956, and served as President Kennedy's special assistant throughout his thousand days.

Chapter 15

Back and Forth to the United States

ARTHUR SCHLESINGER, JR.

The career and character of Roy Jenkins are a standing refutation of the idea that Great Britain must choose between Europe and America. No Britisher of his time exceeded Roy in his conviction that Britain's destiny lies with Europe. And no Britisher of his time exceeded him in his passion for America; at least for liberal America, for the USA of Franklin Roosevelt, Harry Truman, John Kennedy, and Bill Clinton. As John Kenneth Galbraith has said, Roy Jenkins 'more than any other since Winston Churchill has been, effectively, a citizen of both the United States and the United Kingdom'.

Talk about the 'special relationship' too often assumes that mutual regard and even affection have been the case for a long time. This forgets that the oldest political emotion in the United States is Anglophobia. After all, the United States won its independence by revolting against British rule; the British burned the White House in the war of 1812; as recently as 1895 a South American border dispute threatened war between the two nations. 'I rather hope', said young Theodore Roosevelt, 'that the fight will come soon.'

On the other hand, there were blood ties. Some British politicians had American mothers or married American girls. Roy listed them: not only Churchill but William Harcourt, Joseph Chamberlain, George Nathaniel Curzon, Harold Macmillan, Quintin Hogg, Tony Crosland, Keith Joseph, Tony Benn, and David Owen, not to mention the Duke of Windsor. (There were, Roy noted, remarkably few examples of American politicians acquiring British wives. 'Almost the only exception (late in life) was Averell Harriman'—and Pamela Digby Churchill Hayward became an American citizen and ended as an exceedingly competent American Ambassador to France.)

Few British politicians in the nineteenth or early twentieth centuries, even those with American connections, showed much interest in the United States or knew much about American history or institutions. Roy's beloved Gladstone actually backed the slave states during the American Civil War. Sometimes political moods in the two nations ran along parallel lines, but like parallel lines they never met.

The Liberal era in Britain and the Progressive era in the United States coincided in the first years of the twentieth century. But, for all the intellectual and political affinities, personal contact was slight. Asquith never visited the United States. Theodore Roosevelt detested the young Churchill. (I once asked T.R.'s daughter why this should have been so. 'Perhaps because they were so much alike,' Mrs Longworth replied.) Woodrow Wilson distrusted Lloyd George.

Nor did right-wing governments in both countries in the

1920s nurture special relationships. There was no Stanley Baldwin–Calvin Coolidge axis. Baldwin did not cross the Atlantic between 1923 and his retirement in 1937. In the liberal 1930s Franklin Roosevelt found Ramsay MacDonald at once fuzzy and doctrinaire; and he never could understand the post-MacDonald Labour Party, which combined a rhetorical opposition to fascism with a practical opposition to rearmanent. Nor did Labour leaders—Clement Attlee, Herbert Morrison, Nye Bevan—care to inspect the New Deal.

As for the Tories, Neville Chamberlain regarded the United States with a disdain bordering on contempt. Anthony Eden, Chamberlain's vigorously peripatetic Foreign Secretary, as Roy observed, 'spent 2¼ years in that office without ever once thinking of including Washington in his diplomatic tours'. In the vital pre-war years Eden never once met Roosevelt, nor did Churchill. In the past a frequent visitor to the United States, Churchill, after a taxi ran him down on Fifth Avenue in 1931, failed to come for the rest of the decade. (If the taxi had killed Churchill, and if the assassin who, fourteen months later, had aimed accurately at Franklin Roosevelt instead of killing the man beside him, think what the twentieth century would look like now.)

After the Second World War, Truman and Attlee regarded each other with the mutual respect of one astute old pro for another, though Truman, as Roy discovered, much preferred Churchill to Attlee. Ernest Bevin won the respect of his opposite numbers in the field of foreign affairs. But even then the flow back and forth between the Labour government and Truman's Fair Deal was surprisingly meagre.

On the top level, at least; but now the war generation with mid-level experience were rising towards the top. In Britain they were already prepared for a closer American partnership.

F.D.R., as Roy wrote in his memoir, was one of his two heroes (Keynes was the other). With the world grimly divided between laissez-faire and totalitarian ideologies, F.D.R. stood for an anti-ideological Third Way (not invented by Tony Blair and Anthony Giddens)—affirmative government pursuing Keynesian policies in a mixed economy.

As Roy wrote in 1972, F.D.R.'s New Deal and his opposition to dictatorship 'changed the whole European attitude to American politics. Nineteen thirty-six was the last presidential election which appeared to the outside world as a lot of Tammany braves dancing rather incomprehensibly but highly successfully round the wigwam.' Thereafter American presidential elections drew the intense attention of the outside world.

It was after the war that the special relationship emerged. Aspiring young British politicos were naturally curious to see what the American superpower was all about. Travel was eased by jet aircraft that carried visitors to London or Washington in a few hours instead of five days spent in sea travel. New Labour personalities, unlike their predecessors before the war, took care to make the grand tour of America. Denis Healey paid his first visit to the United States in 1949, Hugh Gaitskell in 1950, Roy Jenkins in 1953, Tony Crosland in 1954.

I first met Roy in 1953, a wandering young MP, three years younger than I, soaking up the sights and paradoxes of the one-time British colony. Elective affinity at once took over, and we became lifelong friends. Roy wandered around the land for a couple of months, a beneficiary of the so-called Smith–Mundt programme of bringing 'young leaders' to the States. 'Altogether I adored America,' Roy wrote in 1991, 'and the whole trip made an immense impact on me ... It transformed my thinking and my emotions about the United States . . . The impressions gained in that first and longest visit have reverberated through my seventy or so subsequent visits.' To judge by the frequency of his visits and the number of words he wrote about the United States, he was a good deal more smitten than his Labour coevals.

He claimed in *Twelve Cities* (2002) that 'in the past five decades I have paid nearly 200 separate visits' to New York City. Probably he counted his New York stopovers within his seventy American trips. When he became a minister in the 1960s, he was 'nonetheless able to justify a number of official or semi-official visits to New York'—three as Minister of Aviation, five as Chancellor of the Exchequer, and two as Home Secretary, those last visits requiring 'a little more ingenuity of justification' but rewarded by a meeting with J. Edgar Hoover, during which the FBI director freely denounced the brothers Kennedy.

As for the written word, despite his campaign for the European connection, Roy's political journalism strongly favoured America. He described his *Gallery of 20th Century Portraits* (1988), as 'a fairly dense but by no means complete coverage of twentieth-century political figures of this country [Britain], a much more partial but nonetheless substantial coverage of their American counterparts, and a few isolated forays into continental Europe'. This was an accurate report on the balance of his journalism.

His first book about America Roy in retrospect called the 'somewhat obscurely entitled *Afternoon on the Potomac?*', a title not clarified by the question mark at the end. The book was based on the Henry L. Stimson Memorial Lectures delivered at Yale in 1971 and was preoccupied with international monetary issues—understandably so, since his most recent government appointment had been Chancellor of the Exchequer.

Roy met eight Presidents of the United States, six while they were in office, two outside it, and 'liked Lyndon Johnson the least'. He wrote considerably about American political history, and as a historian I must pay tribute to the skills Roy brought to our trade—the deftness and brilliance of his characterizations, the analytical insights into the burdens of decision, the humane understanding of the agony of choice, the illuminating parallels between past and present.

He displayed those skills in his two biographies of American presidents—*Truman* (1986) and *Franklin Delano Roosevelt* (2003). He was preparing to write a third, on Kennedy, when he died. He drew incisive and perceptive portraits of American political personalities—Johnson, Stevenson, Acheson, Harriman, Robert Kennedy, Joe McCarthy—and showed a knowledgeable and easy familiarity with the American scene unrivalled among European political figures.

How did he reconcile his passion for the United States of America with his passion for the European Union? I imagine that he would stand by the conclusion to the mysteriously titled *Afternoon on the Potomac?* If we see our role as being fully part of Europe, [he wrote]

but a part which, because of our tradition and outlook, is likely always to use its influence so as to make European unity fully compatible with close ties across the Atlantic, we will better serve both our own needs and those of the Atlantic Community as a whole.

The best hope, he continued, is the nearest possible approach to equality between Europe and America.

Such an approach to equality is at least as much in the interests of the United States as it is in that of the European countries. This was true even while the United States was bearing its massive responsibilities with equanimity. It is still more true today, when the equanimity is a little strained.

It is even more true a third of a century later, when the equanimity is sorely fractured.

ANTHONY KENNY

Anthony Kenny was born in Liverpool and educated at the Gregorian University in Rome and at St Benet's Hall, Oxford. After a period as a Roman Catholic curate in Liverpool, he became a Fellow of Balliol College in 1964. From 1978 to 1989 he was Master of Balliol, and from 1989 to 1999 Warden of Rhodes House and a Fellow of St John's College. He was President of the British Academy (1989–93) and Chairman of the Board of the British Library (1993–6). He was knighted in 1992. From 1984 to 2001 he was a Pro-Vice-Chancellor of Oxford University. He is the author of thirty-six books, mainly on philosophy and its history.

Chapter 16

Oxford's Chancellor

ANTHONY KENNY

Roy Jenkins's 1979 Dimbleby Lecture, and the Lime-house Declaration of 1981, were greeted with great interest in Oxford, and perhaps especially in Balliol. In 1963, when I joined Balliol as a young don, I found a college with a mainly Labour SCR and a mildly Conservative JCR. By the end of the 1970s, when I had become Master, the JCR was home to many a Trotskyist and most of the SCR had lost patience with the Labour Party. No one was comfortable with Thatcherite conservatism, and by a number of the dons the creation of the SDP was warmly welcomed.

Roy had been made an honorary Fellow of Balliol in 1969—paired, as it were, with Ted Heath, who was similarly honoured at the same time. When Roy was elected the first

In writing this chapter I have been greatly assisted by conversations with Dame Jennifer Jenkins, Lord Neill of Bladen, Sir Richard Southwood, Sir Peter North, Sir Colin Lucas, Sir Keith Thomas, Dame Ruth Deech, Miss Elizabeth Llewellyn-Smith, Professor Jasper Griffin, Dr Miriam Griffin, Miss Ann Smallwood, and Mr Ted East.

Leader of the SDP, the occasion was celebrated by a party for him and Jennifer in the Master's Lodgings. The College had, in the twentieth century, prided itself on producing leaders of political parties: first Asquith, then Macmillan, then Heath. We wondered whether this latest Balliol party Leader might follow in his predecessors' footsteps by leading his new party to electoral victory and heading a government.

I do not know how far Roy himself entertained such a dream. He did, after all, single out 'liberal optimism' as the characteristic imprint that Balliol had made upon him as an undergraduate. Whatever he may have felt during the initial surging triumph of the new party, by 1987, the year of the death of Harold Macmillan and of the demise of the SDP, he had given his ambitions a gentler form. From his autobiography it appears that the prospect of becoming Chancellor of Oxford had attracted him since 1973, when Chancellor Macmillan had conferred on him an honorary Doctorate of Civil Law. When Macmillan reached his eightieth birthday in 1974, and became ever more visibly frail, there was speculation that he might retire. Roy considered running in the election for his successor. 'I probably saw myself', he tells us, 'as a left-of-centre candidate willing to lose than as a likely winner.' The most likely winner, he thought, would have been Lord Hailsham, repeating the Conservative victories of Curzon over Rosebery, of Cave over Asquith, and Macmillan over Oliver Franks.

In characteristic fashion, Roy took pains to inform himself about the history of the chancellorship. The first Chancellor, he discovered, had been Robert Grosseteste, in 1224, a Bishop of Lincoln heading a line of medieval Oxford clerics. After the Reformation the chancellorship had been held by a succession of grandees, and between the two Cromwells and Harold Macmillan every Chancellor had been a peer spiritual or temporal. But as the grandeur increased, the scope of the office diminished. Macmillan, memorably, had said that nowadays the one reason Oxford needed a Chancellor was that, without one, there could not be a Vice-Chancellor, and without a Vice-Chancellor there would be no one to run the University.

Macmillan did not resign in the mid-1970s as expected, but continued as Chancellor for a period of twenty-seven years. He had a great love for Oxford, always tinged with nostalgia for the golden years before the First World War. In his after-dinner speeches he was equally skilled in provoking laughter and evoking tears. He was a popular Chancellor, loved by young and old; as Roy put it, 'if anything he became better as his venerability made the shuffling gait, the hooded eyes, and the theatrical pauses still more appropriate'.

The University gave a banquet in Balliol in 1984 to mark the ninetieth birthday of the Chancellor, now Lord Stockton. It was a colourful occasion of academic pomp, attended by the heads of house and all the senior figures in the University. The Vice-Chancellor and I, as joint hosts, flanked the Chancellor in the middle of High Table; at either end of the table sat Roy Jenkins and Ted Heath, each wearing the gowns of their honorary doctorates. One topic of conversation that evening was whether it was not high time for the University to give an honorary degree to the Prime Minister, Margaret Thatcher.

Macmillan often stayed in the Balliol lodgings after his cere- monial visits to Oxford. As we would sit together over a long nightcap he would ask me, year after year, whether the time had come for him to resign. Every year I told him that everyone in Oxford would be desolate if he resigned. But at last there came a time when it was clear that he was proving more of a burden than a blessing to the senior officers of the University. I screwed up my courage to give him the answer that it was the time to go. But that year the question was never put. The Chancellor remained in office until his death in the last days of 1986.

It was clear that it would be a difficult task for anyone to take Macmillan's place. The election of his successor was watched with particular public interest because Oxford University had placed itself in the forefront of the opposition, among the academic profession throughout the nation, to the government of Margaret Thatcher. After the Brighton bombing of 1984 the University's Hebdomadal Council had resolved to propose her name for an honorary degree. But a series of measures—the imposition of higher fees for overseas students, the attempt to abolish free tuition for home undergraduates, the cuts in central funding, especially in the sciences—had built up a formidable constituency of opposition. When in 1985 the vote was taken in Congregation, the assembly of the University's senior members, the proposal for the honorary degree was defeated by a substantial majority.

Roy used to tell the story of how the then Chancellor reacted to the news. 'Terrible business, Roy,' he said, meeting him in the Palace of Westminster, 'this insult to the Prime Minister by our old University, terrible.' After much shaking of the head, a certain light came into the old man's eyes. 'You know, it all comes down to a matter of class. The dons are mainly upper-middle-class, and they can never forgive Mrs Thatcher for being so lower-middle-class. But you and I, Roy, with our working-class ancestry, are above that kind of thing.'

Macmillan was not long at rest before speculation began about his successor. I recall the journey back to Oxford from the Sussex funeral in the university car, with Vice-Chancellor Neill and two other Pro-Vice-Chancellors, one of whom was Lord Blake, the Provost of Queen's. Roy's name was mentioned as a possible runner, along with four or five others:

Archbishop Runcie, Sir Edward Heath, Lord Scarman, and Lord Carrington. Soon after the funeral a poll for the chancellorship was arranged for the days of Thursday 12 March and Saturday 14 March.

To the delight of his many Oxford friends, Roy was the first to declare himself a candidate. For a brief period he looked to be a shoe-in. But then Ted Heath announced his intention to stand—against the advice of a number of friends and without the support of the government or the Conservative establishment. Few, in Oxford or elsewhere, thought that he had a strong chance of winning: but clearly he would present Roy with very significant competition. The journalists licked their lips in anticipation of a lively fight.

Not everyone in Oxford was happy to see the chancellorship election turned into a contest between two politicians, and Balliol politicians to boot. The Vice-Chancellor secured the nomination of a third candidate, Lord Blake, believing, mistakenly, that he would be seen as an academic non-political candidate. In fact Blake, though universally respected as a historian, was immediately seen as the Thatcherite Conservative candidate, and was backed by all those, inside and outside the University, who had been outraged by the rejection of the Prime Minister's honorary degree. Heath found that his support came largely from the Left, largely from those who admired his recent activities on behalf of the undeveloped world, but also from those members of the Labour Party who had not forgiven Roy's defection to the SDP. At Balliol, though the College was officially neutral between its two honorary fellows, support for Ted among the dons was stronger than that for Roy. If the chancellorship—as Ted mischievously told Robin Day—was to be decided within *the* College, then he would have emerged from the campaign triumphant.

It was, however, injudicious of Heath to publish a list of nominators with not a single person from any other college. The first Jenkins list contained 120 names against Blake's 60 and Heath's 28. The next week Roy increased his total to 237 nominators and in the third and final list he could count 410 published supporters (against 160 for Heath and 67 for Blake). This number, as he later proudly reported, included eight heads of house, thirteen former heads, five heads of Cambridge colleges, two Nobel Prizewinners, three members of the Order of Merit, and twenty-seven Fellows of the Royal Society or of the British Academy.

Until the last day of the election the outcome was very uncertain. All MAs of the University—about 80,000 of them—were entitled to vote in person and no one had any idea how many would turn up on the day, though colleges did their best to woo their alumni back to do so. A straw vote among the (disfranchised) students, and a late Gallup poll, put Roy ahead by a small margin. The situation was complicated when, at a late stage, Downing Street and the whips began to advise Conservative members of Convocation to vote for Heath as the party member who had collected most nominations and was most likely to win. An exit poll on the first day gave Roy the victory, but that indicated only the degree of support among the resident members of the University—the MAs from the wider world would not be voting until the Saturday.

The two Balliol candidates, however, seem to have had a premonition of the outcome. The College had offered them its premises for post-election parties to entertain their followers. Ted Heath booked the Master's drawing room for a tea-party of twenty-four. Roy ordered evening champagne for eighty in the old Senior Common Room. At the end of a day of glorious spring sunshine, on which 6,000 voters enjoyed luncheon in their colleges, the Proctors announced the result: Jenkins 3,429, Blake 2,674, Heath 2,348. As Roy thanked his supporters in the OCR, he told them that he was doing so on the exact spot where in 1939 he had made his acceptance speech as President of the Balliol JCR.

The election was an object of extraordinary interest to the world's press. As Roy remarked, 'from the *New York Times* to *Le Monde* to the *Frankfurter Allgemeine* it was front-page news'. Many commentators remarked that it was ironic that such an enthusiastic supporter of proportional representation had benefited from the first-past-the-post system, since the Conservative votes, if united on a second count, would have made a majority of three to two. Roy, an enthusiastic if not always impartial psephologist, devoted a not wholly convincing paragraph of his autobiography to arguing that he would have won even on an alternative vote system.

It is, however, very probable that Roy was the favourite candidate of the resident electors, and certainly, once he was elected, Oxford welcomed him warmly. Those who, in advance, disliked his public voice and manner quickly found that he was not at all stand-offish on personal acquaintance. Even those who had voted for other candidates acknowledged that he stepped into Macmillan's shoes with remarkable aplomb. It was perhaps the Chancellor's immediate cortège, such as the bedels, who found it hardest to accept anyone as a successor to the grand old man; but over the years they too came to respect and admire the new Chancellor's punctilious attention to his ceremonial duties.

The principal such duty of a Chancellor is to confer honorary degrees on behalf of the University. In accordance with tradition (invented in 1903 by Lord Curzon), a new Chancellor is allowed to honour his own friends at a special convocation after his election. Roy assembled a distinguished slate of statesmen and academics, which included two heads of state, the King of the Belgians and President Cossiga of Italy, and one recently retired Prime Minister, Garret Fitzgerald. There were two notable Americans—Robert McNamara and Arthur Schlesinger—and among the Oxford residents Isaiah Berlin and Iris Murdoch.

Roy regularly presided at the annual conferment of honorary degrees in the Sheldonian Theatre. The main duty of a Chancellor on such occasions—in addition to processing with a dignified step and sitting in grandeur, swathed in gold lace, on a high and perilous throne—is to present a diploma to each honorand while uttering a Latin sentence of praise. While Macmillan used to bark out the encomium confidently in the highly Anglicized pronunciation popular in nineteenth-century public schools, Roy took great pains to master the current received academic pronunciation. He used to copy the text in his own hand with the stresses marked, and undergo rehearsals with the Public Orator beforehand. His conscientious efforts were not always rewarded with success, and the audience could perceive a sense of relief and a quickening of pace as he arrived at the final unvarying part of the formula: 'auctoritate mea et totius universitatis . . .'

This initial glittering assembly was followed during the chancellorship by the conferment, at the University's request, of degrees by diploma on more than a dozen heads of state, including, most conspicuously, President Clinton. Roy welcomed such occasions as testimony to the international importance of Oxford University. Clearly, however, it also gave him personal satisfaction to receive visiting monarchs in his capacity as the democratically elected president of a modest academic republic.

He was well aware that the statutes and customs of the University allowed him only the customary privileges of a constitutional head of state: the right to be consulted, to encourage, and to warn. Those who served under him as Vice-Chancellor are unanimous in their praise of his conduct in this monarchic role. He was always ready to be consulted and to offer wise advice; but he was very careful not to interfere with the University's management of its own affairs.

Even in the matter of honorary degrees, in which he naturally took a keen interest, he made no attempt to thrust the names of candidates on the University. When he made suggestions they were considered through the normal channels, and accepted or not, in the same way as suggestions from anyone else. He would have liked an opportunity to remedy the distresses of 1985 by conferring a degree on Margaret Thatcher; but he did not press the point when he was advised that any attempt to do so was more likely to open new wounds than to heal old ones.

The one substantial power that statute and custom offers the Chancellor is that of chairing the electoral body which proposes to the University the name of a new Vice-Chancellor. Roy asked Vice-Chancellor Neill to chair the first such election after his installation, but he attended one meeting himself in order to see how it operated. After that election, which led to the appointment of Sir Richard Southwood, he chaired the proceedings which produced the two next Vice-Chancellors, Sir Peter North and Sir Colin Lucas. At the time of his death he was much looking forward to presiding over the election of Lucas's successor, inquiring among his friends for names of possible candidates, and sounding out reactions to suggested runners. Sadly, in the event, it was Colin who presided over the proceedings for the election of Roy's successor.

There was some uncertainty whether a Chancellor, if he wished, had the right to chair the Hebdomadal Council, or effective governing body, of the University. No Chancellor in living memory had done so, and Roy did not seek to exercise the right, if it existed; but he did once attend a meeting, sitting on the Vice-Chancellor's right hand. He reported afterwards that the members had mastered their briefs and spoken more to the point than the members of most Cabinets he had attended.

In addition to the solemn ceremonies of Encaenia, a Chancellor is called on frequently in the course of each academic year to give official orations, and Roy was often asked to attend college feasts. As an after-dinner speaker he was always polished and often brilliant. When asked to preside on formal occasions, he never played hard to get, and he put himself on record as not once having refused a serious invitation to dinner in Oxford. ('God forbid', a journalist commented, 'that Lord Jenkins should ever receive an unserious invitation to dinner in Oxford.') He calculated that in 1987, his first year of office, he fulfilled seventy-three engagements within or on behalf of the University and its colleges.

Roy was in great demand as a dinner guest: as one head of house put it to me, 'when he entered a common room, everything turned into a party'. He was a most informative and entertaining dining companion, and in his turn he enjoyed intellectual conversation with academics. The conventions of placement meant that his immediate neighbours at table were often women. He was a model of respectful gallantry to those he found attractive and intelligent; but on occasion he could make it embarrassingly clear that he felt he had been ill placed. In private, he was commonly very considerate of those he had to deal with—whether it was making a personal telephone call to break the news to an unsuccessful candidate for the vice-chancellorship, or hosting a special party for a retiring bedel.

When a foundation stone is to be laid for a departmental building, or a new wing of a College to be declared open, the Chancellor is often the obvious person to perform the task. Jenkins's period of office coincided with an unprecedented spurt of building activity throughout the collegiate University. He carried out such duties with dignity and aplomb, though he could not always conceal his distaste for some of the recent additions to Oxford's skyline. Opening a building at one of the former women's colleges he was heard to say that there was no good architecture in Oxford north of the Broad. No doubt his predecessor Archbishop Laud turned in his grave as he thought of St John's Canterbury Quad.

All such occasions brought with them the chore of writing a speech, or, as Roy candidly admitted in his autobiography, 'at least the titivation of an old text in order to make it seem more suited to the particular occasion'. Roy's speeches were structured like the liturgy in the Prayer Book: there were parts that were common to all occasions, and parts that were proper to particular feasts and places. Roy took great pains in devising, say, the Bodleian proper or the Somerville proper, gathering titbits of information and moulding suitable epigrams. In the common part of the Cancellarian liturgy there was an oft-quoted sentence from *The Idea of a University*, which celebrated the 'umbrageous groves' of the Oxford colleges. Old hands in the audience, on hearing the name of Newman introduced, listened keenly to hear how, this time, the Chancellor would cope with those two prominent 'r's.

In 1988 Vice-Chancellor Neill launched a five-year campaign to raise funds for Oxford. The Chancellor worked manfully to make the appeal a success, accompanying Vice-

Chancellor North as far as China in search of benevolent philanthropists. He often repeated his conviction that 'unless Oxford raises substantial private funds, it will not, for all the splendour of its buildings and the glory of its history, be able to maintain its position as one of the handful of universities of pre-eminent world class'. But he warned that it would be a tragedy if 'the idea of a university' began to assume a new meaning of being the sighting and pursuit of the nearest rich man.

During the Southwood vice-chancellorship the University set up a new body, the Chancellor's Court of Benefactors, to give public and ceremonial expression of the University's gratitude to philanthropists who give it substantial financial support. This new institution, which met twice yearly, added to the Chancellor's ceremonial and rhetorical burdens. Nonetheless, Roy welcomed its creation, since it allowed the University to make a clear distinction between due formal acknowledgement of beneficence and the recognition of distinction by the conferment of an honorary degree.

During Roy's chancellorship Oxford, and the whole national university system, suffered a number of financial crises. When a Labour government came to power in 1997, there were initial hopes that action would be taken to remedy years of underfunding by Conservative governments. Roy took advantage of his friendship with the new Prime Minister to press on his attention the serious threat to the academic prestige of Britain's great universities. The University of Salamanca, he once reminded him, used to be one of the most celebrated universities of the world. Unless urgent remedies were applied to the financial plight of universities, Oxford, like Salamanca, might altogether fade from global consciousness.

It was reported in the press that it was Roy who had convinced the Prime Minister of the desirability of allowing universities to charge top-up fees, a measure that has, of course, proved highly controversial. I have been assured, however, on good authority that Roy did not recommend any particular reform of the funding system, but restricted himself to emphasizing the universities' serious financial plight and the need for swift remedial action.

In private, in fact, Roy became more and more convinced that only independence from government funding and control would enable universities like Oxford and Cambridge to remain in the same league as the Ivy League universities in the United States. He was unwilling to express this opinion publicly, since it was not the policy of the University, but he once said to me that he was willing to devote the rest of his life to helping to bring it about.

Roy was fascinated by the non-financial aspects of Oxford's fortunes, studying the University's performance in the national Research Assessment Exercise, and watching the ranking of the colleges in the annual Norrington Table of classes gained in Final Honour Schools. He was, indeed, an aficionado of rank orderings and performance indicators: legend has it that he once described someone as 'the third most dangerous Head of House in Europe'. He liked to evaluate his successive Vice-Chancellors in order of efficiency; he ranked his last one so highly that he had to be dissuaded from proposing legislation to allow him to serve for a further term. His favourite party game was to choose players across the centuries for an XI of Oxford all-time greats against an XI of Cambridge all-time greats.

Roy did not, however, take a keen interest in strictly academic debate. One would not expect to hear him discuss, for instance, whether there were too many or too few post-structuralists in the English Faculty, or whether in social sciences we needed more seat-of-the-pants economists and fewer econometricians.

The most important, and the most delicate, feature of Oxford's constitution is the relation between the colleges and the central University—often compared, misleadingly, to the relationships between the individual states and the US government. Lord Franks, in 1965, suggested that the Vice-Chancellor should chair a council of colleges, which would have formalized the relationship. This suggestion was never adopted, and an informal role has been left for a Chancellor, if he wishes, to fulfil. Roy was frequently invited to dine in colleges, where dons felt free to express their concerns to him; and he was able to pass on to busy, non-dining, Vice-Chancellors useful information about which university policies were approved, and which were resented, by the average tutor.

The Chancellor is ex officio Visitor of several colleges, and this entailed special, and sometimes demanding, duties. It was Somerville which most publicly involved its Visitor in college affairs. At the beginning of the 1990s Somerville was one of the only two Oxford colleges reserved for women. Most of its fellows combined their membership of a single-sex college with lecturerships in a mixed university: and the restriction to women of appointments to such hybrid posts was problematic in the light of anti-discrimination legislation. Mainly for this reason, the College's governing body in 1992 voted to amend its charter and statutes to permit men to join the College as senior and junior members.

There was widespread opposition to the change among the College's present and past students, and the Somerville JCR, which had not been consulted about the change, appealed to the Visitor. After a preliminary meeting with Lord Wilber-force, the University's High Steward, senior and junior members of the College submitted their case, through counsel, to the Visitor at a hearing in the University Offices on 11 May 1993. He ruled that the governing body had acted perfectly legally, but had failed to fulfil a moral obligation to consult the resident undergraduates. He urged the governing body to delay the admission of men for at least a year.

Some Somerville dons felt that Roy had been weak, and should have stood up more firmly to student agitation. But it is arguable that his decision averted the danger of lawsuits in the civil courts, brought by women students claiming breach of contract. The year of delay allowed for full consultation, which enabled senior members to bring many junior members to see the merits of their case. When men were eventually admitted in late 1993 for 1994 they were able to take up residence peace-fully, and they were given a gracious welcome by the last purely female generation of students.

During his chancellorship Roy published ten books, including the award-winning biographies of Gladstone and Churchill. Some over-professional dons complained that these were not works of original scholarship, and felt that they insuf-ficiently acknowledged their debt to published sources (par-ticularly if these were their own works). Most of us, however, revelled in the lively and luminous style of the biographies, and the personal reflections and inimitable graces that no full-time academic could have matched. The University was proud to have a Chancellor who practised as well as preached the life of humane endeavour. He, in his turn, was proud of his well-earned honorary fellowship of the British Academy.

Jenkins valued the chancellorship not only as an honour and a public service, but as an opportunity to expand an already extensive network of friendships. In these last fifteen years of his life Roy became close friends with a number of Oxford heads of house and other university figures. He and his wife, Jennifer, offered marvellous hospitality to their friends at East Hendred, and no couple ever took more pains to keep their friendships in good working order. Roy had his moments of pomp and vanity, but one of his endearing qualities was his awareness of his own weaknesses. He never stood on ceremony or minded being teased. Shortly before his death he was commending to his friends a remorseless parody of his last book, *Twelve Cities* (2002), by Craig Brown in *Private Eye*.

Of the seven twentieth-century Chancellors of Oxford, four left little mark on the University. Milner (1925) died in the year of his appointment, and Cave (1925–8) left no mark. The best that the official history of the University can say of their successors is, 'As chancellors, Lords Grey (1928–33) and Halifax (1933–59) kept their distance.' The three who stand out are Curzon, Macmillan, and Jenkins.

Curzon was anxious to play an active part in Oxford's affairs. He resided for a while in the Judge's Lodgings in St Giles, conferred with senior officers, and wrote a whole book on the necessity for reform of the University. His proposals were, for the most part, very sensible, and had the support of senior figures in the administration; but he had no understanding of the arts needed to secure a majority among the college tutors, who formed the majority of Congregation. Even though he was able to hold over the dons' heads the threat of a Royal Commission (which he said he could secure from the Prime Minister by a flick of his little finger), he was unable to overcome the opposition to his reforms, and in 1911 he said, 'I have given up the government of Oxford as beyond hope.' Some of his proposals were put into effect by a Royal Commission after the 1914–18 war; others still await implementation.

Roy Jenkins, with his keen sense of history, made no attempt to emulate Curzon by seeking executive power or obtruding proposals for reform. But under his chancellorship a very significant set of reforms, proposed by Vice-Chancellor North and implemented by Vice-Chancellor Lucas, have altered the governance in Oxford in the direction that Curzon, with his passion for administrative efficiency, would have admiringly approved.

Roy never became an Oxford legend as Macmillan did in his lifetime. However, there are those who believe that if he had lived as long as Macmillan did he would have acquired his stage presence and achieved his iconic status. Whether or not that is true, Chancellor Jenkins worked much harder for the University than Chancellor Macmillan ever did, and inspired much more affection than Chancellor Curzon ever did. He has a good claim to have given more to Oxford than any other twentieth-century Chancellor.

Certainly, very few chancellors anywhere have carried out their duties to their university with such diligent devotion combined with such manifest delight. I once asked Jennifer which parts of the Chancellor's job Roy liked, and which he hated. 'He loved all of it' was the reply. In one of the last chapters of his autobiography, *A Life at the Centre*, Roy recorded that in the years since his election as Chancellor, Oxford had taken up a good quarter of his time and energy. But he went on to say that since in the same period it had provided a half of his happiness, he regarded the balance as a favourable one.

David Cannadine

 David Cannadine is the Queen Elizabeth the Queen Mother Professor of British History at the Institute of Historical Research, University of London. He is the author and editor of numerous books, including *The Decline and Fall of the British Aristocracy* (1990); *G. M. Trevelyan* (1992); *Class in Britain* (1998); *Ornamentalism* (2001); and *In Churchill's Shadow* (2002). He is a Trustee of the National Portrait Gallery, the Kennedy Memorial Trust, and the British Empire and Commonwealth Museum, a Commissioner for English Heritage, and a member of the Advisory Council of the National Archives.

Chapter 17

Writer and Biographer

DAVID CANNADINE

After a long and distinguished lifetime spent in both politics and literature, Roy Jenkins concluded that writing books was a more difficult and demanding activity than governing the country, and in support of this mildly unexpected proposition, he advanced evidence which must surely have been born of personal experience. It was, he insisted, perfectly feasible to transact a morning's ministerial business with a mind-numbing and physiologically debilitating hangover. Yet under the same inhibiting circumstances, it was not possible to cover blank pages with coherent sentences, let alone with vivid and sparkling prose. At its lowest level, he thought Whitehall work was largely reactive and derivative, responding to agendas set, papers produced, and meetings arranged by junior ministers and civil servants, with whom the impetus of official life largely lay. But by contrast, he felt even the most undemanding writing chore was solitary, self-generating, and proactive, requiring substantial resources of energy and momentum, determination and commitment, buoyancy and creativity, which only a non-hung-over author, who was mentally alert and physically vigorous, could hope to provide.

This was an instructive (and unusual) ranking of the relative demands of statesmanship and scholarship, and Roy Jenkins was better equipped to make it than any Briton of his time. For as a politician and a penman, he was doubly pre-eminent, being as much at home in the groves of literature as in the corridors of power. In a public career spanning more than half a century, he held two of the greatest offices of state, he was the Deputy Leader of one party and the founding Leader of another, he was several times spoken of as the next Prime Minister, he was President of the European Commission, and he ended his days as the friend and mentor of the longest-serving Labour premier. But during the same period he was also a prolific, influential, and acclaimed author—of reviews and essays, lectures and pamphlets, histories and biographies—who produced twenty-three books, beginning with an interim biography of Clement Attlee, and ending with his evocation of twelve cities in Britain, Europe, and the United States. At the time of his death he had nearly completed a life of Franklin D. Roosevelt, and he was eagerly looking forward to beginning a biography of John F. Kennedy. While his 'upper-case' ambition was to excel and do good in politics, his 'lower-case' concern was to make his mark as a writer and biographer.

Of course, it was one thing to say that writing was a more demanding endeavour than ruling: it was another to say that it was a more important activity. This Roy Jenkins never claimed; but having surveyed twentieth-century British prime ministers and American presidents, he concluded that those who knew about the past and who were interested in history

generally performed better. This was partly because knowledge of the past implied a curious and well-stocked mind, and
politicians with those attributes were better equipped to govern than those who lacked them. And it was partly because
history helped to lengthen perspective and provide a sense of
proportion, which discouraged excessive partisanship or unrealistic expectations. Put the other way, this meant that politicians
with no knowledge of the past, and no interest in history, were
'likely to be dull men and uncomprehending rulers'. But Roy
Jenkins was neither boring nor blinkered: he was abundantly
endowed with a lively and curious mind which had been
stimulated during the childhood which is the essential starting
point for understanding him as a writer.

In *The Labour Case*, which he wrote for the 1959 general election, Jenkins noted that 'children who come from homes
where there are a lot of books, where a wide range of subjects
are discussed, and where foreign travel is a common activity'
had a much better start in life than those brought up in narrower and more deprived environments; and his own boyhood
environment was comfortable and nurturing in exactly these
ways. His father had worked in the south Wales coalfield, but he
was well educated, well read, and a good linguist. In the family
home at Pontypool he assembled an extensive library, and as an
only child, Jenkins spent much of his time reading. Indeed,
he later recalled that *Harmsworth's Encyclopaedia* furnished him
with many precise and often esoteric facts, including the exact
populations of the great cities of the British Empire, and also
with a lifelong appetite for 'rather useless details'. By the time
he had been through Oxford and the Army, he had devoured
Jane Austen, Hardy, Tolstoy, and Dostoevsky; and he developed
an affection for Trollope, Proust, Evelyn Waugh, and Anthony

Powell. Once begun, the habit of 'omnivorous reading' (one of several characteristics he shared with Asquith) stayed with him: he reread the whole of Proust's *À la recherche du temps perdu* during his first stint as Home Secretary; and when on a brief holiday in the summer of 1980, he consumed three books on Roosevelt, novels by Iris Murdoch, Barbara Pym, Graham Greene, and Angus Wilson, and three essays by Lytton Strachey.

Jenkins's home was also a forum for the discussion of a wide range of subjects, and he was introduced to politics and politicians at an early age. His father was MP for the local constituency, and was Attlee's parliamentary private secretary from 1940 to 1945, which meant he was at the heart of the then Labour establishment. And Arthur Jenkins brought down to Pontypool such figures as Herbert Morrison, Hugh Dalton, and Attlee himself, with whom his son was thus familiar from an early age. As the product of such an environment and the beneficiary of such encounters, Roy Jenkins also came to view history as a gradual process of change, and began to appreciate the importance of particular politicians, usually on the left, in nudging progress forward by peaceful and constitutional means. As a result, he would always be interested in individual people rather than in the impersonal forces of history, and he believed that politicians should concentrate on the next practical move forward rather than vainly and naively striving for the millennium. For an active practitioner of one of the most egotistical and self-absorbed professions, this deep human curiosity was remarkable. Indeed, with the conspicuous and honourable exception of his close friend and near-contemporary Ian Gilmour, Roy Jenkins was unique among politicians of his generation in writing more about other people than about himself.

By the standards of the time, the young Roy Jenkins was also very well travelled, visiting Cardiff, London, Paris, and Brussels while still a boy, in the company of his father. All his life he was fascinated by towns and cities and by their architecture, and the range of his interests extended from the medieval cathedrals of Rheims and Chartres to the skyscrapers of Chicago and Manhattan. But he was especially captivated by the great cities of the nineteenth century: their town halls and museums, and their railway stations and trains. (Although he had no enthusiasm for Victorian morality, he greatly admired Victorian buildings.) Much of his early journalism would contain a strong architectural and topographical component, as did *Twelve Cities* (2002). When he came to write his biographies, he gave special attention to the means whereby his subjects travelled: Gladstone was a very assiduous user of railways; Baldwin was the last British Prime Minister never to fly; Churchill loved his wartime journeys round Britain in the prime-ministerial train; and Truman was the last US President to make much use of the railroad. And he was fascinated by the importance of their country houses in providing the formal setting and logistical headquarters of their lives: The Wharf at Sutton Courtenay for Asquith, Astley Hall near Bewdley for Baldwin, Hawarden in Flintshire for Gladstone, Chartwell in Kent for Churchill, and Hyde Park on the Hudson for Roosevelt.

Having taken the Higher School Certificate in history, English and geography, followed by a term of intensive reading at University College, Cardiff, Jenkins went up to Balliol College, Oxford, to read PPE. He took papers in the history of labour movements in the nineteenth century, European diplomatic history 1870–1914, and international relations 1919–39. But this was only a small part of the syllabus, and in any case, his main interests and activities were extra-curricular, focusing on politics and the Union. When subjected to a viva for a First (which he eventually obtained) he was asked to name the Foreign Secretary in 1868. He suggested Earl Granville; it was a good guess, but the answer was Lord Clarendon. Thereafter, he never had any time for the scholarly obsessiveness and parochial gossip of academic life, he was not interested in abstract theories or general speculation, and he did not see himself as an intellectual in politics in the way that Richard Crossman or Tony Crosland did. Unlike them (and, indeed, unlike Attlee and Dalton and Gaitskell), he never held a university job, and he had no wish to be head of an Oxford college, although he was delighted to be elected to the chancellorship. Yet he did not include Oxford in his *Twelve Cities*, on the revealing grounds that it was a university but not a metropolis. As this suggests, he liked academics to be worldly rather than reclusive, and with a broad range of public interests: Isaiah Berlin in Oxford, Noel Annan in Cambridge, and J. K. Galbraith and Arthur Schlesinger at Harvard.

It was only at the end of the Second World War, during several months of enforced army leisure at the end of 1945, that Jenkins began to become seriously proficient in his knowledge of modern British political history. In rapid succession he consumed John Morley on Gladstone, J. L. Garvin on Joseph Chamberlain, Lady Gwendoline Cecil on Salisbury, Winston Churchill on Lord Randolph, Lord Crewe on Lord Rosebery, Blanche Dugdale on Arthur Balfour, and the standard lives of Harcourt, Campbell-Bannerman, Asquith, Grey, and Curzon. Like Churchill at Bangalore in the 1890s, this was for him a great and formative period of self-education, though Jenkins was clearly starting from a much higher level of general knowledge. Although these tombstone biographies were obviously dated in their style and approach, and were padded out with long printed extracts from letters and speeches, Jenkins found them infinitely preferable to Lytton Strachey's brief and deflating essays in *Eminent Victorians*. As such, they provided him with a detailed knowledge of political history from the 1830s to the 1930s, and they reinforced his conviction that 'individual performance has made, and continues to make, a lot of difference to politics and government'.

Thereafter, Jenkins tended to see modern British history in essentially individualistic and biographical terms. As someone who distrusted abstract ideas, he thought all generalizations to be partly and manifestly false. He did not accept the Marxist view that history was exclusively to be explained in terms of class struggle, or that it was moving inexorably towards some preordained proletarian goal. Nor did he have any time for the Braudelian view that it was the 'longue durée' which mattered, and that political events were merely 'l'histoire événementielle'. (Indeed, French intellectual life seems very largely to have passed him by; he was rather disparaging about it in his *European Diary* (1989), and he made no mention of it in his essay on Paris in *Twelve Cities*.) For Jenkins, history was made, and progress brought about, by individual political actors who, if they were of a radical or reformist inclination, worked slowly towards greater freedom, tolerance, and equality, both domestically and internationally. All Jenkins's major biographical subjects could be described in these terms, and so, too, could his own career. Moreover, and here again the parallel with Jenkins is close, Attlee, Asquith, Gladstone, Churchill (at some stages), and F.D.R. were all radical politicians whose lifestyles were distinctly conservative. And he also had a preference for the 'classical' over the 'romantic' in politics: Peel, Gladstone, Asquith, Attlee, rather than Disraeli or Churchill (in other phases).

But for Jenkins, there was nothing preordained about

progress and reform, however hard it was worked for by politicians in the 'classical' tradition. In so far as the lessons of history taught anything, it was that the Conservatives would always enjoy widespread backing, that radical governments would be relatively rare occurrences, and that they would inevitably run out of steam and support. Not surprisingly, the great reforming administrations in modern British politics were few and far between: 1830 (Grey), 1868 (Gladstone), 1908 (Asquith), and 1945 (Attlee). It was, he believed, absurd for the left to think that it could ever hold power for a long time, or to insist that all Conservatives were knaves or fools. For history also taught that accident and contingency mattered a great deal, and Jenkins's books are shot through with an appreciation of this. If Dilke's divorce scandal had not erupted in 1885–6, he might have kept Joseph Chamberlain in the Liberal Party, and the whole course of late nineteenth- and twentieth-century British history might have been different. If Asquith had not been so downcast when Venetia Stanley told him of her engagement to Edwin Montagu, he might have handled the coalition crisis of May 1915 better than he did. If Churchill had been deselected by his constituency in 1938, because of his 'disloyal' stance over appeasement, he might not have been back in Parliament by 1940. And if 29,000 people had voted differently in the presidential election of 1948, Truman might have lost to Dewey, as the papers, the pundits, and the polls expected him to do.

For Jenkins, chance and contingency were important elements in history and politics alike; and so, too, were character and temperament and intellect. Accordingly, as he saw it, it was the major task of biographers to establish and evoke a personality, to explain how their subject's mind operated, and then to follow this unique personage through its allotted span. This was a very different sort of biographical approach from both the pious prolixities of the traditional tombstones (notwithstanding his own personal debt to them), and the revelatory and deflating ironies of Strachey (though he was obliged to go into some detail with the private lives of Dilke, Asquith, and Gladstone). As such, his biographical approach had much in common with that of Harold Nicolson, Philip Magnus, Elizabeth Longford, Robert Rhodes James, and John Wheeler-Bennett. Like him, they were amateurs, they were not iconoclastic, they did not break new ground in form or style, they accepted the social and political assumptions of the worlds in which their subjects lived, and they had a discerning eye for the sort of detail which would interest the general reader. And they concentrated on the letters and diaries of their subjects, rather than trawling through a wider variety of personal and official papers in (as Jenkins saw it) the mistaken and naively obsessive academic belief that all primary sources were of equal value.

This was Jenkins's notion of biography, and he was markedly modest in the claims he made for what he insisted was essentially a craft rather than 'a high literary art form'. For past precedent suggested that even the best of biographies dated quickly, whereas the greatest histories and most resonant fiction did not. Even Froude's *Carlyle*, Morley's *Gladstone*, and Ward's *Newman* were not in the same category of 'artistic excellence' as Gibbon's *Decline and Fall*, Carlyle's *French Revolution*, the poetry of Tennyson or Browning, or the novels of Jane Austen, the Brontës, Trollope, or George Eliot. Yet Jenkins also took it for granted that biographies came in the category of 'good books', which he believed were one of the essential components (along with better food, better buildings, better music, and greater personal freedom) in the more civilized society which he hoped Britain might become, and which as a politician he would help bring about during the 1960s. He had no doubt that there was an educated, moderate reading public for whom he was writing: the people who bought the weekly journals and the quality Sunday newspapers; those who later became the supporters of the Social Democratic Party; and (if a more precise example were necessary) also comprised the highly educated electors of what would briefly but happily be his own Glasgow Hillhead constituency.

In addressing such an audience, Jenkins rapidly developed into an accomplished and unusually fluent writer, who rarely revised his first drafts extensively, and there can have been scarcely a day when he was out of front-line politics which did not see several hundred words (he always counted his output) committed to paper. And what words they sometimes were. He loved them if they were long and slightly old-fashioned: 'periphrasis', 'clamant', 'areopagitical', 'rodomontade', 'pharisaical', and 'eleemosynary' (a particular later favourite, often applied to Gladstone). When, in 1987, he settled on the full title of Baron Jenkins of Hillhead, of Pontypool in the County of Gwent, he described it as 'a piece of Cymro-Scottish miscegenation'. He liked illuminating oxymorons: F.D.R. regarding crowned heads of state as 'slightly inferior equals'; Churchill being 'magnificently unfitted' for office when he returned as Prime Minister in 1951. And he excelled in summing up careers in one sentence, often with two halves which made a surprising, unexpected, and yet very satisfying whole. Thus Campbell-Bannerman: 'since Pitt, he was the only Prime Minister to die in 10 Downing Street, and he timed it rather well.' Thus Cripps: 'his sympathy embraced the world, without understanding most of the people in it.' And thus Leopold Amery: 'he would be ill at ease in any party today, and he was altogether rather admirable.'

Jenkins's writing also abounds in memorable aphorisms: 'the judgment of those who hate is rarely good'; 'municipal elections do not determine political destiny'; 'biographers, unlike mathematicians, get better as they get older'. He liked vivid metaphors: Wilson's style of leadership was 'more like that of an acrobat skilfully riding a bicycle than of a ringmaster imperiously cracking the whip'; and Healey's belligerent wavering amounted to carrying 'light ideological baggage on a heavy gun carriage'. He was adept at situating his subjects, both comparatively and sociologically. If John Maynard Keynes had not written the *General Theory*, he would have occupied a place in British life that would have been an amalgam of Harold Laski and Lord Cherwell. And while the Roosevelts and the Harrimans were the aristocratic American equivalents of the Salisburys or Churchills, Adlai Stevenson had more in common with the British service gentry, as exemplified by Sir Stafford Cripps or R.A. Butler. He also produced 'lightning flashes of insight' which not only illuminated the subject but were sometimes self-revealing as well. Here is Jenkins on Dilke: 'whether in London or the country nothing would divert him from the most accurate and minute apportionment of his days'. Here he is on Truman: 'he absorbed many facts, and he thought about them a good deal, but his conversation involved no spinning of general theories'. And here he is on Gaitskell: 'he left a memory which shows that honest speech and a warm heart are no obstacles to success in politics'.

The young Roy Jenkins who left the Army on 1 January 1946 knew much more modern British political history than when he had confronted his Oxford examiners four and a half years earlier. But his primary aim was 'success in politics', and to this end he sought election to the House of Commons as a Labour

MP. There was an appropriately historical dimension to this ambition: partly family piety (he attempted to follow his father as MP for Pontypool when he died in 1946); and partly a recognition that he would be taking his place at the centre of national life in the traditional arena of British politics (in 1948 he was elected as MP, first for Southwark in London, then for Stechford in Birmingham). As befitted a young and ambitious MP, he established a reputation as an expert (in his case on economic issues), and he wrote political tracts: *Pursuit of Progress* (1953), which insisted that the Left could not realistically expect to win elections every time; and *The Labour Case* (1959), which put forward many of the arguments Anthony Crosland had recently advanced in *The Future of Socialism*, although with more style and in a much less self-consciously intellectual way. But as an opposition backbencher who understood the need to bide his time, and who later described himself as having been 'a semi-detached MP', most of his writing during these years, although politically informed, was more historical and biographical than polemical.

Indeed, Jenkins had already declared himself as a writer when he entered Parliament, with the publication of *Mr Attlee: An Interim Biography*, in April 1948, the very same month that he was elected for MP for Southwark. It was a substantial book of 85,000 words, and a major commission for a young man who had never produced anything before. It owed much to personal connection (his father), and depended on access to particular documents (Attlee's 'fairly exiguous private papers'), and in both these ways set the pattern for his later biographical works, especially *Dilke* and *Asquith*. Indeed, it is one of the more intriguing ironies of Roy Jenkins's career as a stylish and prolific writer that it was Clement Attlee, one of the least verbally expansive of prime ministers, who effectively launched him on it. He produced the book in the twelve months from November 1946, writing in the evenings or at weekends, but lacking the time for sustained periods of composition that only became available once he was an MP. In retrospect, and given his 'complete lack of experience', Jenkins thought it 'not a bad book'. He took a liking to Attlee's father, 'a man of great tolerance and considerable breadth of view'. He showed a stronger preference for Attlee's practical socialism than for MacDonald's vaguer and more Utopian ideals. And he showed how central a figure Attlee had been during the great Second World War coalition, where he alone with Churchill remained a member of the War Cabinet throughout.

But at least in retrospect, this first biographical venture was important for other reasons, too. Although Attlee was a predictably uninterfering subject, Jenkins resolved that he would never again write about a living person. 'There are', he later observed, perhaps with his experience of writing *Asquith* in mind, 'enough problems in dealing with the susceptibilities of relatives, without taking on those of the subjects themselves.' In describing Attlee's preference for political activism rather than secluded reflection, Jenkins was very much expressing his own views: 'a life of strict scholarship was not so much beyond his ability as outside his interests.' And when he wrote that 'facts have always been more important to Attlee than either theories or expediency', there was the same sense of identity between subject and author. It was clear that Jenkins had already taken against Lloyd George, and thought that Asquith was the Prime Minister Attlee most admired, and was 'most comparable in character to himself'. And there was also one piece of inadvertent (and, by later standards, not all that well phrased) autobiographical prescience: 'it is important to remember that however easily the deputy leadership of the

Labour Party fell into his hands, his future accession to the Premiership could in no way be regarded as a necessary concomitant of this office.'

The publication of *Attlee* earned Jenkins a modest literary reputation (although very little money), and in 1952 he was invited to write the official life of Ernest Bevin. But he wisely concluded that it was not the right project for him: partly because there was no single archival collection on which the biography could be based; and partly because, although he greatly admired Bevin, their backgrounds and styles were very different. It is not possible to imagine Jenkins writing at ease and at length about someone whom he would subsequently describe as resembling, when Foreign Secretary, 'a rather truculent liftman on the verge of retirement'. Meanwhile, Jenkins was beginning to make a reputation as a journalist as well as a biographer. During the late 1940s he wrote regularly for *Tribune*, producing generally cautious articles on economic and financial matters, and from 1951 to 1956 he contributed weekly essays to the Indian newspaper *The Current*, on British politics and the wider national scene. As with the Attlee biography, this opportunity owed much to personal and family connections, for the paper was owned and edited by D. K. Karaka, an Oxford-educated Indian politician who had married Jenkins's cousin. But it also provided an excellent apprenticeship: for Jenkins learned to write regularly, promptly, and to length on a wide variety of topics, including the Oxford and Cambridge boat race, Teddy boy fashion, Princess Margaret's romance with Peter Townsend, and the Coronation of 1953.

Meanwhile, Jenkins had returned to more sustained writing, and in 1954 he produced his first (indeed, only) work of narrative history, *Mr Balfour's Poodle*, which described the clash between the Lords and the Commons in the aftermath of

Lloyd George's 'People's Budget' of 1909. The book was based on a careful analysis of the tombstone biographies of the principal characters, topped off with some judicious quotations from *Hansard*, and it made repeated comparisons between the great Liberal landslide of 1906 and the Labour triumph of 1945. Indeed, it was partly inspired by the renewal of this controversy in 1949, when the Labour government passed a second Parliament Act, reducing the peers' powers of delay from the two years allowed in the Parliament Act of 1911 to one. Here was a clear continuity between the Asquith and Attlee administrations (and, indeed, with the Grey and Gladstone governments before them), as both were obliged to confront the same anti-democratic obstruction of hereditary Toryism in getting their reform measures through. And although this was by no means a polemical book, there was no doubting whose side Jenkins was on: Balfour possessed 'a conceit not unusual in those whose party had been long in office'; Lansdowne was as 'stubbornly obscurantist' over the Lords in 1910 as he had been over Ireland in 1885; the 'unthinking section of the Unionist Party' was, as usual, 'a formidable force'; whereas Asquith, by contrast, was 'a conservative-minded man' who was also 'a great radical prime minister'; and the Parliament Act of 1911 was 'the last monument of triumphant Liberalism'.

Despite his evident partisanship, Jenkins was by the mid-1950s making important cross-party friendships with three people who were to be of great importance in his development as a writer. The first was Mark Bonham Carter, whom Jenkins had known at Balliol, and who was briefly Liberal MP for Torrington in 1958–9. He was also an editorial director of Collins, persuaded Jenkins to move there from Heinemann, and continued to be his publisher for the next thirty years. In addition, Bonham Carter was at the very centre of the

Liberal Party establishment: his brother-in-law was Jo Grimond, and his mother was Asquith's daughter (and most redoubtable champion) Violet. The second was David Astor, whose brother Jakie was Jenkins's 'pair' in the Commons. From 1948 to 1975 David Astor was both the owner and the editor of *The Observer*, which he made into the outstanding liberal Sunday paper of its time. From the late 1950s Jenkins began to write and review for *The Observer*, and it remained his most enduring journalistic billet for the best part of forty years. The third of these literary-cum-political friends was Ian Gilmour: another Balliol graduate, a coming man in the Tory Party, a stylish and discerning writer of history and biography, and from 1954 the owner and editor of *The Spectator*, which became under his direction the most exciting and broad-ranging weekly of the time. By the late 1950s Jenkins was writing a regular political commentary in its pages and also reviewing those modern political biographies and autobiographies which he missed out on for *The Observer*.

Mark Bonham Carter had been impressed by the mastery of late Victorian and Edwardian politics which Jenkins had shown in *Mr Balfour's Poodle*, and suggested that for his next book he should write a life of Sir Charles Dilke, the radical, republican politician whose political career had crashed in ruin in the aftermath of a controversial divorce case in 1885–6. There was a two-volume tombstone life, by Stephen Gwynn and Gertrude Tuckwell, which had been published in 1917, six years after Dilke's death; but it had made scarcely any allusion to the divorce, and Dilke's personal papers had subsequently been placed under wraps in the British Museum. That embargo was lifted in 1955, and the papers provided the crucial source for the book. It was an ideal subject for Jenkins's first historical biography. Dilke's disgrace weakened the Liberal Party at a critical moment, with Gladstone about to embrace Home Rule, and intensified those divisions which kept it out of effective power for the next twenty years. And the divorce case itself was a prime example of the intolerance and hypocrisy of the nineteenth-century moral code, to the overturning of which Jenkins was increasingly concerned to devote his political energies. Aside from Mrs Crawford, who seems to have been determined to ruin Dilke, but for no particular reason, the other character who emerged with little credit was the crusading journalist W. T. Stead, revealingly described by Jenkins as possessing 'to an unusual degree the essential ingredients of moral intolerance—he was a puritan fascinated by sex'.

Although the final truth of the matter will never be established, Jenkins was almost certainly right to conclude that Dilke was more sinned against than sinning, and was the victim of a conspiracy. Hence his subtitle: *A Victorian Tragedy*. The book was widely and favourably reviewed (although it did dwell disproportionately on the divorce, and gave scarcely any attention to Dilke's subsequent career), it was made into a television programme and a stage play, and, as Jenkins later recalled, it 'was a further notch in my movement towards being a professional writer'. It took him virtually the whole of the 1955–9 Parliament to complete, and during the same period he was also working hard politically in the cause of literature, by campaigning for the reform of the law of censorship, under which reputable publishers were still at risk of prosecution. He led a cross-party Commons campaign, and Jenkins's allies included Hugh Gaitskell, Jo Grimond, Mark Bonham Carter, Hugh Fraser, and Lord Lambton. He was further assisted by A. P. Herbert, who provided much publicized outside support, and by R. A. Butler, who became Home Secretary in 1957, and was noticeably more liberal than his Tory predecessors. Jenkins skilfully steered his Obscene Publications Bill through the Commons, and it received Royal Assent in July 1959, just before Parliament was dissolved for the general election.

By the late 1950s Jenkins had carved out for himself a serious reputation as an author, and after the literary-cum-legislative successes of *Dilke* and the Obscene Publications Act, he consolidated his position during the long Parliament of 1959–64. In this sense, he was lucky that the electorate were insufficiently persuaded by his arguments in *The Labour Case*, for he could not have accomplished this if (as would surely have been so) he had been holding junior office in a Gaitskell government. Instead, he was able to establish his reputation as a biographer and man of letters so securely during these five years that it readily survived the long middle phase of his career, when politics came to occupy so much more of his time. Indeed, during the early 1960s he seemed to many to be an author first and a politician only second. He was writing and reviewing regularly for both *The Spectator* and *The Observer*, and at David Astor's suggestion he produced lengthy special articles on the Cuba missile crisis, the failed takeover bid for Courtaulds by ICI, the election of Pope Paul VI, and the problems of the British aircraft industry. In addition, he was also contributing to the *Sunday Times*, the *Daily Telegraph*, the *Evening Standard*, *Encounter*, and *History Today*. And shortly after Hugh Gaitskell's death in 1963 he was invited to become editor of *The Economist*. It was a signal tribute to his literary standing, and he took a long time to make up his mind to refuse.

But his main authorial preoccupation during the 1959–64 Parliament was his biography of Asquith. After Dilke, he wanted to write about a major late Victorian or Edwardian political figure, preferably on the left, and there had been no life of Asquith since the two-volume biography of 1938. As

Jenkins's friend and publisher, and as the subject's grandson, Mark Bonham Carter was eager and encouraging, and he made available the letters which Asquith had written to Venetia Stanley between 1910 and 1915. But he also worked his way systematically through the Asquith papers in the Bodleian, which meant this became his most fully researched biography. As the lifelong keeper of her father's flame, Lady Violet was not wholly happy with the result, and she was astounded to learn of Asquith's epistolary relationship with Venetia. But Jenkins's portrait was favourable and admiring, and his identification with his subject was complete. Like Jenkins, Asquith was a provincial who had made his way via Balliol to the House of Commons. Like Jenkins, Asquith was liberal, tolerant, civilized, fastidious, humane, optimistic—a self-conscious upholder of the 'classical' political tradition. Like Jenkins, Asquith was a radical in politics, who lived a socially conservative (and very active) life. And like Jenkins, Asquith worked with great speed and efficiency, leaving ample time for leisure, which made it easy to underestimate his energy and ambition.

In later life Jenkins insisted that *Asquith* was the book by which he would most wish to be judged (though at that point he had written neither *Gladstone* nor *Churchill*). And it remains, nearly forty years on, the best single-volume life, in part because no one has attempted another biography on a similar scale. Like its subject, it has not escaped criticism: for being too discreet about Asquith's drinking and private life; for failing to admit his mistakes in handling House of Lords reform and Irish Home Rule; and for insisting he was, at least at the outset, a better war leader than his opponents alleged. To the very end, Jenkins remained unmoved by such criticisms. But he had identified with Asquith more closely than he would ever do with any other biographical subject. It is impossible to imagine him regarding Asquith as either tragic (as he had Dilke) or comic (as he would Gladstone and Churchill). But it was also the case with *Asquith* (as, earlier, with *Dilke* and *Mr Balfour's Poodle*) that Jenkins was a pioneer in a field which would soon become intensively ploughed, as academic research into the politics of the nineteenth and early twentieth centuries boomed during the 1960s and 1970s. Inevitably, this meant that some of his opinions and interpretations would need to be modified, and that *Mr Balfour's Poodle* and *Dilke* would be superseded. But that does not diminish the originality and importance of the books in their time.

From 1964 to 1988 the balance of Jenkins's activities between politics and authorship changed dramatically, as he became a virtually full-time public figure in the aftermath of Harold Wilson's electoral victory, and he retained this commanding, and often controversial, position for a quarter of a century. Inevitably, this meant that much of his published writing during these years was the by-product of his official life and political activities: *Essays and Speeches* (1967) contained his most eloquent statements as a liberal reforming Home Secretary; *What Matters Now* (1972) set out his agenda for the Labour Party in the aftermath of his resignation as Deputy Leader in 1972; and *Partnership of Principle* (1985) was a collection of his speeches as the founder of the Social Democratic Party in the early 1980s. But high office and high politics also left him with little leisure for the sort of large-scale writing projects and original research that had preoccupied him during the 1950s and early 1960s. He declined the invitation to write the official biography of Hugh Gaitskell with much more reluctance than he had refused the earlier Bevin commission. And he made little progress on what he hoped would be his next big book, where he hoped to explore and interleave the lives of three twentieth-century British prime ministers and three twentieth-century American presidents.

But Jenkins was eager to keep up his literary presence, both as a liberalizing and as a creative force. As Home Secretary, he supported legislation to abolish the Lord Chamberlain's powers of theatre censorship. He continued to lecture and review, and these activities resulted in two books, *Afternoon on the Potomac?* (1972; derived from a series of lectures on Anglo-American relations in the twentieth century delivered at Yale in the same year), and *Gallery of Twentieth Century Portraits* (1988; an assemblage of his recent reviews and essays). And while out of office from 1970 to 1974, he completed a series of pen portraits of near contemporaries, most of whom he had seen, and some of whom he had known, which were eventually published as *Nine Men of Power* (1974). They originally appeared in *The Times*, and were longer than the reviews he was regularly writing of the biographies and autobiographies of politicians. They allowed space for comment and analysis, but did not require anything by way of original research, and they enabled him to venture beyond the Left and beyond Britain in his search for subjects. There were three studies of Labour figures: Cripps, Gaitskell, and Bevin. There was another trio, of Americans: Adlai Stevenson, Joseph McCarthy (the black joker in the pack), and Robert Kennedy. And to balance the book, there were Lord Halifax (liberal Conservative), John Maynard Keynes (liberal most of the way), and Léon Blum (the sole but significant European).

Jenkins clearly enjoyed writing these essays, and he would later produce another six (on R. A. Butler, Aneurin Bevan, Iain Macleod, Dean Acheson, Konrad Adenauer, and Charles de Gaulle). But he was also eager to get back to something longer, and when his term as President of the European Commission drew to a close, he revisited his earlier idea of presidential and prime-ministerial biographies. But instead of trying to produce a *magnum opus* with six studies standing side by side between the same hard covers, he decided to produce two brief, stand-alone lives: longer than his *Men of Power* pieces, but extended essays rather than full-dress biographies. The two figures on whom he finally settled were Truman and Baldwin, and the books appeared in 1986 and 1987 respectively. At first sight, they seem very un-Jenkins-like figures for him to have selected. Truman lacked F.D.R.'s 'style, his resonance, his confidence, his occasional sweep of innovative imagination, his tolerance and understanding of diverse human nature'. Moreover, he played poker, he was very untravelled, he did not like New York, he was never enthused by Adlai Stevenson, and on the basis of one brief meeting, Jenkins was convinced they would not have got on. As for Baldwin: he was a Conservative, he presided over unprecedented periods of high unemployment, and he was also an appeaser.

Yet it says much for Jenkins's growing breadth of vision that he was attracted to both figures. His Truman showed an enviable capacity to distinguish between great issues and small ones, and on the former (though not the latter) he was almost invariably right. He stood up to McCarthy and he sacked MacArthur. He was responsible, with Acheson and Marshall (and with Attlee and Bevin), for the creation of the post-war settlement built around the Marshall Plan and NATO. And like Attlee (whose period of prime-ministerial power coincided almost exactly with Truman's presidency), he suffered much contemporary derision during the late 1940s, before his reputation began its seemingly inexorable rise. This was a brave and bracing choice of subject in the high noon of

Reaganism; but perhaps for that reason, *Truman* did not sell all that well in America. Jenkins's Baldwin was a very different character. He 'sought to govern by mood creation rather than by decision', and 'the general habit of his mind was ruminative rather than executive'. He greatly admired Asquith's 'urbane liberal gravitas', and his benevolent and tolerant Toryism was in marked contrast to the narrow-minded and partisan politics of Bonar Law and Neville Chamberlain, which came before and after. It was also very different from the confrontational Conservatism of Margaret Thatcher, who in 1987 was still riding very high. Like *Truman*, Jenkins's *Baldwin* carried with it an clear contemporary political message, namely that things could be managed differently, and could be managed better.

This was a substantial output during a quarter-century when Jenkins was occupied almost full-time in politics and public life. He may have been concerned with the voting public more than with the reading public, but he did not neglect the latter. To be sure, he produced nothing during this period to compare, in scale or originality or impact, with *Asquith*, and after 1964 he never undertook original archival research again. Inevitably, then, this meant his work was in some ways 'slighter', even as he extended his range into Europe and the United States. Had Jenkins died after the publication of *Baldwin* (and after his defeat at Hillhead in 1987), he might have been remembered as a biographer (and as a politician) who had never quite lived up to the great hopes of the early and mid-1960s. There might have been a definite sense of things tailing off. But as it was, his departure from the House of Commons turned out to be both the prelude to, and the precondition for, a last phase of extraordinary literary activity and public renown. 'One of the most difficult feats for a successful politician', he would later write, 'is to manage a semi-retirement so that it gives at least as much satisfaction as, and maybe more happiness than, the battles to which it is a post-script.' It was a feat which he himself was to manage brilliantly, and writing would turn out to be the major feature of it.

Jenkins's defeat at Hillhead may have spelt the effective end of his political career, but it opened up a last phase of his life in which literature occupied an even more prominent place than it had when he was writing *Asquith*. Sensing that his front-line contribution to politics had been accomplished, and feeling in a correspondingly 'ending up' mood, Jenkins devoted the next few years to writing, for the first and last time, almost exclusively about himself. To be sure, he continued to lecture widely, especially at and on behalf of Oxford University, and to review modern political biographies and autobiographies in *The Observer* and elsewhere, and a final collection of these occasional pieces, *Portraits and Miniatures*, appeared in 1993. But his prime preoccupation during this period was not biography, but autobiography. He began by publishing his *European Diary, 1977–1981*, the detailed (but much-abridged) journal he had kept during his years as President of the European Commission. It provided vivid vignettes of politics in Brussels and Britain, and showed Jenkins's continuing determination never to let professional life interfere with social life. Its most memorable entries described the places he visited, among them Salisbury Cathedral ('too much of a ship and too little of a shrine'); Namur ('slightly reminiscent of Aylesbury or Gloucester, without the cathedral'); and Mysore ('there is a striking similarity between English late-Victorian and Edwardian pier architecture and the style favoured by Indian maharajas a little later').

European Diary was but a prelude to his full-dress autobiography, *A Life at the Centre*, published in 1991. It was an enterprise which he approached with considerable trepidation: partly because, after a lifetime reviewing such works, he well knew the pitfalls of the genre (inaccurate recollection combined with excessive egotism); partly because it represented a return to writing on a scale which he had not attempted since *Asquith* (the two books were of almost exactly equal length); partly because he was 'intimidated by the prospect of finding a tone of voice' in which to write about himself; and partly because, for the most recent period, 'the wounds from the break-up of the SDP were still raw', albeit more so for some of his colleagues than for him. On the other hand, he had accumulated extensive records: beginning with his father's diaries, there were 'substantial chunks of memoir raw material' for his years on the Labour front bench, and he had abundant documentation from his European diary and from the latest phase of his life. And so there was never any likelihood that he would lack for interesting and important things to say. He began by writing about the period from 1964 to 1976, which was the part of his life most closely akin to a conventional political biography; next he 'swallowed twice' and got down to his early years, 'beginning with the dreaded childhood chapter'; and only then did he take the story from 1976 to 1990.

The result was an autobiography widely acclaimed as one of the four best single volumes of post-war political memoirs, in the same league as Duff Cooper's *Old Men Forget*, R. A. Butler's *The Art of the Possible*, and Denis Healey's *The Time of My Life*. Despite his initial qualms, he got the 'voice' exactly right, avoiding both the oratorical grandiloquence of Churchill (appropriate for war, but not for peace), and the embittered belligerence of Thatcher (who assumed all her opponents were either knaves or fools). As a result, the book was remarkably free from regret or rancour or resentment (except, perhaps, against David Owen); it showed a broad-ranging sympathy for a wide spectrum of people and politics; there were some very funny stories, often told against himself; and it was clearly the work of someone with a remarkable capacity to see his life in sane perspective and realistic proportion, and who had come to terms with what he had (and hadn't) achieved. 'I always sensed', Jenkins wrote by way of conclusion, 'that I would enjoy being Prime Minister more when it was over than while it was taking place.' It was a revealing confession—of someone who was too much of a politician ever to be a full-time biographer, but also too much of a biographer ever to be a political obsessive.

For most politicians, the publication of their autobiography effectively brought their career to a close. Yet for Jenkins, *A Life at the Centre* was not so much a matter of 'ending up' as of beginning again—but as a writer, rather than as a man of power. For his next biographical endeavour, 'a full-scale but not multi-volume biography of Gladstone' was by far his 'rashest literary enterprise'. It was, he explained, 'like suddenly deciding, at a late stage in life, and after a sedate middle age, to climb the rougher face of the Matterhorn'. As such, it was as much of a risk biographically as leaving Labour to form the SDP had been a risk politically. For Gladstone's career dwarfed that of Asquith in terms of its length and its scope, and the array of archival and published material was not just correspondingly but almost exponentially greater. Moreover, Gladstone was dominated by religion as much as by politics, and Jenkins admitted to possessing 'an inadequately spiritual mind'. And two-thirds of his life was lived before 1868, a period of British politics about which Jenkins had never written. But there was one means by which these risks could be minimized, and the whole enterprise made manageable, and that was by basing his account very closely on the Gladstone diaries, which had been impeccably edited by M. R. D. Foot and H. C. G. Matthew in fourteen volumes published between 1968 and 1994.

The result was the best single-volume study of Gladstone since Philip Magnus's life of nearly half a century before, and it won for Jenkins the Whitbread Prize for Biography. He gave particular attention to Gladstone's pre-prime-ministerial career, especially his religious and sexual crises of the 1840s; he reaffirmed his view that his 1868 administration was one of the great reforming governments in modern British politics; he showed real sympathy with his later efforts to bring Home Rule to Ireland; and he was far from complimentary about the petty and narrow-minded obstructionism of Queen Victoria and Lord Salisbury. This was not a Gladstone to everyone's taste, and Tory historians felt it paid insufficient attention to what they regarded as his increasingly frenzied and partisan opportunism. But it was a beautifully proportioned and real-ized book, as sympathetic to its subject as *Asquith*, yet also, and perhaps to its advantage, more detached. And it carried a powerful (if initially implicit) contemporary political plea: for a unified Left, which Home Rule had regrettably shattered; and for the completion of still unfinished business concerning both Ireland and the House of Lords. Two years later Tony Blair's election held out the prospect that these pleas might become policies, and for a time this gave *Gladstone* a political resonance which reinforced its popular appeal.

Gladstone's pre-prime-ministerial reputation substantially depended on his labours as Chancellor of the Exchequer—an office whose pivotal and prestigious position in government was largely his creation, which had also been held by two of

Jenkins's other biographical subjects (Asquith and Baldwin), and which he himself had come to occupy one hundred years later. And so it was an almost natural progression from writing a life of the Grand Old Man to producing a collection of essays on the nineteen chancellors between Gladstone's last appointment to the office and Attlee's first. They were a diverse bunch: Liberals such as Sir William Harcourt and Sir John Simon; Tories such as Lord Randolph Churchill and Austen Chamberlain; and two Labour men in the form of Philip Snowden and Hugh Dalton. Some were well known, in part because they went on to higher things: not only Asquith and Baldwin, but also Lloyd George, Winston Churchill, and Neville Chamberlain. Some were deservedly obscure: C. T. Ritchie, Reginald McKenna, and Sir Robert Horne. But some were less well known than they ought to be: Sir Michael Hicks Beach, Sir Kingsley Wood, Sir John Anderson. 'Taken together,' Jenkins concluded, 'the post-Gladstonian Chancellors were a disparate lot, with no very obvious sinews of provenance, style or policy connecting them.'

Once again, Jenkins saw this as bearing out his belief that the only generalization in politics and history is that no generalizations can or should ever be made. They all had 'somewhat more than average ability and substantially more than average ambition', but beyond that, they were 'almost, but not quite, as variegated as a random selection of any nineteen reasonably successful men'. Put more positively, this meant that Jenkins had ample scope for evoking personalities, and judging their politics. He believed Lord Randolph Churchill's besetting weakness as a minister was 'his constant addiction to partisan demagoguery'. He likened Sir William Harcourt to 'an amalgam of attributes subsequently possessed by Hugh Dalton, Willie Whitelaw, Richard Crossman and Roy Hattersley'. As ever, he found Austen Chamberlain the most unexpectedly agreeable member of his clan: 'he had managed with dignity and decency to span the political world from Gladstone to Attlee more comprehensively than had anyone else'. He had no time for Bonar Law ('his way of life was almost aggressively joyless'), and never warmed to Neville Chamberlain ('he lacked any breadth of tolerance'). But he was both impressed and amused by Waverley (formerly Sir John Anderson, and 'the only peer of the railway age to be called after a station'), and by his one-time mentor Hugh Dalton (about whom he felt 'there was more than a touch of Anthony Powell's Widmerpool').

The Chancellors (1998) was Roy Jenkins's most comprehensive attempt at collective biography; but it was also an almost relaxing diversion between two titanic tasks. After *Gladstone*, he turned away from the medium-scale biographies of Truman and Baldwin, and 'came to be attracted rather than inhibited by big subjects', in terms of both their historical significance and their expositional scale. There would have been some limited pleasure in reappraising John Morley, or Hicks Beach, but as a sequel to the life of the GOM, such a project would have been 'the equivalent of trying to get excited, after a Himalayan expedition, by an amble up Snowdon'. And after Gladstone, that unique but quintessentially nineteenth-century figure, the only twentieth-century successor was Winston Churchill. But even more than Gladstone, Churchill was not an immediately obvious subject for an author approaching 80. The relevant secondary material was as much in excess of that on Gladstone as the materials on him had exceeded those on Asquith. Moreover, Churchill had been a Conservative for most of his life, and had often been more belligerent and intransigent than Baldwin. And much of his career was taken up with waging war, a subject and an activity that were no more congenial to Jenkins than they had been to Asquith or Gladstone.

If anything, then, a biography of Churchill represented an even greater risk than a life of Gladstone. But Jenkins was encouraged both by his appointed biographer, Andrew Adonis (who rightly thought that such an enterprise would add colour and climax to his subject's old age), and also by Mary Soames (Churchill's only surviving child, whose late husband, Christopher, Jenkins had come greatly to admire). Moreover, in the companion volumes to Martin Gilbert's official biography, which printed a mass of original material, there was a single source that resembled, but was in some ways superior to, the Gladstone diaries. Jenkins's Churchill was, like his Gladstone, a figure larger than life: by turns heroic and comic, magnificent and idiosyncratic. In thus portraying him, Jenkins paid especial attention to Churchill's metabolism and morale—subjects about which historians care little, but which politicians rightly recognize are of supreme importance in setting the bounds to what they can realistically achieve. He recognized that Churchill's method of writing books—with a team of researchers forming a cottage industry, and with dictation far into the night—was very different from how he himself did things, and was a way of re-creating the excitement of office in opposition. But he also understood that for Churchill, as for himself, good living was not the denial of public duty, but the necessary precondition for its successful discharge and sustained fulfilment.

Jenkins's *Churchill* was a remarkable triumph for an author of 80 who was not by then in the best of health. For it conveyed (in the words of one reviewer) 'an absorbing sense of one member of a rare species minutely dissecting another of its own kind', as the greatest author–politician of one generation celebrated and saluted the greatest author–politician of another, with a rare mixture of deep appreciation, mellow affection, occasional exasperation, and amused detachment. The biography sold in hundreds of thousands on both sides of the Atlantic, and it received the Wolfson Prize for History, not just in recognition of this particular volume, but also as a fitting tribute to Jenkins's whole lifetime's œuvre. Yet despite worsening health, he kept writing. Having contributed a well-balanced and well-disposed entry on Harold Wilson to the *Oxford Dictionary of National Biography* ('he kept the train of government on the rails over difficult stretches of country'), he began another book of essays, dealing with places rather than with people, describing the great cities of Britain, Europe, and North America he had known. This was partly a second instalment of autobiography, but by another name; it was partly a means to indulge his lifelong interests in history and topography, buildings and architecture; and it was also a way of evoking the 'purpose and personality' of his favourite cities, which furnished the essence of sophisticated living.

As such, the book contained memorable vignettes: of Cardiff (the nearest big city of his boyhood, which evolved in his lifetime from coal metropolis to Celtic capital), Paris (the first great European metropolis he got to know, and where he would later have some hilarious misadventures in the British Embassy), Birmingham (whose Stechford constituents sustained him in Parliament for twenty-five years, but which was 'not a city which easily clutches at the heart strings'), Brussels (where he spent much the most time, having lived there for four years as President of the European Commission), and Glasgow (whose Victorian splendours, unrivalled setting, vibrant civic culture, and highly educated Hillhead electors he came late in life so much to admire). But there was more to these essays than urban evocation and autobiography. The essays on New York and Chicago, the 'two skyscraper capitals of the world', were not only vivid portraits of these uniquely high-style, high-rise cities: they also expressed his lifelong love of liberal and metropolitan America. Those on Bonn and Berlin were additionally a paean of praise to the singular success of post-war German democracy under Adenauer, Erhard, Brandt, Schmidt, and Kohl. And those on Barcelona and Dublin celebrated the emancipation of Spain and Ireland from the narrow-minded, authoritarian, and theocratic regimes of Franco and de Valéra, and their subsequent blossoming as more liberal and cosmopolitan members of the European Community.

One unexpected consequence of this book, the last to be published in Roy Jenkins's lifetime, was that it inspired a gloriously perceptive parody from Craig Brown in the last issue of *Private Eye* for 2002, which caught his later tone and cadences perfectly, and in which Jenkins was writing, not about his favourite cities, but about his preferred stations on the London Underground:

Hainault is, one might almost suggest, the most oxymoronic of tube stations, being on the Central Line, but very far from central. East of Woodford, yet due south of Grange Hill, it is not a station with which I would claim an instinctive and intimate relationship, rather one which I would say has always greeted me most warmly, offering to carry my bag, whilst stopping short, as it were, of asking me in for a bottle of half-way-decent claret.

By then, Jenkins had nearly finished a brief life of Franklin Roosevelt, on a similar scale to his earlier studies of Truman and Baldwin, and he was looking forward to beginning his biography of John F. Kennedy. *Franklin Delano Roosevelt* (2003) was a predictably vivid evocation of his patrician social milieu, of his protean, charismatic, and star-quality personality, of the improvised twists and often uncertain turns of the New Deal, of the importance of his 1940 electoral victory for the fate of the free world, and of the lesser significance of his decision to run again in 1944. The last chapter was entitled 'Death on the Verge of Victory', and Jenkins died while still working on it, having just written to Craig Brown thanking him for his 'very funny, un-wounding and even affectionate' parody.

In his writings, as in his politics, Roy Jenkins constantly stressed the need for perspective and proportion. How does his life and work as a writer look when assessed from these appropriate vantage points? Whether it was his prime concern (as from 1959 to 1964, and again after 1988) or his second-string activity (as in the years in between), he wrote prolifically in three different, but complementary, modes: as a journalist, essayist, lecturer, and reviewer; as a political pamphleteer and polemicist; and as a formal, full-dress biographer, autobiographer, and, occasionally, historian. As a journalist, he kept his name regularly before the reading public, he assimilated most recent political biographies and autobiographies as they appeared, and he was able to set out his more general thoughts on history and politics, albeit in an unsystematic but highly revealing way. As a more engaged political polemicist, he constantly wrote from a historical perspective, drew illuminating parallels from the past, and repeatedly (and increasingly) recognizing that partisanship had its limits. And as a biographer, he was unusually wide in his sympathies, though they stopped well short of Salisbury, Bonar Law, Neville Chamberlain (and Thatcher) on the one side, and Rosebery, McKenna, MacDonald (and Benn) on the other.

Yet there were also changes and developments across the three phases of Jenkins's career, reflecting both his progress as a writer and his evolving political experiences. Between 1945 and 1964, when he was establishing his reputation as an author no less than as a politician, his biographies of Attlee and Asquith were those of impeccably loyal party men, the two most important leaders of the British Left during the first half of the twentieth century. From 1964 to 1988 Jenkins's interests widened, both politically and authorially, as he began to write about British Conservatives, European leaders, and American presidents. And during the last phase of his career he gave most attention to figures who were often, as he himself had by then become, ill at ease with rigid, over-dichotomized party divisions. For this was not only true of Gladstone and Churchill, but also of both Roosevelt presidents. In democracies, Jenkins noted at the end of his first chapter on F.D.R., those who never accepted the discipline and necessity of party were left 'flapping their wings in impotence'. But that had to be balanced against the fact that 'the politics of party loyalty from time to time make monkeys of all who accept them'.

So much for perspective and proportion: but what of posterity? Beyond question, Roy Jenkins's literary output was massive and varied: but how much of it will still be read in fifty years' time? Journalism, lectures, and reviews are by their nature ephemeral, political polemic and pamphleteering is no less time-bound, and collections of essays rarely remain in print for long. Much of Jenkins's writing came within these categories, and seems likely to share the same fate, while among his more substantial works, both *Dilke* and *Mr Balfour's Poodle* have already been superseded by more recent and comprehensive studies. In future, these writings will be read, if at all, because Jenkins was a significant political figure, and for the light they cast on his attitudes and opinions, rather than because of their enduring literary distinction, biographical standing, or historical stature. But that still leaves four of his books which do seem likely to live and last: *Asquith* still unsurpassed after forty years as a work of liberal empathy and fastidious appreciation; *A Life at the Centre*, one of the few outstanding political autobiographies of the twentieth century; *Gladstone*, which has superseded Philip Magnus as the best single-volume account of the greatest Liberal of them all; and *Churchill*, as the most remarkable tribute ever paid by one Grand Old Man of British politics to another.

To have produced four such major, enduring works was a literary achievement unrivalled by anyone else of Roy Jenkins's political generation. If comparisons are to be drawn, they may most fittingly be made with those figures from an earlier time who had also combined liberal politics with literary endeavour in a similar blend of 'upper- and lower-case' ambition and activity: Lord Macaulay, Sir George Otto Trevelyan, James Bryce, John Morley, and H. A. L. Fisher—all of them both Cabinet ministers and influential authors. To be sure, there was nothing in Jenkins's œuvre to rival their most substantial works: *The History of England*, *The American Revolution*, *The American Commonwealth*, *The Life of Gladstone*, and *A History of Europe* respectively. By comparison, even his best books may have seemed to some to be no more than 'upper middlebrow'. But he belonged to an age in which the mode of writing for an educated public had changed and become more compressed, he was as much a master of that mode in his day as they had been in theirs, and he was, in addition, far more politically influential in his prime than any of them had ever been. Throughout his later life Roy Jenkins was widely and rightly recognized as the last upholder of this great liberal and literary tradition; and one of the saddest aspects of his death has been that there is no successor in sight.

Robert Harris

Robert Harris was born in Nottingham in 1957 and took a degree in English from Cambridge University, where he was President of the Union. After working at the BBC as a reporter on *Newsnight* and *Panorama*, he became political editor of *The Observer* in 1987. He has also been a columnist on the *Sunday Times* and *Daily Telegraph* and in 2003 was named Columnist of the Year in the British Press Awards. He is the author of four novels, *Fatherland* (1992), *Enigma* (1995), *Archangel* (1998), and *Pompeii* (2003).

Chapter 18

A Late Friendship

ROBERT HARRIS

On 5 September 1995 my publishers threw a party at the Travellers' Club in Pall Mall to celebrate the publication of my second novel, *Enigma*. Roy Jenkins was invited at short notice on the strength of a generous review he had given it in the previous week's *Sunday Times*. Slightly to my publishers' surprise—and certainly to my everlasting good fortune—Roy came, thus initiating a friendship that was to last for more than seven years. During the course of that first conversation I happened to mention that I had an Enigma machine, lent to me for a promotional tour. He expressed his curiosity and almost before I knew what was happening he had pulled out a Smythson's pocket diary and arranged to come for lunch the following Sunday to have a look at it. Two weeks after that we lunched again. And then, two weeks after that, again. And somehow, it seemed, we never stopped lunching. I reckon we must have met at least a hundred times in all.

The practical foundation of our friendship was that we were

neighbours in the country, he at East Hendred, where he came to spend every weekend from Friday to Monday, and we at Kintbury, near Hungerford. Our two villages, separated by the wide grey river of the M4, were closer than they looked on the map—'only twenty-six minutes between us', as he would occasionally remark. (He had a freakish memory for journeys and their precise durations; once, in the middle of nowhere, navigating from the back seat, he announced: 'You can either turn left here, which is nought-point-six of a mile longer, or turn right, but that entails passing over ten sleeping police-men ...'.) Sometimes we would meet at my house, sometimes at his, but most often at a series of country pubs midway between the two. If British politics and letters are the poorer for Roy's passing, so, too, it must be said, are the landlords of the Blue Boar at Chieveley, the Harrow at West Ilsley, the Royal Oak at Yattendon, the Red House at Marsh Benham, the Fish at Sutton Courtenay, the White Hart at Hamstead Marshall, and a large number of other congenial establishments spread across Oxfordshire and West Berkshire.

If this sounds a frivolous way to remember a great man, I do not think he would have objected. Lunching, dining, social life, travel, gossip—these were at least as important to Roy as his political activity and his writing. In this, he left himself wide open to caricature, for we live in a dreary age of professional politicians, who measure their effectiveness by the number of hours they work, and their virtue by the number of lunches they take at their desk. But Roy worked hard at his leisure: he never wasted a second of it. One of his aims in life was to avoid passing a mealtime alone, and in this, as in much else, he was triumphantly successful.

Our lunches followed a set pattern. His preferred ren-dezvous time was 1.15. First, a glass of wine or champagne.

Then a bottle of red wine—almost invariably a Bordeaux, although he was not (contrary to myth) a fanatic about this, and was generally willing to settle for a Chianti or Rioja if they looked reasonable. (What he couldn't abide, at least in my experience, was Beaujolais: 'Beaujolais with fish? I think not.') He had a Churchillian capacity to combine drinking with working: on most days after lunch he returned to his study and wrote another 1,000 words. We took it turns to pay the bill, the record kept meticulously in his neat handwriting in his tiny diary. As for the quality of the food, that did not concern him much. It was the conversation, the human contact, which he relished.

There was something Roman about his capacity to operate on all these levels—political, literary, social—with equal energy. He was omnivorous in his appetite for experience. When I came to write the character of Pliny the Elder in my fourth novel, *Pompeii*, I recognized—and incorporated—elements of Roy in the personality of that formidable administrator, polymath, and wine expert. But Roy was a much greater statesman than Pliny ever was: Cicero, perhaps, would be a better match. For example, when Cicero, in old age, wrote to his friend Papirius Paetus, urging him to abandon his stern resolution to avoid all dinner parties, the sentiments could have been Roy's exactly:

Really, my dear Paetus, all joking apart, I advise you, as something which I regard as relevant to happiness, to spend time in honest, pleasant and friendly company. Nothing becomes life better, or is in more harmony with its happy living. I am not thinking of physical pleasure, but of community of life and habit and of mental recreation, of which familiar conversation is the most effective agent. And conversation is at its most agreeable at dinner parties . . . because at dinner parties, more than anywhere else, *life is lived in company* . . . (my italics)

Conversation was essential to Roy. Someone once said that, in listening to his voice, one heard the authentic echo of English as it was spoken in the 1930s. He practised conversation, too, as an art from a golden age, in the way that Evelyn Waugh once defined it: the apt joke, the shared confidence, the mutual building of a privately shared fantasy. His memory was prodigious, and he was generous in sharing it. Here was a man—is there another left?—who was in the gallery of the House of Commons to listen to Churchill's great speeches in the summer of 1940, and who bumped into Ernest Bevin on the promenade at Sidmouth in 1937 (the leader of the Transport and General Workers' Union announced: 'I'm 'ere on 'oliday with Flo'). He could talk with first-hand knowledge of the great Labour figures of the mid-twentieth century: Attlee, Morrison, Cripps, Gaitskell. He knew all the Kennedys—Jack, Jackie, Bobby—and once described how he had asked Richard Nixon if he had ever considered contesting the result of the 1960 election. ('Consider it?' replied Nixon, 'I thought about nothing else for a month. But I decided it would all run away, like rivulets into the sand.' Roy loved that phrase; he repeated it lovingly: '*like rivulets into the sand . . .*')

But, for all his stories, and despite his age, he never relapsed into anecdotage: the names either arose naturally in conversation, or they did not arise at all. This perhaps helps explain why, although there was a gap of thirty-seven years in our ages, I was never conscious of it. He had that quality which many obituarists mentioned in connection with the late Queen Mother: he would talk about the past, but he refused to live in it; he was always eager for the latest gossip, or to discuss the latest book or film. (I remember I gave him William Boyd's *Any Human Heart*; he gave me Justin Cartwright's *Half in Love*.) Dozens of his oldest friends must have died during the course of our acquaintance, but he never sighed after them, or dwelt on details of their passing. Whether this was a reflection of his generation's attitude to illness and death, or the necessary ruthlessness of the determined survivor who has lived to bury most of his contemporaries, I am not sure. Perhaps it was both. 'Most lives end pretty badly when you stop to think about it,' was all he would say. In the face of his own heart trouble, in the final two years of his life, he was entirely stoic—Roman again—with never a trace of self-pity. It did not stop him travelling, working, or lunching right up to the end. As Jennifer said, when she rang me to tell me he had died: 'He would never give in.'

If he was not at all like an old man, he was most emphatically not like an old politician. His outlook was sophisticatedly liberal: nothing shocked him, little surprised him. He thought, on the whole, there were too many laws and too much interference in how people lived; for that reason he instinctively opposed the government's proposed ban on fox-hunting. There was no bitterness about him in his retirement. He spoke warmly about most of his former colleagues, including Harold Wilson, for whom he felt more affection as years went by. He never had much time for the fashionable notion that the politicians of the past were all giants, and those of today, pygmies. He was undoubtedly disappointed in some of what Tony Blair did—or, more accurately, failed to do. 'I have three great interests left in politics,' he told me in November 1999, 'a single currency, electoral reform, and the union of the Liberals with Labour. And all three are languishing.' But he remained on warm terms with the Prime Minister. I have never forgotten how, when I once complained that Mr Blair seemed to be all things to all men, he gently replied that this was not necessarily a mark of insincerity, that 'the human heart has many chambers—if I may put it that way', and that perhaps people were more complex creatures than I was willing to recognize.

He did have a couple of *bêtes noires*, of course. Norman Lamont, for some reason, was one. David Owen, more understandably, was another. At lunch at East Hendred in 1997 my wife once announced that she had almost reversed her car over Lord Owen in Hungerford High Street. 'Almost!' exclaimed Roy. 'Don't you ever come to this house and say that you *almost* ran over David Owen.' On another occasion, on a summer's evening, looking out over the cricket pitch at West Ilsley, he told me that he had recently had a hankering to make his peace with Owen. But then he had had a dream in which he and Owen had finally sat down together, and Owen had said, 'Roy, it really is wonderful to see you again, especially as you now agree that on everything we disagreed about I was right and you were wrong.' And that, said Roy, had put him off seeing him for good.

One of the keys to Roy's contentment in his final years was that, at heart, he was a writer at least as much as he was a politician, and writers do not have to retire. Even at 80 he had more work—offers to write columns, ideas for books—than he could cope with. And this work was not, for him, a poor substitute for politics. Surely no other contemporary politician would have maintained, as Roy did when he was Home Secretary in 1966, that it was actually harder to be a writer than a minister: that whereas 'ministerial work has a momentum' which can carry one through the day, however jaded one feels, 'the sheer deadweight effort' of getting up in the morning and trying to fill a blank page with words 'is the hardest sheer intellectual work, harder than anything in a minister's life, which I've ever done'.

This shared daily battle with the blank page was another

strong element of our friendship, especially after he retired as Leader of the Liberal Democrat peers in the House of Lords. To break the solitariness of the working day with a lunch is one of the joys of the writing life. We would exchange news about publishing, publicity, sales figures, translations. Comparisons of daily output was a more contentious matter, since his was always so much greater than mine. He would return from a week's holiday and announce that he had added another 10,000 words; he produced three books to my one. And yet I do not think I had a friend who took a livelier interest in what I was writing. He read a lot of fiction—more than I did—and found the process of making up stories and characters particularly fascinating: perhaps because it was the one area of writing that was closed to him.

I remember once being startled by his description of how he had rescued a daddy-long-legs from his bath that morning, and had put it—'very bedraggled'—on the window sill, and how, when he came back an hour two later to find it had flown away, it had 'really made my day'. He had that kind of novelist's eye for detail, and a novelist's curiosity about human beings: as long as he considered them decent or interesting, their political affiliations were irrelevant to him. His table was regularly open not only to Liberal Democrats like Paddy Ashdown and Charles Kennedy but to politicians from the Labour Party (Tony Blair, Jack Straw, Peter Mandelson, Lord Irvine) and to Tories (Sir Edward Heath, Lord Carrington, and Michael Heseltine). He liked Neil Kinnock and wished that he had won the general election in 1992. He took John Major out to lunch a couple of years ago and reported that Mr Major had asked him whether he ever regretted not being Prime Minister. 'I said "Not really" and was tempted to ask him whether he ever regretted that he had been.'

Did he really not regret his failure to reach the very top? I only knew him well in his final years, when political ambition was spent, but I believe that he did not. 'I rather think I would have liked being Prime Minister in retrospect, rather more than I would have enjoyed it at the time' was how he often put it to me. As a historian, he would have enjoyed seeing his name in the record books; as a politician, he was all too aware of the price. What made him such a wonderful friend and companion—the lack of rancour, the broad toleration of all points of view, the unhurried pleasures in food and drink and conversation—were the very qualities which in the end held him back from achieving the supreme office. He was not ruthless enough, or nasty enough, or willing enough to stoop to conquer. He was the most clubbable Coriolanus British politics has ever produced.

We had our last lunch together on 16 December 2002, at the White Hart in Hamstead Marshall. Mentally, he was as sharp as ever, but physically he was manifestly ailing, hoarse-voiced, and walking with the aid of a stick. He said he was going into hospital straight after Christmas for electric shock treatment on his heart, and then immediately changed the subject. He inquired after *Pompeii*, and when I told him I'd finally written the first fifty pages, he asked if he could see them. In the air, for the briefest moment, hung the unspoken possibility that he might not survive to read the finished novel. We arranged to have lunch in the first week of January and I promised to bring along the completed pages. But the day we were due to meet turned out to be the day of his funeral and I never saw him again.

Jenkins and Blair, patron and protégé, as seen by
The Guardian shortly after Roy Jenkins's death

Chapter 19

A Biographer's Tale

ANDREW ADONIS

Roy Jenkins's *Asquith* was the first political biography I read, stuck in boarding school at the age of 15 during the 'winter of discontent'. I remember the vivid excitement, awe, and sense of drama at the unfolding story, and my admiration in equal measure for Asquith and Jenkins. The date I recall precisely, because I reached the last chapter and Asquith's condemnation of the General Strike, his last political act, just as the campaign of strikes and union intimidation paralysed Britain in the spring of 1979. It seemed to me at the time that this marked the final destruction of Asquith's liberal idealism and I was puzzled by Jenkins's continuing allegiance to the Labour Party. My admiration was for his combination of the statesman and the biographer, re-creating so brilliantly the classical age of British parliamentary politics. I immediately went on to read *Mr Balfour's Poodle*, Jenkins's account of the struggle between Asquith's government and the reactionary House of Lords, and immersed myself in political history.

Such were the seeds of an association which ultimately led to my becoming his biographer. The historical and political strands were to intertwine to an improbable degree. On the historical side, *Mr Balfour's Poodle* began in me a fascination with the House of Lords and the remarkable blend of radicalism and tradition which characterized Gladstone and his successor twentieth-century reformers, Liberal and Labour. In time this became the subject of my doctoral thesis, published as an academic monograph in 1993.

By then I knew Jenkins slightly from political and Oxford connections.[1] But we had never had a proper conversation and it was with surprise bordering on amazement that in October 1994 I received a handwritten letter out of the blue from him—sent to the *Financial Times*, where I was then industrial correspondent—praising my book effusively. He ended, endearingly, with the remark that he had read it while writing his biography of Gladstone 'at the instigation of Mark B.C. [Bonham Carter] and found it as enjoyable as it was profitable—to me, I mean, probably not vastly so to you, I fear' (which was true enough).

The letter and my reply led to lunch, appropriately under Gladstone's statue in the National Liberal Club dining room. The conversation flowed back and forth across nineteenth- and twentieth-century politics. 'Tony Blair has made a first-rate start,' he said. 'Good bold decisive moves on the run at the outset, which is almost invariably the key to success in politics.' We agreed that Blair's election as Labour Leader might come to be seen on a par with the famous assembly in Willis's Rooms

---

[1] I was one of the band of enthusiasts who canvassed and ferried gowns around the Sheldonian Theatre to get him elected Chancellor of Oxford in 1987. The successful Jenkins camp ran its own gown service for the voting electorate of Oxford Masters of Arts over the two days of the poll, with those on 'gown duty' wearing 'J' labels on their lapels.

in June 1859 which formed the mid-Victorian Liberal Party as a broadly based progressive governing party lasting two generations. The lunch went so well that over coffee I plucked up courage to remark that I had long had at the back of my mind the idea of writing the Jenkins biography. 'Well,' he replied with his Cheshire cat smile, 'I have been having the same idea myself.' With precision and emphasis he explained that he wanted a biographer 'a generation or more younger than me; empathetic but with detachment; able to tell a tale well; and it must be written by the Berlin rules so the whole story can be told complete and in the right proportions'. I had never heard of the 'Berlin rules': they meant observing the agreement between Michael Ignatieff and Isaiah Berlin, of full access to papers and interviews so long as the biography did not appear in the subject's lifetime. That was fine by me, I said with alacrity.

Somewhat deflatingly, what followed was a further letter in his crablike hand—all his personal letters and book manuscripts were produced by (left) hand, his writing the hardest I have had to decipher besides Joe Chamberlain's—ending: 'I will take seriously the proposition you were good enough (that is almost Gladstonian!) to put to me. I hope you will not mind my taking a few years to think it over.' And by years he meant years. We met only four times over the next three years. One lunch in 1995 was to have a bearing on my personal career (related later), but there was no further discussion of the biography until December 1997, when I broached the subject again. This time there followed a swift New Year lunch invitation to East Hendred with my wife to meet Jennifer. Agreement was pronounced as we got up to leave.

'Here's a key to the house,' he said as we got into the car. 'Come and go as you please when we are not here to look at the papers; just let Gimma [his secretary] know when you are coming.' With that disarming gesture began many a (mostly freezing cold) day and occasional week in the loft, cellar, and study of St Amand's House, East Hendred, sorting through piles of barely arranged papers. He offered no guide and rarely enquired after progress. Two prize finds in the voyage of discovery were Roy's father's diaries stashed in Krug champagne boxes at the bottom of a cupboard—continuous from 1912, when Arthur Jenkins was a young Abersychan miner with dreams of a better life, until his death in 1946 as a minister in Attlee's government—and piles of wartime letters from Jennifer, Tony Crosland, and others stuffed in unmarked brown envelopes under the stairs.

I assumed our relationship would continue cordial but distant. But two events set it on an entirely different track. The first was that East Hendred lunch itself. The main topic of conversation was not his biography but his next book. He had just finished his somewhat recherché essay collection *The Chancellors* (1998), on all nineteen chancellors of the exchequer between Randolph Churchill and Hugh Dalton, and was thrashing around for a new subject. Another set of essays—on cities, or chancellors of Oxford University since the Duke of Wellington—was on his mind; so too were single lives of Macmillan or Balfour, 'both somewhat underestimated and about the scale I have in mind'. I instead suggested Churchill; tentatively at first, but by coffee I had persuaded myself and got a long way towards persuading Roy—as he had by now become—that this was a feasible, not foolhardy, project, now that Martin Gilbert's printed volumes of the Churchill papers were available. Churchill was not only a fitting progression from Gladstone, but would also fill a huge biographical gap, there not being a good single-volume life then available; and was in some ways easier to accomplish because Churchill came without religion (never Roy's strong suit) or the GOM's fearsome complexity of motive and expression.

Within a day or two Roy was on the phone to say that Churchill was 'growing on me' and discussing his proposed reading schedule. 'I'll also call Mary Soames [Churchill's daughter] to see what she thinks' (she was strongly encouraging). From then on barely a week passed without some communication back or forth on Churchill. The draft chapters started arriving in the post at regular intervals from April 1999. The rate of composition was remarkable: barely a day passed without another 500–800 or so words (Roy kept a precise daily tally); by late September 2000 he had completed thirty-five chapters, reaching 1942. The approach to the Second World War slightly unnerved him that summer—'It's like approaching Mount Popocatepetl from a distance, knowing that before long you are going to have to try and get up it somehow'—but there was no writer's block or slowing of pace.

A different block then intervened, in the form of a heart-valve operation he had to undergo on 13 October. Roy had convinced himself that this would take him out of action for only a week or two. But the recovery took far longer, and during the first few days in the Wellington Hospital, St John's Wood, his condition and morale were so poor that he wasn't sure he would finish the book at all. I was a regular visitor—by now he had become one of my closest friends—sharing half-bottles of champagne, which his consultant permitted as 'the best medicine in his state'. On my first visit he asked, with evident preparation, whether I would finish the book for him 'if I can't do it'. I parried this as best I could; but it introduced a new complicity between us and most of my weekends thereafter were immersed in the manuscript and later the proofs. But that was nothing compared to the renewed energy which Roy brought to the writing when out of hospital and allowed back to his desk in early December. Between then and 3 January, when we met for a first day-long editing session at East Hendred, he had completed 20,000 words. He continued at that pace until, on Tuesday 27 February, he phoned to say he had written the final words, comparing Churchill with Gladstone, 'at 9.45 last night, having done 4,200 words on Sunday and Monday and 82,000 since 7 December'. 'And now,' he added, 'I have to get on to my *DNB* [*Dictionary of National Biography*] essay on Wilson: I'm not sure what I shall say about him but as you know I will be fairly favourable.'

As well as that 10,000-word essay on Wilson, two further books, *Twelve Cities* (2002) and *Franklin Delano Roosevelt* (2003), were (largely) completed in the remaining twenty-two months of Roy's life. Our penultimate phone conversation, four days before his sudden death, was devoted to his plans for his next book: a biography of John F. Kennedy, 'who, with his circle, were for me the glamour of the Sixties, and whose reputation is I think in need of rerating upwards'. He had already agreed terms with his agent, Michael Sissons, including a 2006 publication date. On the morning of his death he was rereading Ted Sorensen's biography of JFK.

So my observation of Roy's literary life, at its final and most productive phase, was extraordinarily close. However, the literary was only the first thread of our relationship; it intertwined with a second, political strand, which was equally unexpected at the time of the 'vetting lunch' at East Hendred in January 1998.

Then a columnist and leader-writer on *The Observer*, I had become a strong supporter of New Labour, having in 1995 moved across from the Liberal Democrats after Tony Blair succeeded in replacing Clause IV of Labour's constitution.

Roy was encouraging when I mentioned this intention over a lunch that year: 'In terms of leadership, Labour and the Liberal Democrats are now basically the same party; so at your age you should join the larger one,' he said. But I was not expecting an early move away from journalism and writing; hence the desire to nail down the Jenkins commission. However, within a month I was approached about joining Tony Blair's staff, and by May had moved into a box-sized office on the second floor of Downing Street overlooking the garden—a room which had been part of the No. 11 flat when Roy was Chancellor and which his father had often slept in during the War when PPS to Attlee (who lived in no. 11 as Deputy Prime Minister).

Once in Number Ten I became both an observer and periodic conduit in perhaps the closest and most fascinating friendship of recent times between a Prime Minister and a political giant from a previous generation. The only parallel that comes to mind, but not a close one in terms of the actual relationship, is Baldwin including the 77-year-old Arthur Balfour in his Cabinet in 1925, twenty years after Balfour's premiership. On becoming his biographer I naturally assumed that Roy's political career was long over, and that in that respect at least I would be chronicling the past as a historian. In fact there were still five years of political career to come and I was to be a bit-player, beginning with his report on electoral reform, commissioned by Tony Blair and Paddy Ashdown, which was his main preoccupation throughout 1998.

By mid-1998 we were frequently meeting for lunch or dinner. Robert Harris's lunching odyssey was to be mine too, except that as a London not a country friend our lunches mostly rotated around clubland—Brooks's mainly, sometimes the Reform, the National Liberal, or the Athenaeum, particularly its garden terrace in the warm summer. The lunchtime conversation took on a pattern almost as standard as the fare: political and social gossip (sometimes real business) over the champagne and hors d'œuvres; moving on to Churchill or his other writing during the main course and claret; and then, by the dessert and coffee (if there was time), me trying to steer the conversation to two or three biographical points I had thought about beforehand. Despite one or two early attempts, I did not manage to secure a single structured interview for the biography; it was to be interview by luncheon. After lunch it was an equally hit-and-miss process of noting down the results after dashing back (often late) to meetings in Downing Street.

The Blair–Jenkins relationship will be a major theme of my forthcoming biography. Suffusing it all was Roy's passionate continued commitment to the political game and the goals of his political life, which he identified intimately with the success of Tony Blair. Roy's sustained political and emotional engagement constantly surprised me; so too the range of his continued preoccupations, whether Europe, Lib–Labbery, electoral reform, Cabinet personalities, Iraq, or Oxford (to name the first half-dozen that come to mind), all of them fuelled by a dense web of information and contacts assiduously maintained across politics, the media, and the Establishment at large. By 9.30 a.m. daily, as well as a good chunk of Churchill reading and writing, he had scoured all the broadsheets—much more thoroughly than I—and was often on the phone with some point or other. He attended the Lords most afternoons and was an amusing raconteur of its doings. Politics retained the capacity to make him angry—more angry, I suspect, than under the Tories because he felt he had some capacity to influence it for the better. I was increasingly struck by how much his relationship with Tony Blair mirrored that of forty years previously with Hugh Gaitskell, whose photograph dominated the East Hendred dining room. In both cases intense loyalty, admiration, frustration, and disillusion vied in equal measure.

To give just one incident—the coda. When I phoned Tony Blair to tell him the sad news of Roy's death (it was a Sunday morning), he was in a meeting on Iraq and I said I'd happily draft a tribute. It was an hour or two before I got back with a draft. By then he had written his own tribute in longhand, which went out unchanged. 'Roy Jenkins was one of the most remarkable people ever to grace British politics,' it began. The rest says so much about their relationship and the final productive phase of Roy's political career:

His influence on politics was as great as many who held the office of Prime Minister. He had intellect, vision and an integrity that saw him hold firm to his beliefs of moderate social democracy, liberal reform and the cause of Europe throughout his life. Even those of us who disagreed with the decision to form the SDP admired the way he never wavered from the view that the British people should have the chance to vote for a progressive politics free from rigid doctrine and ideology and one that stood in the tradition of Lloyd George, Keynes and Beveridge as much as Keir Hardie, Attlee and Bevin.

He was a friend and support to me and someone I was proud to know as a politician and as a human being. As his brilliant biographies demonstrate he had extraordinary insight and a naturally unprejudiced mind. He was above all a man of reason. I will miss him deeply.

And what of my view of him, as the relationship of biographer and subject developed in this unusual way?

In one respect my view changed fundamentally. I had previously thought him a bit of a dilettante, and that this had been perhaps his critical weakness as a politician and also in his later writing career. It took only a few weeks of engagement with him on Churchill and Blair to realize that dilettantism was the opposite of the truth. Roy was a dedicated professional, but not in one sphere alone. Politics, literary endeavour, and his wide social circle were pursued with a passion and assiduity which few devote to any one of those activities. It was the sum of these parts which made him what he was. Churchill, Roy liked to joke, 'combined a puritan work ethic with a great capacity for pleasure, even self-indulgence, a combination I find very attractive'.

I soon realized the extent to which his success and lifestyle, including his remarkable peripateticism, constantly travelling until within weeks of his death, were made possible largely by Jennifer's extraordinary support, forbearance, and self-identification with his political and literary projects. Equally important was a perpetual campaign to extract maximum value from time—his diaries parcel out the days in quarter-hours like Gladstone's, including the time of waking and starting work (rarely after 6 a.m. in his later years)— together with supreme economy of effort. A standard criticism was that he sought the palm without the dust, both in politics ('all Westminster, no grassroots' in one barb) and in his writing, where apart from *Asquith* and *Dilke* he never wrote a book requiring archival research. His secretaries all have stories of impossible demands to tell. But economy of effort was not absence of effort: the effort was widely spread, but could also be focused on a single immediate object in great bursts. He in fact became a formidable local campaigner when this was essential to success in his SDP by-elections and his continued survival in Hillhead. So too with his later writing. *Gladstone* and *Churchill* could not have been written without the published archival endeavour of others, yet neither book was remotely a one- or two-source work. In each case his mastery of a wide range of published material, sharpened by intermittent reviewing throughout this last phase, was as remarkable as his capacity to weave it together with his first-hand political and social experience, and (mostly apposite) application of analogies from one context to another, into compelling and fresh narratives.

The valuation of one masterly politician by another gave some of his best insights and judgement. I recall him reading aloud, with great verve, this passage he had just written on Churchill the day after the fall of France in 1940:

There was a routine War Cabinet at 12.30, and Cadogan [the Foreign Office Permanent Under Secretary], with the faint air of disapproval which he always employed when dealing with the political activities of politicians, wrote: 'Winston not there—writing his speech.' He might as well have complained that Lincoln did not apply himself to some minor piece of White House business on the morning of the Gettysburg Address. Churchill's 18 June forty-minute oration was however somewhat longer than Gettysburg but parts of it were almost as memorable: '*The battle of France is over. I expect that the battle of Britain is about to begin. Upon this battle depends the survival of Christian civilisation . . .*'

'Chamberlain', he added, 'would of course have chaired the War Cabinet.'

Equally engaging were his social judgements, the fine calibration (from one whose life had been spent experiencing the gradations of class) vying with self-parody. Churchill, 'the most clearly upper-class Prime Minister since Balfour', invited a roll-call of the intermediates and their family credentials. Perfectly quintessential was Roy's last review, of *The Asquiths* by Colin Clifford. Asquith, by birth 'unstably in the middle middle class', was described by Roy in his family setting thus:

Asquith's first family was a remarkable brood. They were not entirely free of the alcoholism which (speaking from a by no means puritanical position) I regard as one of the most consistent 20th-century legacies of both British Prime Ministers and American Presidents to their children: one Lloyd George offspring, one Baldwin, most Roosevelts, one Attlee, several Churchills and Macmillans amount to a formidable alcoholic roll-call. The children of those who just missed the highest office—Joseph Chamberlain, Rab Butler, Quintin Hailsham—seem to be somewhat steadier, which could be regarded as one of nature's compensations.

It is hard to think of anyone but Roy Jenkins who could have conceived such a passage. It was of a piece with his benign tolerance, even welcome, for his cartoon and gossip column image. 'All first-rate politicians are figures of fun: better to be a figure of fun than not a personality at all,' he would say. He particularly liked Steve Bell's Michelangelo of the celestial Jenkins tossing claret bottles at Blair below (Fig. 10.16). But for all the self-parody, and extraordinary use of language, there was little pretence. His pretensions were for real: he really did understand wine, with a keen eye for a bargain, and he really had read Proust, twice.

I also came to understand that it was misleading to think of Roy's three spheres—politics, writing, and social life—as *separate* spheres. For Roy, biography was politics by other means, as was a large part (but not the entirety) of his social life. One of his favourite metaphors for his career was that it had an 'upper' and 'lower' case: writing the 'upper case' before 1964 and after 1983, politics the 'upper case' for the two decades in between. But in truth, the great game of politics was upper- and lower-case throughout; apart from enforced war service, it was the main preoccupation of his life from adolescence until death. Roy was a player when he could be, a critic when he couldn't, and a historical observer of politics, with a biographer's flair and commitment, throughout. The only change, across the different phases of his career, was the balance between forms of political engagement. All his biographies were of politicians, all but two of them (*Truman* and *Franklin Delano Roosevelt*—neither of them extended works) British parliamentary politicians of the mid-Victorian age and after, performing on the stages of Westminster, Whitehall, and mostly Oxford before they got there, which he knew and loved so intimately. Even his final biographical selection of J.F.K. came only after an iterative process with friends and agent: Balfour was, yet again, his initial preference.

My most enduring impression is one of intensifying admiration for Roy's singular steadfastness and boldness, with a strong dash of courage and an immense strength of political personality. We usually agreed, though not always. On many of the social reform concerns of mine he evinced an indifference, and in some cases a conservatism, which made conversation pointless. Yet on the big political issues of the day, and a number of constant preoccupations including Europe, relations with the United States, and political alignments at home, his view was always definite and often passionate, informed by liberal and internationalist principles essentially unchanged since his pre-war Oxford days. He could be maddeningly dismissive of detail (as opposed to anecdote), although perfectly capable of mastering it. But at his best, he had had the four ultimate qualities of the successful liberal political leader—rational optimism, deep humanity, a bold plan for the future, and inspirational perseverance.

I came to well appreciate the boldness—with courage at key junctures—which characterized his periods as Home Secretary, Chancellor, President of the European Commission, and creator of the SDP, for I unexpectedly saw it at first hand in the production of *Churchill*. It was a perilous enterprise, vast and daunting in scale and almost fatally terminated by ill health. Roy was 77 at the outset and 80 at publication. He had been very uncertain about taking it on, and at times I felt guilty for having urged it upon him, which bound me still more closely to the project and to him personally (plenty of others, several of them authors of the preceding essays, forged similar relationships in previous Jenkins enterprises). But once embarked upon it—apart from the immediate aftermath of his heart operation—he never flinched, rarely doubted his judgement and capacity, and set and met a regime of work and deadlines which I found astonishing. By the end there were frayed nerves all round: his brilliant copy-editor, Peter James, solemnly announced that he could not go through the same again. But none of us doubted that it was a monumental achievement: the best one-volume life of Churchill, a stimulus to liberal political idealism every bit as powerful as *Asquith* forty years earlier and of far wider appeal.

Roy also had a good general sense of proportion—a rare quality in politics—and was especially strong on the rebound, when so many fail. Etched on my mind is one of his last public lectures, on Churchill at the Guildhall. The lecture itself was his by now standard canter through Churchillian themes. But then came the questions. What, asked the first questioner, did Lord Jenkins make of the recently published diaries of Alanbrooke, Churchill's Chief of the Imperial General Staff, with their bitingly critical comments on the great man's capacity as war leader? Without even stopping to consider, Roy responded that Alanbrooke also wrote much praise of Churchill, which needed to be seen alongside his reactions to his leader's 'often extremely exasperating behaviour'.

However [he continued], the difference between Alanbrooke, a very considerable CIGS, and Churchill, the great world statesman, is summed up by their respective reactions to Pearl Harbor at the end of 1941. Alanbrooke, who had been worried about a Japanese attack on British positions without bringing in America, recorded: 'O dear, so we have wasted seventy-two hours of intensive staff work on a false appraisal.' Churchill simply said: 'So we have won the war after all.' Which was the great statesman? [Laughter.][2]

Roy Jenkins was in the statesman's mould, worthy of his own closing words on Asquith: 'He had always been faithful to liberal, humane ideas, and to civilised, even fastidious, standards of political behaviour. He never trimmed for office … And with him there died the best part of the classical tradition in English politics.'

[2] A paraphrase of Alanbrooke's actual words, and it was forty-eight hours of wasted effort he complained of, not seventy-two (*War Diaries* (2001), 209). But this captured the spirit perfectly.

Acknowledgements

Our greatest debt is to the contributors, who have produced their texts at very short notice and have good-humouredly endured our editorial interventions. We are grateful to Dame Jennifer Jenkins for much help, and to Michael Sissons for freely giving his services as literary agent, to Laurien Berkeley for her sensitive copy-editing, to Humaira Erfan-Ahmed for secretarial assistance, and to Ruth Parr, Anne Gelling, Kay Rogers, and Louisa Lapworth at Oxford University Press for their ready advice and their speediness.

A.A.
K.T.

Picture Acknowledgements

Plates were reproduced by kind permission of the following: Bundesbildstelle Berlin and Helmut Schmidt 14b; Gillman & Soame 16c; Hulton Archive 3, 7, 9, 11, 15a, 15d; Lawson Gibbs & Co. 16b; Norman McBeath 16a; Topham Picturepoint 17; *The Times*/NI Syndication 12. We are grateful to Dame Jennifer Jenkins for the supply of personal photographs.

We would like to thank the Centre for the Study of Cartoons and Caricature, University of Kent, which supplied many of the cartoons for Chapter 10. We are also grateful to the cartoonists and newspaper groups who waived fees, supplied prints, and granted permission to reproduce their work in this book.

Efforts have been made to trace and contact all copyright holders prior to printing. Oxford University Press apologizes for any errors or omissions in this list and, if notified, will be pleased to make corrections at the earliest opportunity.

Index